"For Christians, the biblical command to seek justice is a core element of our faith. But in a world rife with complex issues of injustice, it can be difficult to know where to begin. For those of us who are parents, teachers, or others influencing children, bringing kids along on this journey can seem even more overwhelming. That's why I'm so grateful for Lisa Van Engen's superb *And Social Justice for All*, which examines a broad range of justice issues in age-appropriate ways for children, teenagers, and adults, combining biblical analysis, helpful explanations of the issues, questions for discussion, and a plethora of suggestions for diving deeper. My family and I will be referring back to this resource frequently."

—Matthew Soerens, US director of church mobilization of World Relief and coauthor of *Seeking Refuge* and *Welcoming the Stranger*

"In her debut book, Lisa Van Engen presents an educational manual that not only identifies justice issues, universal but immediate, but also offers both hope and resources to engage these life-and-death issues in our everyday living and learning. Very rarely do we find a combination of passion for the gospel so deep, commitment to justice so contagious, and language and style so accessible in one volume. A valuable resource for adults and children alike!"

—James Taneti, director of the Syngman Rhee Global Mission Center and assistant professor of world Christianity at Union Presbyterian Seminary

"There's much discussion in Christian circles about whether or not we should be concerned with social justice. Lisa Van Engen lends her voice to the conversation with *And Social Justice for All*. Van Engen encourages us that justice is the action of a good neighbor, who is mindful of her duty to those on the other side of the globe as well as across the fence. Not just another book about the ills of this world, *And Social Justice for All* gives resources custom fit to various ages, social groups, and faith communities to effect change in the world around us.

"At its core, this is a book about hope. Hope that our God cares about those to whom he gave breath, and hope that he can use us to make a difference for those who need it most."

—Susie Finkbeiner, best-selling author of the Pearl Spence novels

"*And Social Justice for All* is a thoughtfully curated collection of resources for families, classes, and small groups. Lisa Van Engen weaves a rich tapestry of Scripture, activities, questions, and ideas to provide a valuable guide for following God in seeking justice. The stories Van Engen tells and the insights she offers provide a beautiful image of the diverse, and sometimes surprising, ways that Christ is at work in communities today."
— **Rev. Shannon Jammal-Hollemans,** racial justice team leader of the Christian Reformed Church in North America

"A wonderful read. This is a great resource to help folks understand basic social justice issues in their community and around the world. Even more importantly, it gives practical ways for people of faith to get engaged. *And Social Justice for All* is an essential read for Christians who want to live out their faith and be the hands and feet of Christ in their neighborhood and across the globe."
— **Chris Palusky,** president and CEO of Bethany Christian Services

"Lisa Van Engen has a beautiful heart for sharing God's love. Through *And Social Justice for All*, she has given us an accessible, practical guide for families to meet our communities' deepest needs. With activities geared for children of all ages, your family can begin to live out God's love in a hands-on, life-changing way. This is a book you will refer back to for years to come! The devotionals will shape your family conversations deeper into the heart of Christ. I highly recommend it!"
— **Amelia Rhodes,** author of *Pray A to Z: A Practical Guide to Pray for Your Community*

AND
SOCIAL JUSTICE
FOR ALL

AND
SOCIAL JUSTICE
FOR ALL

Empowering Families, Churches,
and Schools to Make a Difference
in God's World

Lisa Van Engen

Kregel
Publications

ISBN 978-0-8254-4506-4, print
ISBN 978-0-8254-7457-6, epub

Printed in the United States of America
19 20 21 22 23 24 25 26 27 28 / 5 4 3 2 1

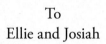

To
Ellie and Josiah

Contents

Preface: Proximity

In a fourth-grade storytelling class, I was asked to choose a fairy tale to recite to a first-grade classroom. Being a timid, quiet girl, I paged through the pile and found the shortest tale. The story, "The Princess and the Pea" by Hans Christian Andersen, covered three-fourths of a piece of paper. The illustration showed twenty colorful mattresses and twenty feather beds haphazardly stacked atop one another. When I thought about that story, I did not imagine a princess precariously perched upon the mattresses, tossing and turning through the night because of the pea below. I imagined the fragile pea underneath the weight of the mattress layers.

Our personal stories are built of many layers, like those mattresses stacked atop one another. Unless we truly know someone, we have no way to fully grasp the weight of the layers they carry. We do not know how even one more paper-thin sheet might cause the whole pile to go toppling, or how hard people battle to keep all their layers upright.

The challenges people face became real to me growing up in Oceana County, one of the ten poorest counties in Michigan. In the little village of Shelby, I grew up with my brother and parents in a redbrick house. Through my parents' work—my dad was a foundry manager and my mom an advocate for at-risk families at the public school—I witnessed what the compassionate response of Christ looked like.

My dad's workers arrived on our porch steps and were welcomed into our living room. Dad listened to their struggles and worked through those challenges with them. That compassion allowed his workers to hold their jobs and provide for their families.

When my mom made home visits and deliveries, my brother and I would ride along. We would set up games and food for family nights, and we sat in my mom's office after school, coloring with her students.

At an early age, I understood the strain and trauma of poverty. There was an air register in the north corner of my bedroom's floor, directly above the living room of our home. I used to listen. Oh, did I listen. I wanted to understand what was real. For me, Jesus resided not so much in the church pews but among the people in my community.

> **Justice. Making sure everyone is cared for.**
> **—Nora Claire, age 7**

Real stories of abuse and neglect worked their way into my heart. These were not just stories but real families and real children. What they experienced was enough to smash flat a million delicate peas and topple one thousand mattress piles. My parents perhaps worried my brother and I were exposed to too much, too soon. Looking back, I know those experiences shaped my heart and changed my life. I processed what I witnessed by writing stories. They did not have tidy endings or beautiful characters. Already I knew the answer to injustice was not simple to solve nor easy to obtain.

The summer before my senior year, I went on a mission trip with my high school youth group. We weaved through the Appalachian Mountains to a camp in Spencer, Tennessee, called Mountain-TOP. Some say that it is more difficult to breathe at higher altitudes, but I felt like I started to breathe for the very first time. The largest project my group completed was building a porch to replace a rickety half-ladder that a family used to enter and exit their beat-up mobile home. Four young children lived there. When rain fell heavily and we weren't

> **You don't have to move somewhere to make a difference.**
> **—Caleb, age 9**

able to work, I played with the kids. They showed me their worm farm and held my hand. When we went back to work, the kids helped me carry water, hammer nails, and steady boards. We circled up and prayed for those children before we left. By the door of the van, they hugged me tight. Their mom looked me in the eye and said, "They don't take to nobody, not even my sister." I felt a little fissure in my heart.

After high school, I went on to study social work at Grand Valley State University. There I was exposed further to people and their intricate layers. Like the mattresses stacked on that little pea, I was struck by the layered complexity of justice issues. That first college summer, I realized my long-held dream of becoming a camp counselor. I sat in my interview at Camp Geneva with the tough but gentle-hearted camp director, Jon Mark. He asked me to talk about someone who had made a differ-

**Adults should pay attention to kids. We have good, if not better, ideas.
—Mackenzie, age 12**

ence in my life. An answer emerged that I was not expecting. I shared about the kids I had known from my mom's work and MountainTOP. They had changed me. Loving them had given me hope and inspired me to be more.

I spent three summers in cabin 7B on the shore of Lake Michigan. A shy, uncertain girl, I had found a place that felt like home. Sometimes a camper would arrive in my cabin with clothing in a garbage bag or share a situation in her life that would challenge an adult. I felt my heart stretching wide open to those kids. On Thursday nights the camp held consecration services in the chapel. The counselors would form a tunnel while campers walked underneath. As they exited, we sang about God preparing us to be a sanctuary. A *sanctuary* can be defined as a place of refuge or safety. I wanted desperately to be that for others.

Without my ever seeking it, a nearness to justice became the natural bent of my life. At Camp Geneva, I met a caring and smart young man from northwest Iowa. Kris and I married and entered into a decade-long journey of youth ministry. We found youth who were ready to tackle tough issues, serve, and welcome others. They were brilliant. In that space, I began to understand how, when equipped, young people were gifted in engaging justice issues.

One fall, after school, the sound system in our church balcony was vandalized. The scrappy middle school student who tampered with the equipment returned to the church to complete community service hours, but

> **Kids have an overly active imagination and can learn more than people ever thought possible. We can use our imaginations to bring our dreams to life.**
> **—Eli, age 10**

when the hours were completed, he remained. He brought friends to youth group, and those friends brought friends. They brought language and backstory. They brought loud voices and questions. They brought damaged and fractured families. They brought school drama and brokenness. The landscape of our church group changed, but the kids of the church knew their own gifts and struggles and recognized the same in the new kids. They included the new kids and offered quarters for popcorn, cans of pop, slices of pizza, and spaces in their small groups. They prayed with them, greeted them in their school hallways. Their acceptance was unconditional and humbling.

Throughout my life, I continue to witness the surprising ways kids pursue justice when guided and empowered to do so. Being in proximity to justice all these years has been what has kept me going. In my life, depression and anxiety have had a way of obscuring my hope. When dark days seep in, I remember this is a life worth living because proximity to justice has given

> **What advice would I give to adults about making the world a better place? Just try.**
> **—Auburn, age 13**

me far more than I have contributed. I know that I myself am in need as much as anyone else.

Being a parent and working with children in education every day, I understand how parents and teachers long for children to be humble in their actions and sensitive to how those actions affect the world around them. We hope for children to embrace kindness and grow courage to challenge injustice. If we offer young people references and markers to anchor their lives in seeking justice,

they will soak that up. When we expose young people to the realities of injustice, they will rise to meet the challenge. The Word of God and the life of Jesus provide us with examples of this love in action.

When I began blogging about justice issues, I found that families were struggling with the same roadblocks mine did in making a difference. Families find themselves busy and lacking resources and appropriate opportunities that would involve children of all ages. In response to this need, in the summer of 2015, I launched Talk Justice Playgroups. We organized partnerships and invited families to serve together in community with one another. Families responded wholeheartedly and embraced the opportunity to talk about tough issues and join together to contribute to justice causes.

Over the past three years, Talk Justice Playgroups have opened the doors for many partnerships where families of different backgrounds, churches, and neighborhoods join together to learn, serve, and play. We decorated lunch bags and packaged trail mix for a local nonprofit that provides sack suppers to area students, made cards for veterans through our public library's community reading program, and loaded up backpacks for kids in foster care through a local nonprofit. We learned from immigrants during a local Blessing Not Burden campaign to honor the contributions of immigrants in our community, created collaborative art, and shared children's books. In community we have found greater strength.

> There is a whole world out there searching for help.
> —Aliyah, age 16

In my work in education, I travel to many classrooms and have the privilege of seeing many children each day. One morning I entered a third-grade classroom in the midst of a pajama-and-stuffed-animal day. The students were working on personal narratives, and I noticed one little boy struggling to finish. I knelt down to help him, and he immediately introduced me to his stuffed Yoda. He turned his head toward me, and his little voice rose up an octave. He announced, "He's so ugly and so beautiful at the same time." His eyes brimmed with tears as if that deeper understanding of life had just occurred to him.

Life is beautiful and ugly at the same time. Heartbreaking justice issues pervade our world. They should deeply disturb and unsettle us. When we are not in proximity—either naturally or intentionally—it is easy to pretend it's not really happening: *I can't see it. It doesn't touch me. It doesn't affect my family.* We become numb to injustice and suffering. First John 3:16–18 says, "This is how we know what love is: Jesus Christ laid down his life for us.

And we ought to lay down our lives for our brothers and sisters. If anyone has material possessions and sees a brother or sister in need but has no pity on them, how can the love of God be in that person? Dear children, let us not love with words or speech but with actions and in truth." Do we have the courage to love with actions and in truth, and do we teach the children in our lives to do the same?

> Kids can change the world by not doing the terrible things that adults do now.
> —Zac, age 15

One year the foundry my dad had worked at his whole life closed. My parents spent a summer in Cincinnati, where Dad had a short-term position. My husband and I and our children went to visit, and our family took a trip to the Cincinnati Zoo. My son, Josiah, was about three years old at the time, and he fell in love with a polar bear at the Kroger Lords of the Arctic exhibit. Below the exhibit, you can stand in a cave-like area and see polar bears swimming under the water. One polar bear kept swimming up to the window, its white fur moving in the blue water. He would push off the glass and come back, over and over again. Josiah was delighted. "He swam right up to me." He told the story to anyone willing to listen. Josiah was delighted because zoo critters typically keep a careful distance from people and the potential danger they bring.

I think people can be a lot like zoo creatures when it comes to issues of injustice; we like to keep a comfortable distance. But Josiah's polar bear broke all the norms and drew close. He swam right up to Josiah over and over again. How can we, like the polar bear, put our families in proximity to the uncomfortable and unfamiliar? How can we swim right up again and again to the hurt in our world?

When my kids were young, I would sometimes stash Junior Mints in the kitchen. I'd occasionally sneak off to eat some. When I returned to whatever we were playing on the living room floor, my kids would inevitably say, "I smell something on your breath and it's mint and chocolate. I want some." When we are living life with others, we should have the same magnetic effect. *I see you fighting injustice. It's improbable love. It makes me look to God, and I want that.*

When we rise, they will rise too.

Introduction

Each chapter in *And Social Justice for All* covers one of fourteen global justice issues and follows a similar structure to allow the reader quick and easy access to the information and resources.

The chapters open with general information on the subject, which might include history, statistics, illustrative stories, context, current events, and projections. The introductory material only touches the surface of the issue; use it to foster further exploration into one or more aspects you find relevant, interesting, or challenging. Most issues are multifaceted and interrelated. A few global and next-door concerns are highlighted to lead to further understanding of the issues. Finally, hope is offered through exciting and encouraging work being done in each field and a call to make a difference.

> We should think a little more about each other.
> —Jiyun, age 17

Features You'll Find in Each Chapter

Innovation to Explore: Learn about innovative ideas in each justice category. Talk to your kids or students about the solutions people have created to everyday challenges. Think about what area of study those creators used. Encourage young people that no matter what gifts they possess or what field of study they go into, they can use their gifts to extend justice.

Talk Justice: Use these conversation starters as a way of gently introducing these complex subjects to young children and pressing older children to dig deeper into the subject. The more we draw justice issues into everyday conversations, the more we equip children—and ourselves—to respond. Be willing to ask hard questions, and be all right with not having all the answers. Commit to listening to children and, whenever possible, put actions behind the words to affirm that you value their contribution to the conversation.

Study God's Word: Henri Nouwen said, "The spiritual life does not remove us from the world, but leads us deeper into it."[1] We turn to God's Word to equip us to be effective as God's hands and feet to his people. A brief devotional covers each topic with a Scripture verse, thoughts, challenge questions, and prayer.

Explore Justice: Activities are grouped for three age ranges: 3–6, 7–11, and 12 and up. From relay races to artistic reflection, children will actively engage by reading, playing, observing, experimenting, gathering, creating, and connecting. All the activities make connections to justice issues and provide opportunities to deepen understanding. Though the children's books I suggest throughout are helpful in nurturing awareness of the fourteen featured topics, not all suggested titles contain the gospel message. This is due to the limited number of children's social justice books in the Christian marketplace. And while I've suggested age ranges for each book, as a caregiver I encourage you to preread each book in order to determine if and when your child is ready for a particular title.

Challenge and Extend Awareness at Home: Especially useful for families, this section offers more options for exploring justice cross-generationally, from a thirty-day prayer challenge to a YouTube video to an outing.

Making a Difference: This section includes various ideas for making a tangible difference as a family, group, or classroom. These are just suggestions, and their inclusion here is not an endorsement of each organization's overall faith or mission. Do the research to find those projects that best reflect your biblical convictions. Many religious organizations do amazing work. But don't be afraid to support a nonreligious organization; just because a mission is not preaching the gospel does not mean that they will be ineffective at using money wisely to dig wells or feed the hungry. Also, there's room to personalize this list, as most areas have amazing local organizations.

Throughout the book, you'll notice that I've included web addresses for organizations and links to helpful information. If the URLs become outdated, as all online information is prone to, there is no need to worry. Just visit my website (lisavanengen.com) and click the And Social Justice for All tab for direct links to both featured organizations and material, plus more that I become aware of.

While all of the material in the book can be used as stand-alone suggestions and ideas, I have included in appendix A information for how to organize social action groups in your own community, church, or school.

My Prayer

My prayer is for this book to be an encouragement to you and a resource to help you take small steps to fight injustice in your busy life. I hope you will mark up this book. Circle ideas. Put checkmarks next to the things you try. Write questions in the margins. Add your ideas. Dream. I hope you will visit my website and share the stories of what your family, classroom, or group talks about and tries.

My favorite part of this book ended up being the kids' quotes. They are brilliant, as we would expect. As I wrote this manuscript, the United States experienced discord. Kindness disappeared into the background, and the need for justice seekers became even more pronounced. Sometimes I desperately wanted to give up. I did not feel adequate. We received messages about not being "real Christians" due to my husband's work with refugees and immigrants. But each time I wanted to quit, another kid's survey response came in. I would be left stunned again by each young person's thoughtful response, wise insight, and simple profundity. Each time I was renewed. I wanted to do them justice.

> Making a difference means helping someone see something they have not seen before.
> —Rysa, age 13

Clean Water and Sanitation: Cracked Cisterns

When the well's dry they know the worth of water.
—BENJAMIN FRANKLIN, AMERICAN DIPLOMAT AND INVENTOR

Raise Awareness

March 14—International Day of Action for Rivers
March 22—World Water Day
October 15—Global Handwashing Day
November 19—World Toilet Day

Water refreshes and revives. Everyone can relate to desperate thirst and the quenching relief of a glass of water. Or to the irritation of dirt and grime and the pleasure of being clean once again. Or to the oppression of heat and the restorative comfort a dip in cool water can bring.

Or can they? Does everyone have ready access to clean water?

Our need for water weaves into our everyday life and is a necessity for survival. We use water for hydrating our bodies, cooking food, laundering clothes, washing dishes, practicing personal hygiene, cleaning our homes, watering our lawns and plants, and maintaining our sanitation systems, fire protection, and power generation within our homes. Health, agriculture, energy, sanitation, manufacturing, and livestock all rely on accessible, clean water. For every living species, water is life. Without water we cannot survive. The average adult body is made of 50–65 percent water.[1] You can live upward of three weeks without food, but on average only three to four days without water.[2]

Understanding the Issue

When kids look at a globe, they see an abundance of water. We need to educate them that in reality, 97 percent of that water is ocean water, leaving around 3 percent as fresh water. Within that fresh water, 68.7 percent is locked in glaciers and icecaps, 30.1 percent is groundwater, and about 1.2 percent is surface water such as lakes, rivers, and swamps.[3] If we look at those numbers, we realize that we have a responsibility to protect potable drinking water for ourselves as well as generations to come. As the population of the world increases, so will the demand for clean water.

> Dirty water is sick. It would make you die.
> —Landon, age 3

The per capita availability of drinking water is diminishing in all developed and developing nations.[4] Physical water scarcity occurs when the demand for clean water exceeds the earth's ability to provide fresh water for all its inhabitants. Drought, changes in climate, overuse of resources, and pollution can all contribute to physical water scarcity. Population growth makes it difficult for certain areas to have access to all the clean water they need. In the western United States, many states have faced water shortages and have had to adjust life accordingly. Limits are placed on the amount of water farmers can use, and in a trickle-down effect, this can result in increased food prices.

> To make a difference, be proactive.
> —Dineo, age 11

Economic water scarcity occurs when water distribution is allocated inequitably. The governments of some nations do not invest in infrastructure that allows for clean water access for everyone. Regions that are unstable due to war and conflict do not have reliable sources of water to meet the needed demand. Globally there are 263 transboundary lakes and river basins.[5] For example, the longest river in the world, the Nile, flows through Egypt, Ethiopia, and Sudan. Water sources that cross international boundaries are often at risk. Different nations do not always work together to preserve water, share water, or create quality regulations for water. Many people in poverty receive an unequal distribution of water. They live where there is no infrastructure to provide clean running water or sanitation facilities. In other areas, private companies can take over water systems and charge prices too high for those in poverty to afford their water bills.

Bringing clean water to every nation in the world looks different in each community. To reach aquifers, some places need to hand dig or drill wells. Other neighborhoods might use pipe networks, rainwater catchments, gravity-fed systems from elevated spaces, purification systems, biosand filters, rooftop rainwater harvesting, or water purification tablets. In Tanzania, Concern US uses the Moringa tree to purify water. Community members grind the tree's nuts into a powder that collects pollutants as it sinks down in a container, leaving the drinkable water on the surface. Nations that face conflict over water supplies are encouraged to work together to make water treaties before they find themselves in dire need.

Global Concerns

Although global statistics are improving each day, 2.1 billion people still lack safely managed drinking sources.[6] Every day, 600 children die due to diarrhea caused by unsafe water or poor sanitation.[7] Children under the age of five are particularly vulnerable to waterborne illnesses. Each year, children lose 443 million school days because of water-related illness.[8] Imagine serving young children lunch and placing cups of dirty water beside their plates. They are thirsty and must drink, yet you know they might become ill from the invisible bacteria that swim within. In developed nations, people do not even fill the bowls of their pets with unclean water. Yet the reality of waterborne illnesses surrounds many families around the world.

> I like clean water. Dirty water has yucky germs. Clean water doesn't have germs.
> —Jack, age 7

In developing nations, lack of education contributes to the consumption of unclean water as well. People drink whatever water is available and may not understand that contaminated water can lead to disease or even death. Diarrhea is a common result of drinking unclean water and can lead to dehydration and death. Other waterborne illnesses include cholera, typhoid, Guinea worm, and hepatitis E. Lack of clean water then becomes a huge health-care issue and cost. Education as simple as hand washing makes a difference. When relief organizations bring latrines to communities, simple features like door locks, labels for women's and men's spaces, and toilet lids make a difference.

Imagine inadequate bathrooms for the children in your life. Many girls in the developing world are unable to continue schooling because of the lack of safe, private sanitation. According to the Gates Foundation, 40 percent of the world's population—2.5 billion people—lack adequate sanitation facilities or practice open defecation.[9] Not everyone has a toilet to use or a faucet to wash his or her hands afterward. In areas of poverty, water tainted with garbage and human waste can run right through neighborhoods. Outbreaks of deadly diseases like Ebola and cholera are more likely to occur in these areas. The cost to build toilets, sewers, and wastewater treatment facilities are high but essential for the health, dignity, and safety of so many.

Consider the long walk for water many take in the developing world. Women and children tasked with water collection are not able to attend school or provide for families through paying work. Their walk for water also brings them to areas that make them vulnerable to human trafficking. The average steel jerrican holds five gallons of water, the equivalent of forty pounds.[10] Imagine the stress on a woman's body making multiple trips throughout the day carrying water. Drought forces entire families and communities to walk for water through displacement. The UN Refugee Agency estimates 766,000 people were displaced in Somalia from drought since November 2016.[11]

Next-Door Concerns

The water crisis in Flint, Michigan, shattered the assumption that all Americans have access to clean water. Two and a half hours from the city I live in, a new water pipeline in 2014 delivered highly polluted water with detected E. coli and total coliform bacteria to the residents of Flint. Citizens had to present jugs of discolored water, children with rashes, and reports of mysterious illnesses before anyone would listen. The Environmental Protection Agency found high levels of lead in the water. Lead poisoning can severely affect mental and physical development, especially in children under six years old. Flint, an economically depressed city in the richest nation in the world, did not have access to clean water.

Other local waterways show stress as well. Due to a sixteen-year drought, "demand for Colorado River water is already stretched thin."[12] The water level of the biggest reservoir in the western Unites States, Lake Mead, continues to decrease. In many cities, aging pipes are a growing concern. "In New York City, for instance, over eight million citizens rely on drinking water delivered primarily by two tunnels, one of which was completed in 1917 and the other in 1936."[13] Beaches and waterways close for a period due to polluted water with high levels of bacteria. Even in the United States we feel the strain of providing clean water for all citizens.

The 1974 Safe Water Drinking Act protects public drinking water through federal law. "In 2015, nearly 77 million Americans lived in places where the water systems were in some violation of safety regulations."[14] Our local water sources are at risk through chemical spills, aging infrastructure, and severe weather. Flooding can cause water contamination by fecal matter from farming areas running into water systems. During drought, farmers often turn to groundwater to irrigate their crops.

> I like clean water because I can drink it.
> —Felix, age 5

Since 2015, California has experienced periodic mandatory statewide restrictions of water usage. A study in 2012 by the California State Water Control Board found that drought "raises the concentration of nitrates in the water left in the ground."[15] These local water concerns bring the global need for clean water and sanitation into even greater focus. Access to clean water will continue to be a concern into the future for the developing world and your community.

Hope

The organization Blood:Water, founded by the music group Jars of Clay and activist Jena Lee Nardella, focuses its efforts on providing access to clean water and on training grassroots organizers and leaders in the areas where they work. They teach these leaders how to maintain and complete maintenance on their water systems. The work they do is then sustainable even when Blood:Water is not on-site. A charity called The Last Well models innovation by partnering with ten different organizations that bring water and the hope of Jesus to the country of Liberia. Working together, the ten groups and The Last Well demonstrate that partnerships make clean water efforts stronger and more sustainable over the course of time.

And while many organizations that work toward clean water focus efforts on rural areas, an organization called Splash has a different focus. Splash studies international hotels and restaurants that provide clean water to tourists around the world. When they find supply chains and resources that work well, they seek to replicate those solutions and bring clean water to citizens without access in those same areas. The founders of Splash firmly believe that everyone deserves equal access to clean water.

The prophet Amos lived during a time of economic prosperity. The rich forgot their calling and oppressed the poor. In Amos 5, the prophet reports that "the Lord, the LORD God Almighty, says: . . . 'Let justice roll on like a river, righteousness like a never-failing stream'" (vv. 16, 24). God compared justice with the beauty of flowing waters. Fresh water brings with it health, hope, and the means for surviving and thriving. We can bring justice by fighting for access to clean water and sanitation for all of God's people.

INNOVATION TO EXPLORE

- *Using Science*: Explore LifeStraw, a straw-like filter that purifies contaminated water.
- *Using Physics*: The Hippo Roller allows people to collect clean water by pushing five times more water than what a single bucket could hold.
- *Using Microfinance*: WaterCredit offers small, easy-to-repay loans through Water.org to help global families realize their dream of clean water and sanitation. When repaid, the loan passes to another family in need.
- *Using Technical Studies*: Check out the work of Plumbers Without Borders. Plumbers install water purifiers for those in need of clean water.

- *Using Climate*: In foggy climates, mesh nets have been used to trap and collect water from the moisture in fog. The largest harvesting project produces 6,300 liters of water per day on Mount Boutmezguida, Morocco.

Appreciate the Beautiful Waters of Our World

Check out books from your local library or use the internet to explore:

- The blue lagoons of the Cook Islands in the South Pacific
- Victoria Falls in Zimbabwe
- The turquoise Peyto Lake in Alberta, Canada
- Perito Moreno Glacier in Argentina
- The colorful river Caño Cristales in Colombia
- Mekong River in Southeast Asia

TALK JUSTICE

Ages 3–6

What do you use water for in your life? Name everything you need water for.

_____

_____

How many water faucets are in your house? How many toilets?

_____

_____

Where is your favorite place to play in water (a lake, river, pool, splash pad)?

_____

_____

How often do you take a bath? Why is it important to take a bath?

_____

_____

How would drinking dirty water make you feel?

_____

_____

Ages 7–11

How would your life change if you only had one water faucet in your house?

_____

_____

How much time would it take, and what challenges might you face, gathering water every day at a community well half a mile from your home?

_____

_____

Where does your water come from?

_____

_____

Can you describe a time when you were really thirsty and didn't have water with you?

_____

_____

Why do you think clean water is so important to the people of the world?

_____

_____

Ages 12+

How would you use water differently if it took time and effort to obtain it?

_____

_____

How can you use the resource of water in a way that honors God?

_____

_____

When a country shares its source of water, what challenges might they face?

_____

_____

_____

What actions could you take to conserve water in your own home?

_____

_____

_____

How are water and sanitation connected?

_____

_____

STUDY GOD'S WORD

Jeremiah 2:13

My people have committed two sins: They have forsaken me, the spring of living water, and have dug their own cisterns, broken cisterns that cannot hold water.

A cistern is a tank for storing water. A cracked cistern is useless because water leaks out and soaks into the earth, where it cannot be used. Our heart can either be full of Jesus's "living water" or it can be a "cracked cistern." When we do not focus on Jesus, we think more and more about ourselves. The more we think about ourselves, the less we think about the people God has put in our lives. Our world becomes narrow and focused inward. Keeping the gifts we have been given for ourselves only results in cracked, broken hearts. Our love for others leaks out, and we become much like a cracked cistern, dried up and unusable.

When we fill our hearts with love for Jesus, however, we become more like a fountain of living water. Our love overflows, and we can offer it to others. We learn that we have more than enough to give. When we give our hearts fully to Jesus, he will help us open them up to others. When we help others—working, for example, to give them access to clean water—they can also know the living water of hope that is Jesus.

Extend Study of God's Word

Read different translations of Jeremiah 2:13.

What does it mean to forsake God? How could we do the opposite in our daily lives?

_____

_____

_____

What is one way you could focus on following Jesus every day?

_____

_____

_____

What crack could you repair in your own heart?

_____

_____

_____

Where could the love of Jesus spill out in your own life?

_____

_____

_____

Choose an organization that supports clean water and sanitation that your family or group can pray for:

_____

Choose a specific community or place in need of clean water and sanitation that your family or group can pray for:

_____

God, thank you for the clean water we have to drink and use. We pray for clean water for everyone on our planet. Help us care for the water we have. Show us where we can make a difference in the work of bringing clean water and sanitation to those who don't have access. When we offer the gift of clean water, help others feel your light and hope. Amen.

EXPLORE JUSTICE

Ages 3–6
Read: *Clean Water for Elirose* by Ariah Fine
Maria and her friends learn about a young girl without clean drinking water and decide to help.

> *Connection—A simple story with sweet illustrations, enabling even the youngest children to understand they can make a difference by helping kids have access to clean water.*

Read: *The Water Princess* by Susan Verde
Princess Gie Gie longs to bring clean water to her small African village. Based on the childhood of supermodel Georgie Badiel.

> *Connection—Children learn about the struggle for clean water and the hope that someday all who need it might receive access.*

Play: Toilet Paper Toss
Gather supplies: a five-gallon bucket, five toilet paper rolls, clear packing tape.
- Set a five-gallon bucket a few feet from where you intend to play the game.
- Completely wrap five rolls of toilet paper with clear packing tape.
- Instruct kids to stand a certain distance from the bucket (experiment ahead of time to find an appropriate range).
- Mark the distance with sidewalk chalk if outside or masking tape if inside.
- Give each child three chances to toss the toilet paper roll into the bucket.

Connection—If you did not have water, how would you flush your toilet? What would happen if you couldn't flush your toilet? Children understand how water impacts sanitation.

Play: Pin the Bucket on the Well

Gather supplies: poster board, double-sided tape, construction paper, poster putty, blindfolds.

- Draw a large water well on poster board and tape it to a wall.
- Make numerous five-inch buckets out of construction paper; affix double-sided tape or poster putty to the back of each bucket.
- Blindfold participants one at a time to see who can pin the bucket closest to the center of the well (experiment ahead of time to find an appropriate starting distance from the wall).

Connection—Without a water well, villagers need to walk long distances to collect water from streams, rivers, or lakes. Wells make it easier for families to collect water in buckets to bring home to use. Water from wells is also clean, so families don't need to worry about getting sick from using it.

Observe: Dirty Water Visual

Gather supplies: clear plastic bottle with cap, water, various "pollutants" such as food scraps, dirt, oil.

- Fill a clear bottle with water and pollutants.
- Show the mixture to the children.
- Pass the bottle around and let each child have a turn to take a closer look and move the things inside.

Connection—This is what unclean water looks like. Could you wash a cut with this water? Would you drink this water? What about taking a bath in it?

Experiment: Germ Monsters

Gather supplies: glitter, paper towel, water, hand soap.

- Sprinkle glitter on kids' hands. Tell them to imagine the glitter is germs.
- First, encourage the kids to get the glitter off by wiping their hands together.

- Second, give them each a paper towel and see if they can get all the glitter off.
- Finally, have them use water and soap to remove the glitter.

Connection—Water and soap are necessary for cleaning our bodies and getting rid of germs. What do you think people would do if they did not have water for washing hands or taking a bath? If you did not have water for washing hands or taking a bath, how would you complete these tasks?

Play: Water Sensory Box
Gather supplies: shallow plastic tub, water, craft sticks, small cups, various "pollutants" such as glitter, sand, rocks, dirt, shredded paper, feathers, beads, leaves, or pom-poms.
- Create a sensory box using a shallow tub.
- Fill the tub with water.
- Provide children with various "pollutants" to add to the tub.
- Give each child a craft stick and small cup to observe through play.

Connection—We started out with fresh, clean water in our tub. After we add more and more objects, the water becomes polluted. Could you drink the water? Would you take a bath in this water? Would you boil macaroni noodles in the water?

Ages 7–11
Read: *One Well: The Story of Water on Earth* by Rochelle Strauss
"All water on earth is connected, so there really is just one source—one global well—from which we all draw our water." *One Well* studies the interconnectedness of water.

Connection—The way we protect water will affect our planet into the future. One Well *helps children understand the urgency of conserving and caring for our global water supply.*

Read: *Ryan and Jimmy: And the Well in Africa That Brought Them Together* by Herb Shoveller

As a six-year-old, Ryan raised money for a well in Agweo, Uganda. Jimmy from Uganda hopes to thank Ryan for the village well. They eventually meet and form a lasting bond.

Connection—An example of how one boy helped a community and made a difference—and how, in the process, his own life was changed.

Play: Transporting Water Relay Race
Gather supplies: two jerricans or two five-gallon buckets, water.

Most hardware stores carry jerricans for purchase. They provide a great visual representation for kids.

- Create two teams of children.
- Fill up two jerricans or five-gallon buckets about halfway with water (experiment ahead of time, but a full jerrican is usually too heavy for children to lift).
- Have each child take a turn carrying the jerrican to a predetermined spot.
- The child turns around to carry the can back to the next person in line.
- The first team to have all its participants carry the jerrican completes the mission.

Connection—Globally many women and children must walk to collect clean water. They walk a long way to fill up their jerrican, and then must carry it home for drinking, bathing, and cooking. How would you like to do this every day?

Experiment: Water Cycle in a Baggie
Gather supplies: clear resealable baggies, tape, permanent markers, water, blue food coloring.
- Give each child some permanent markers and a baggie.
- Instruct children to use their markers to decorate their baggie with water, sun, and clouds.
- Carefully pour about two inches of water into the bottom of the baggie, add 1–2 drops of blue dye, and fully seal the baggie.
- Tape the baggie (along the seal) to a window that is exposed to sunlight.
- Watch water droplets form and try touching them to create rain.

Connection—Talk about the water cycle. How is all water (groundwater, rain, rivers, lakes, oceans) connected? If our water is constantly recycled, why do we need to take good care of it?

Create: String Art
Gather supplies: foam board, pushpins, colorful thread.
- Artists design a wave of pushpins inserted into foam board.
- Weave string around the pins to create string art.

Try string art with other symbols of justice issues.

Connection—Artists use their creativity to feature water in an art piece. Encourage them to add a message to the artwork by sharing a statistic or a call to action to contribute to the work of providing clean water for those without.

Create: Writing
Gather supplies: paper, pens and pencils.
- Prompt: My water has been . . .

Connection—Encourage writers to imagine where the water they drink has been: a far-off country, a layer of a glacier, a swimming pool across the world, a water fountain in a school.

Always provide a time and place for writers to share their work if they wish to.

Create: Clean Water and Sanitation Story Stones
Gather supplies: flat stones, acrylic paint of various colors, paintbrushes, decoupage, magazines, scissors.
- Use flat stones and paint or decoupage clean water images on each rock.
- Ideas: well, jerrican, fire with a bucket hanging over it, raindrops, waves, faucet, a village, a toilet, little girl or boy carrying water. Encourage children to use the story stones to tell a story about clean water and sanitation.

Find story stone ideas for all the chapter themes at lisavanengen .com.

Connection—Telling stories helps children explore, learn, and apply what they are learning about the need for global clean water.

Ages 12+

Read: *A Long Walk to Water* by Linda Sue Park
Alternating stories of two eleven-year-olds from Sudan, one a refugee who walks the African continent seeking safety and the other who walks two hours twice a day for clean water.

Connection—Readers are exposed to the reality of refugees and the daily collection of water, concluding in an inspiring ending that offers hope.

Observe: Study Art
Study *Under the Wave off Kanagawa* (also known as *The Great Wave*) by Katsushika Hokusai. (Images are easy to find on the internet.)

Connection—Contemplate the power of water through this woodblock print of Japanese art. Besides being physically powerful, how else does water have power in our lives?

Create: Writing
Gather supplies: paper, pens and pencils.
- Prompt: Water is . . .

Connection—Writers express their ideas about what water means to the world and its people.

Find a list of social media posts for all the topics in *And Social Justice for All* at lisavanengen.com.

Connect: Clean Water Social Media Blast
Find a list of ready-to-go social media blasts on my website.

Connection—Young people use their social media accounts for good by advocating for clean water and sanitation globally.

Experiment: Rain Gauge
Gather supplies: empty two-liter pop bottle, marker, small stones, masking tape, ruler, scissors or knife, paper, pencil or pen.
- Cut the top off the bottle.
- Put a piece of masking tape up the side of the pop bottle, beginning at the top and ending near the bottom. Using your ruler and a marker, mark inches or centimeters on the tape, beginning near the bottom and working your way up.
- Fill the bottom of the bottle with stones.
- Fill the bottle with water until it is level with the bottom of the masking tape.
- Place the rain gauge outside where falling rain will not be affected by buildings, trees, or anything that would hinder its collection.
- Make a chart to keep track of the rain levels. Read and record the level of water in the gauge each day.

Connection—Analyze and better understand the rainwater data in the area you live in. How does this data compare with other parts of your state, other states, or other countries?

Connect: Beverage Challenge
Gather friends for a beverage challenge. Set a goal to drink only water for one week—no other beverages. When the week is over, tally up the money you saved by not purchasing soda, coffee, or juice during that week. Combine those resources and donate them to an organization that supports clean water.

Connection—Students learn how much on average they spend on beverages other than water during a week. Students share resources to support a cause. Is this challenge something you would repeat in the future?

Study: The Nile River
Research the transboundary Nile River and the Entebbe Agreement of 2010. Consider the challenges nations that share water sources face.

Connection—Students learn about transboundary water conflicts and the challenges they present to all nations to receive equal access to clean water.

CHALLENGE AND EXTEND AWARENESS AT HOME

- Read "30 Mealtime Clean Water Facts," found at lisavanengen.com.
- Practice "30 Days of Prayer for Clean Water," found at lisavanengen .com.
- Calculate your water usage as a family at watercalculator.org.
- Complete challenges from "100 Ways to Conserve Water" on the Water: Use It Wisely website (wateruseitwisely.com).
- Make the kitchen faucet in your home off-limits for water usage for a day. To get water, family members need to use an alternate tap in your home or outdoors. Talk about how it feels to have to work extra for your water, and remember families that have to walk for miles to obtain clean water.
- Look through photo galleries of the stories of water through Blue Planet Network.
- Read stories, accompanied by photography, on the Charity: Water website (charitywater.org).
- Introduce younger children to Raya, the sanitation global ambassador for Sesame Street (sesameworkshop.org).
- Watch the short video "The Long Walk" and others at the Blood:Water Mission YouTube channel.
- Watch videos from the Water.org YouTube channel.

We have the ability to provide clean water for every man, woman and child on the Earth. What has been lacking is the collective will to accomplish this. What are we waiting for? This is the commitment we need to make to the world, now.

—JEAN-MICHEL COUSTEAU, FRENCH EXPLORER

MAKING A DIFFERENCE

- Work with your church, school, or community building to identify leaky faucets and inefficient toilets.
- Bring safe water to an individual through Water.org.
- Encourage personal reusable water bottles instead of bottled water at events.
- Host a Water:Walk to raise funds for Blood:Water Mission (blood water.org).
- Take the Ryan's Well Foundation School Challenge with your school (ryanswell.ca).
- Fund a project through Blue Planet Network.
- Purchase a latrine through World Renew gift catalog (worldrenew.net).
- Support water and sanitation through World Vision (donate.world vision.org).
- Take the water challenge from The Water Project by drinking only water for two weeks to free up money to give one person access to clean water (thewaterproject.org).
- Contribute to the UNICEF Tap Project, providing clean water to more than 100 countries (unicef.org).

For direct links to any of these resources plus additional materials, go to lisavanengen.com and click the And Social Justice for All tab.

Local Ideas

- _____
- _____
- _____
- _____
- _____

2

Creation Care: An Open Window

One has to be alone, under the sky, before everything falls into place and one finds his own place in the midst of it all.
—THOMAS MERTON, TRAPPIST MONK AND ACTIVIST

Raise Awareness

April (week surrounding Earth Day)—Faith Climate Action Week
April (last Friday)—Arbor Day
April 22—Earth Day
May (third Friday)—National Bike to Work Day
June—Great Outdoors Month
June—National Wildlife Federation's Great American Campout

As Christians, we believe God called creation into being, and therefore it is sacred. The beauty that surrounds us without human summoning deserves a gentle hand. The night sky full of mystery asks us to take time to think about our impact. Kids are fascinated by the natural world—the legs of a fuzzy caterpillar, the darting path of a butterfly, clouds shifting and changing shape against a bright blue sky, vivid colors of falling leaves.

Children move their fingers over the bark of a tree, dig knee-deep holes in the sand, gather pebbles to skip across the surface of water, and cradle a fallen robin's egg in their hands. They examine photographs of the big eyes of a deer peering from the wood's edge, the lithe pounce of a lion, the stretching neck of a giraffe.

Think about the moments in nature that have steadied you. Creation is worth our investment a thousand times over. In the Bible, God lovingly provides for us and all he has created. Genesis 1:28 tells us that God blessed the people he created, and he said to them, "Be fruitful and increase in number; fill the earth and subdue it. Rule over the fish in the sea and the birds in the sky and over every living creature that moves on the ground." God entrusted creation to our care and stewardship. The topic of creation care is something children can connect to. They enjoy climbing the limbs of broad trees, splashing in the waters of a lake, and using natural supplies to make a forest fort. They see a photograph of an endangered leatherback sea turtle and hope for its survival. Children take interest in creation: frogs with transparent skin, naked mole rats, pink dolphins, and silly sloths. When we teach them to care for God's creation, they will respond.

Understanding the Issue

Our resources from nature become depleted when people use them faster than they can be replaced. The US Census Bureau features a world population clock whose numbers are continually shifting up. Currently, there are approximately seven billion people populating the earth. With the beauty of each new life, we need to consider the need for creation that can sustain it. Depletion of resources occurs due to many factors, including overpopulation, overconsumption, deforestation, development, mining, and pollution. The fewer natural resources our planet has, the more tension we face as they are distributed.

Carbon dioxide emissions from transportation, deforestation, and the growing consumption of fossil fuels affect our climate. The average weather over a thirty-year period describes a location's climate. When significant changes occur over many thirty-year periods, scientists call it a *changing climate*. The term *global warming* means that the atmospheric and oceanic temperatures globally are increasing. When businesses and individuals shift to clean energy sources like solar, wind, and geothermal energy instead of fossil fuels, they invest in the future.

Pollution and climate change threaten biodiversity. God created a planet full of wonder. Did you know there are more than 350,000 species of beetles alone?[1] In 2014, almost 1,500 new creatures were discovered in oceans.[2] Biodiversity is the variety of life on the planet: the different species of animals and plant life and variety of ecosystems. Life depends on biodiversity; having varying species helps food supply, purifies air and water, modifies climate to changing needs, controls erosion, detoxifies soil, and even helps provide medicines. The concept of creation care encourages sustainable development. As the global population continues to grow, we are cautioned to meet the needs of this generation without depleting the resources of future generations.

Global Concerns

Creation care concerns greatly affect those in poverty, especially in underdeveloped countries. While their homes are often already in fragile spaces, they are at risk of facing displacement due to changes in climate and weather patterns.

People groups around the world have found the need to resettle because their homelands are affected by nature. Flooding, rising sea level, drought, freshwater shortage, and earthquakes can all necessitate resettlement. The global sea level has risen 0.13 inches a year, nearly twice the rate of just twenty years ago.[3] The extent and thickness of Arctic sea ice has declined rapidly over the past several decades.[4] Displacement adds to the already heavy burden of refugees fleeing their homeland due to conflict.

When we do not care for God's creation well, the results can be devastating for every individual on the planet, but they routinely harm the most vulnerable among us. Ninety-two percent of the world's population live in places where air quality levels fail to meet the World Health Organization's safety limits.[5] Air quality disproportionately affects the poor in urban areas with health problems such as heart disease and severe asthma.[6] Weather extremes lead to mosquito- and tick-borne illnesses that strain health-care systems. The poor do not have as much access to immunizations, mosquito nets, and medicines to protect themselves from these diseases.

I don't throw trash out the window.
—Ruby, age 7

Creation care and consumption are irrevocably linked. The United States creates enormous amounts of e-waste as 5–7 million tons of electronics become obsolete each year.[7] Electronic waste that makes its way into landfills is not like regular trash but is, in fact, toxic waste. Those who dig through the landfills for their livelihood are exposed to toxins such as lead and mercury, which also seep into groundwater and soil and create pollution. The discarded waste is also sorted, stripped, and burned, which releases carcinogens and toxins into the air. Those in poverty often scavenge for their survival and are exposed to the harmful health effects.

Next-Door Concerns

Even in the United States, people face consequences of not caring for God's creation. Vulnerable people groups experience displacement. Conflict emerges when immediate needs are not balanced with long-term vision. The toll of consumption continues to weigh down and stress resources. A Native American tribe in the Louisiana bayou of Isle de Jean Charles has experienced displacement due to the environment. They have lost 98 percent of their land to the Gulf of Mexico.[8] Rising waters will force the remaining residents of the island to relocate farther inland. Land anchors communities to their identity, and losing land is a physical and emotional hardship.

Standing Rock was a historic gathering of Native American tribes and allies seeking to halt the construction of the Dakota Access Pipeline that runs 1,100 miles across the Great Plains. A treaty between the Standing Rock Reservation and the United States government assures the tribe hunting and fishing rights on their reservation land. The tribe won a legal battle in federal court in June 2017.[9] The court ruled that the US Army Corps of Engineers failed to study the environmental consequences of the pipeline. An investigation was ordered to take place before construction can resume. Standing Rock stands as an example of the need for those who care for creation to weigh long-term environmental consequences with development.

According to Worldwatch Institute, the United States makes up just about 5 percent of the world's population but uses nearly a quarter of the world's coal, oil, and natural gas.[10] American society thrives on consumerism, and we need to contemplate its effect on the care of our creation. "Our willingness to part with something before it is completely worn out is a phenomenon noticeable in no other society in history. . . . It is soundly based on our economy of abundance," said J. Gordon Lippincott, an industrial designer.[11] Americans have more material goods than at any other time in history. We live in a culture of disposable coffee cups, food waste, technology upgrades, and fast fashion. Marketing surrounds us and urges us that we need more things and better models of what we already have. In our acquiring and caring for what we own and consume, we lose something of our natural world, both literally and, on a deeper level, in our connection to creation. Consumeristic lifestyles add stress, isolation, work hours, and busyness to our lives.

> **If we didn't have trees, I wouldn't be writing on this paper.**
> **—Nayeli, age 7**

The Great Pacific Garbage Patch spins garbage in two massive oceanic vortexes—one near Japan and one between Hawaii and California. The amount of debris is so vast that it is not easily measurable. I imagine the vortex pool at our local aquatic center and the immense strength it takes to move against the water current. People, including Christians, have done significant damage to the planet, but there are ways to halt and reverse that impact. Can we shape our thoughtless consumption into mindfulness? Is it possible for us to slow down enough to contemplate what we use from God's creation?

Hope

On a personal level, we champion creation care when we weigh our purchases by what is durable, repairable, recyclable, and adaptable. The creator of *The Story of Stuff*, Annie Leonard, encourages those who care for the environment to "replace the culture of consumerism with one of community and civic engagement."[12] There are so many ways to contribute to a creation care mind-set by caring for the resources we have been given. From that mind-set, we can look outward and apply the same principles to our churches, schools, communities, and the greater world.

You can start in your own family by reducing your waste stream and leaving a smaller carbon footprint—the amount of carbon dioxide released into the atmosphere by an individual's activities—through recycling, donating, repairing, and upcycling. You can use reusable bags when shopping and reusable lunch packaging and water bottles. At home, you can adjust thermostats, use CFL or LED light bulbs, and replace old appliances with energy-saving models.

> Climate change is a real thing, and we have to make sure that the problem is better for future generations.
> —Harris, age 13

Kids love to load themselves onto bicycles and cruise the sidewalks and neighborhoods. Try challenges like leaving the car in the garage for a day and only biking. Start small by adding one creation care habit to your daily routine, then add on when you are ready. Think about how much extra you possess and whether anything could be shared or given to someone in need. "Every no impact hour that you live per week cuts your carbon emissions by .6% annually."[13] You can go no impact by eliminating all technology usage, driving, electricity use, and purchasing. Start with an hour and work your way up. See how many no impact hours in a row your family can complete.

In Michigan, when the winter temperature breaks 35 degrees, most kids throw off their winter coats and run for it. Often they refuse boots so they are not hindered in their running, opting for soggy sneakers the rest of the afternoon. Nor is it odd to see people in flip-flops and shorts when springtime brings temperatures up to the low forties. We learn to adapt to our environment. What happens when our resources become utterly depleted, though?

> I use a reusable water bottle.
> —Rylee, age 8

How do we adapt then? In our "now" culture, it's hard to think about the future. Right now there is enough—for us. But many people in our global world face lack, and the time may come when we will too. Citizens in developed nations are not used to facing depleted resources and the challenges that would bring.

Psalm 8:3–4 says, "When I consider your heavens, the work of your fingers, the moon and the stars, which you have set in place, what is mankind that you are mindful of them, human beings that you care for them?" Even though creation amazes our heart and senses, God is still mindful of us.

How can we, in turn, be mindful of what God has gifted us with through creation? The organization Interfaith Power and Light provides resources for faith communities to take the Ecumenical Lenten Carbon Fast. They encourage congregations to fast from carbon as a Lenten discipline. They encourage people of faith to participate in activities like planting trees, riding bikes, sharing rides, and fixing water leaks as a direct connection to their faith as it relates to God's creation.

If we don't care for the planet, we'd have to live on a random planet like Jupiter.
—Micah, age 8

Globally, community-led committees help direct the work of relief agencies by sharing their challenges with changing weather patterns. Communities in Niger face drought, and Concern Worldwide US has distributed drought-resistant millet and cowpea seed to farmers in response. World Renew works with farmers in Mozambique to diversify their crops; then if one crop is ruined by drought or flooding, the farmers might be able to harvest another for their food source or to sell for profit. In Bangladesh, a country dealing with unprecedented flooding, World Renew works with farmers to create floating gardens made from water hyacinth and straw to form a raft.

In the book *The Dream of the Earth*, Thomas Berry writes about how disconnected people have become from nature. That disconnect is especially true in the age of video gaming and electronic devices. He encourages people to get back out into nature and affirm our connection to it. Think about all the unexpected beauty and life you find in nature. I think of a vast concrete lot with a flower emerging out of the tiniest crack. Wherever we make space for life, it will grow.

Trees help us breathe.
—Jayden, age 12

Have you ever knelt by a tree stump and touched the delicate lines that measure decades? A person can learn a great deal about past climates from the patterns that lie within. The wider rings reveal years of warmth and rain; the thinner belong to years that were cold and dry. Tree rings mark history. When you imagine generations into the future, what will the stories of the circular lines reveal? I hope they expose a people that cared enough to protect the gift of creation for the generations to come.

INNOVATION TO EXPLORE

- *Using Design*: The Medebar in Eritrea is a market of recycled objects. Discarded objects most would throw in the trash are converted into usable goods.
- *Using Community Planning*: In Chicago, bike racks filled with Divvy blue bicycles line streets. City dwellers rent a bike and ride it around the city.
- *Using Nature Conservancy*: Portland, Oregon, has 92,000 acres of public green space for people to explore and use.
- *Using Alternative Energy*: Currently, the largest offshore wind farm is the London Array in the Thames Estuary.
- *Using Alternative Energy*: Solar-powered parking meters line the streets of Salt Lake City, Utah.

Appreciate the Diversity of Creation

Deep inside a mountain on the remote island of Svalbard archipelago between Norway and the North Pole lies the Global Seed Vault. One hundred fifty countries adopted the Global Plan of Action, and the idea for the seed vault was born. To protect food security, almost 969,000 seed samples are stored in the vault.[14] Think about how many different pieces of creation that represents. Take an interactive tour at croptrust.org.

TALK JUSTICE

Ages 3–6
What items do you recycle in your home?

_____

_____

_____

Does your school or church recycle?

_____

_____

_____

Where is your favorite place to play outside?

_____

_____

What animals have you discovered in nature?

_____

_____

What is one way you can help your family care for God's creation?

_____

_____

Ages 7–11

What is one thing your family can recycle this week that you haven't thought to recycle before?

_____

How many bags of garbage do you fill each week? How can you reduce that amount?

_____

_____

Is there anything you can reuse or pass on to others who are in need?

_____

_____

What kind of food do you waste most often? How can you eliminate that food waste?

_____

_____

What would you think of being a part of a car-sharing or tool-lending program in your city?

_____

_____

Ages 12+

If we don't care for the environment now, how might our neglect of it affect our future?

_____

_____

What is one more way your family could conserve energy?

_____

_____

How would you present the concept of creation care to your church community?

_____

_____

How is the amount we consume connected to creation care?

_____

_____

Creation care points to God as our creator and the creator of the earth. How then could creation care be a starting point to introducing others to Jesus?

_____

_____

STUDY GOD'S WORD

Psalm 19:1–4

The heavens declare the glory of God; the skies proclaim the work of his hands. Day after day they pour forth speech; night after night they reveal knowledge. They have no speech, they use no words; no sound is heard from them. Yet their voice goes out into all the earth, their words to the ends of the world.

A quiet night sky declares beauty—the pinpricks of far-off starlight, the changing shape of the moon. The works of God's hands proclaim how big he is. Did you know it takes millions of years for the light of distant stars to reach our eyes? There are eighty-eight officially recognized constellations. Astronomers estimate there are one hundred billion different galaxies. The vastness of space exceeds our ability to comprehend its size. And that immense expanse declares the glory of God.

God's creation transcends language and speech. No matter your nationality or location, you can understand God's greatness through nature. God as the Creator is a starting point that people groups from all nations can identify with. God cares for the entire world and all the people in it. In response to God, we can care for his creation.

Extend Study of God's Word

Read Psalm 19:1–4 several times until one word stands out. Write that word below. How might it relate to your study of creation care?

_____

_____

_____

How have you seen God in creation?

_____

_____

_____

Where could you look for God in nature?

_____

_____

_____

Read Deuteronomy 10:14. What does this verse tell us about creation?

_____

_____

_____

Choose an organization that cares for creation that your family or group can pray for:

_____

Choose a specific place or community that needs their creation to be cared for that your family or group can pray for:

_____

_____

> *God, thank you for what you have created all around us. Thank you*
> *for showing us things about yourself through what you've created.*
> *Help us dwell on the word that stood out from Scripture. Guide us in*
> *how to slow down and be thoughtful in what we use. Teach us to live*
> *in a way that takes into account everyone else who shares our planet.*
> *Help us think about our impact and the footprints we leave. Teach us*
> *to thoughtfully care for your gift of creation. Amen.*

EXPLORE JUSTICE

Ages 3–6

Read: *Let the Whole Earth Sing Praise* by Tomie dePaola

Using Old Testament Scripture and artwork from Puebla, Mexico, readers learn to sing praise and give thanks to God's for his good creation.

Connection—Readers think about the connection between creation and God.

Read: *Seeds of Change* by Jen Cullerton Johnson

A picture biography of Wangari Maathai of Kenya, winner of the 2004 Nobel Peace Prize, who promoted the right of education and saved the environment, one tree at a time.

Connection—Learn about a woman who made a huge difference through creation care.

Read: *The Tree Lady* by H. Joseph Hopkins

Katherine Sessions started a green movement in San Diego, California. A true story of how one person changed a city forever.

Connection—Readers are inspired to make a difference and given an example of someone who fought against adversity.

Read: *I Imagine* by Rachel Rivett
This picture book connects emotions children experience and prayers they pray with God's creation.

Connection—Children learn prayers that relate to God's creation.

Read: *All About God's Animals: Colors* by Janyre Tromp
God's creation is witnessed in the variety of colors God used to make animals.

Also read: *All About God's Animals: Around the Water* **by Janyre Tromp.**

Connection—Little readers begin to connect God's creation with beauty.

Observe: Nature Scavenger Hunt
Gather supplies: Nature Scavenger Hunt printable (find it at lisavanengen .com) and pencils.
- Break participants up into small groups. This is a great opportunity to pair older kids with younger ones.
- Provide each group with a Nature Scavenger Hunt printable and a pencil.
- Give participants ten minutes to search for items listed on the printable.
- Have participants mark off the nature items they find.
- Come back together and share about their discoveries.

Read Psalm 24:1: "The earth is the LORD's, and everything in it, the world, and all who live in it."

Connection—Learn about nature in the specific place where we live.

Create: Nature Painting
Gather supplies: white paper, natural "paintbrushes" (e.g., stick with leaves

attached to the end, pine cones, feathers, flowers, long blades of grass), paints.

- Give students freedom to create art with supplies from nature.

Connection—Children express themselves through art with natural materials. Encourage them to display and share their creations with others.

The Jesus Storybook Bible by Sally Lloyd-Jones is a wonderful resource for little readers.

Play: Noah's Ark
Set up free play at a table or on a blanket on the ground or floor. Ask participants to bring toys related to the ark and the animals that were a part of the story. Share the story of Noah's ark.

Connection—Learn about the Bible story of Noah's ark, God's care for us, and creation through play.

Create: Leaf Necklaces
Gather supplies: leaves of various types, string, small stick.
- Tie the string to one end of the stick, and use the stick as a needle.
- Kids can thread the string through the leaves to make a leaf necklace.

Connection—Kids connect with nature while practicing fine motor skills.

Observe: Bug Hotel
Gather supplies: rectangular box, natural materials (e.g., twigs, leaves, pine cones).
- Gather a rectangular box and fill it with natural materials.
- Set the box in a backyard or an outdoor area.
- Watch for bugs to take up residence.

Connection—Kids observe nature up close.

Ages 7–11
Read: *Planet Ark* by Adrienne Mason
Planet Ark shows readers how to care for the environment and preserve the world's biodiversity by making small changes.

Connection—Children can make connections about the diversity of the earth and our ability to conserve and protect it.

Read: *Tree of Life: The Incredible Biodiversity of Life on Earth* by Rochelle Strauss
This book introduces the biodiversity of the planet and the five kingdom classifications. Perfect for science-loving kids.

Connection—Children learn about the complexity of living species on earth.

Read: *The Boy Who Harnessed the Wind* by William Kamkwamba
When his village and family experienced drought, William was determined to build a windmill to harness electricity and water. Using junkyard scraps, he succeeded in bringing water to his village.

Connection—Children learn that no matter how young they are or what obstacles they face, they can still make a difference.

Read: *One Plastic Bag: Isatou Ceesay and the Recycling Women of the Gambia* by Miranda Paul
Details how a group of women in Gambia tackled an overabundance of plastic bags through income-bearing upcycling.

Connection—Children learn how creativity and community can help solve problems.

Observe: Art
Study the painting *Looking Down the Yosemite Valley, California*, by Albert Bierstadt.

Connection—Kids contemplate the beauty of creation.

Gather: Field Trip
Gather a group and visit a nature area in your community. Use the website Nature Find (naturefind.com) to locate options in your geographic location. A planetarium is also a great field trip to ponder creation in space.

Connection—Students learn about nature areas that are close to where they live. Talk about features that are unique to your area.

Gather: Cloud Watching
Lie down on the grass and let the clouds roll by.
- Talk about the shapes of things you see in the clouds. Talk about what kinds of clouds you are looking at: stratus, cumulus, cirrus, and so on.
- Visit the National Weather Service (weather.gov) and search for the ten basic cloud types.

Connection—Kids contemplate the beauty of creation and that God brought great diversity to something as simple as clouds.

Create: Reusable Shopping Bag
Gather supplies: reusable canvas shopping bags, fabric paint, paintbrushes.
- Give each student a reusable canvas shopping bag and access to fabric paint and paintbrushes.
- Provide students with ideas for decorating the bags, such as a recycle sign, a tree, or a nature scene.
- Consider adding a message such as "Save trees," "Care for creation," "Conserve," or a verse such as Job 12:10: "In his hand is the life of every creature and the breath of all mankind."

Connection—Students design their reusable bags to use when shopping or to give as a gift to others. Consider donating some handmade shopping bags to a local food pantry.

Ages 12+
Read: *Same Sun Here* by Silas House
River, in Kentucky, and Meena, in Chinatown of New York City, become pen pals. River shares about his experiences with mountaintop removal in his community. Meena writes about her undocumented immigrant status.

Connection—Readers experience intercultural friendship and environmental activism.

Read: *It's Easy Being Green: A Guide to Serving God and Saving the Planet* by Emma Sleeth

In *It's Easy Being Green*, Emma Sleeth explores the theology behind creation care and encourages young people to protect the creation God gave us.

Connection—Students learn about God-centered environmentalism and the justice issue of creation care.

Create: Writing

Gather supplies: paper, pens and pencils.

- Prompt: The biggest change I can make to help the environment is . . .

Connection—Writers explore practical ways they can implement changes in their habits that would benefit the environment.

Connect: Photo Booth

Gather supplies: backdrop for the photo booth (e.g., a wall, colored paper, fabric, balloons, lights, or natural outdoor elements), poster board, markers.

- Create a backdrop for your photo booth. An 8' x 10' backdrop is a good starting point to photograph groups.
- Using the poster board and markers, students can create signs for props. Some ideas: #gogreen, hold up a globe, recycle sign, handful of seeds, #cleanenergy, #climateaction, #endangered, #greenliving, #recycle, #reuse, #sustainable, #actonclimate, #optoutside.
- Encourage young people to share their photo booth pictures on social media.

Find photo booth ideas for all the justice issues in the book at lisavanengen .com.

Connection—Raise awareness about creation care through advocacy.

Create: Upcycled Art Contest

Host an upcycled art contest or art show. Anything entered must be made entirely with upcycled materials. Display the works of art and invite others to see what can be made from upcycled goods.

Connection—Students experience upcycling firsthand and use their creativity to make new things. Sharing their work can help educate the community about upcycling.

Create: Newscast
Gather supplies: paper, pens and pencils, video recording device.
- Gather a group of friends to write a script and tape a newscast about creation care.
- Share facts, find people to interview, and consider on-the-spot reporting. Participants can take on different roles such as writer, editor, anchor, reporter, interviewee, camera operator, producer, or director.
- If all participants agree, share the video on social media.

Connection—Participants focus on one aspect of creation care and work with a team to make its importance something newsworthy and worthwhile to share with others.

Connect: E-Waste Recycling
Organize a community event like a big game of capture the flag, a free-throw contest, or a pickleball tournament. Before the event, organize Recycle It Right information to educate participants on how to recycle electronics in your area. Get started at electronicstakeback.com/how-to-recycle-electronics.

Read Nehemiah 9:6: "You alone are the LORD. You made the heavens, even the highest heavens, and all their starry host, the earth and all that is on it, the seas and all that is in them. You give life to everything."

Connection—Students encourage the community to recycle e-waste, educate them on ways to do so, and foster community through a shared event.

Study: Biodiversity of Rain Forests
Study the unique species of plants and animals of tropical rain forests. Research why they are home to such great biodiversity. Consider how amazing it is that God gave life to so many different creatures and such a huge variety of plants. Learn why biodiversity strengthens the environment.

Connection—Students appreciate the creativity of God, the complexity of creation, and the fact that God gives life to it all.

Gather: Thrift Store Fashion Show
Challenge participants to put together an entire outfit from clothing found at any thrift store, such as Goodwill. (Make sure you give them a spending limit.) Set up a runway and invite others to see the final creations. Consider giving audience members action steps to upcycling their belongings.

Connection—Participants learn about upcycling in fashion.

CHALLENGE AND EXTEND AWARENESS AT HOME

- Read "30 Mealtime Facts for Creation Care," found at lisavanengen .com.
- Practice "30 Days of Prayer for Creation Care," found at lisavanengen .com.
- Visit a local greenhouse, recycling center, community garden, or farmers market.
- Plant a tree seedling somewhere in your yard and read the creation story in Genesis 1.
- Add one new item to recycle in your home, such as your batteries and light bulbs at any Batteries Plus Bulbs (batteriesplus.com) location or old sneakers at Nike Reuse-A-Shoe at any Nike or Converse retail store.
- Watch a video from *The Story of Stuff* at storyofstuff.org.
- Earn points together from RecycleBank while learning great facts about the environment (recyclebank.com).
- Snuggle in for an earth-themed movie night. Suggested films: *March of the Penguins, FernGully, Wall-E, Whale Rider, Happy Feet, Hoot, The Lion King, The Lorax,* or *Arctic Tale.*
- Work through the Energy Star Kids interactive website (energystar .gov) to see how you can lower your energy consumption. Play Recycle City to learn new ways your community can recycle at www.epa.gov /recyclecity.

- Find numerous resources at Interfaith Power and Light (interfaithpower andlight.org).

Some people, in order to discover God, read books. But there is a book: the very appearance of created things. Look about you! Look below you! Note it. Read it. God, whom you want to discover, never wrote that book with ink. Instead he set before your eyes the things that he had made. Can you ask for a louder voice than that?

—Augustine of Hippo, bishop and theologian

MAKING A DIFFERENCE

- Through World Renew, purchase vegetable seedlings for families to grow in Malawi (worldrenew.net).
- Go to a local park, playground, or beach with a garbage bag and pick up trash.
- Plant trees through the Eden Reforestation Projects (edenprojects.org).
- Support a village through Plant with Purpose (plantwithpurpose.org).
- Give the gift of tree seedlings to a family through Heifer International (heifer.org).
- Do you have teens? Get involved in the many projects of Turning Green.
- Calculate your church congregation's carbon footprint at Cool Congregations.
- Purchase carbon offsets through Trees of Hope Project in Malawi (clintonfoundation.org).
- Take an interactive tour of the Svalbard Global Seed Vault (croptrust .org).
- Learn how Thread uses plastic bottles to make fabric (threadinter national.com).

For direct links to any of these resources plus additional materials, go to lisavanengen.com and click the And Social Justice for All tab.

Local Ideas

- _____
- _____
- _____
- _____
- _____

Disabilities: A Place for Everyone

I am conscious of a soul-sense that lifts me above the narrow, cramping circumstances of my life. My physical limitations are forgotten—my world lies upward, the length and the breadth and the sweep of the heavens are mine!

—HELEN KELLER, AUTHOR, ACTIVIST, AND LECTURER

Raise Awareness

January—National Braille Literacy Month
March—National Cerebral Palsy Awareness Month
March—National Developmental Disability Awareness Month
March 1—International Wheelchair Day
March 21—World Down Syndrome Day
April 2—World Autism Awareness Day
May—Better Hearing and Speech Month
May—National Mental Health Month
June 16—Disability Awareness Day
August (begins the first Sunday)—International Assistance Dog Week
September 10—World Suicide Prevention Day

October—National Disability Employment Awareness Month
October (second Sunday)—Disability Awareness Sunday
October (second Thursday)—World Sight Day
October 10—World Mental Health Day
December 3—International Day of Persons with Disabilities

An elderly woman sits on a white plastic lawn chair perched on the rusting frame of a used and aging wheelchair. A young man with a missing limb leans on one metal and one plastic crutch, uneven in height. According to the World Health Organization, over a billion people live with some form of disability. In the United States alone, 56.7 million people have a disability.[1] An estimated 90 percent of children with disabilities in developing countries do not go to school.[2]

Being in proximity to disability opens up understanding and empathy. A fourth-grade class had that experience in 2017 when they visited ArtPrize. Every fall, Grand Rapids, Michigan, hosts an art contest across the city at various venues. The competition has grown into one of the best-attended public art events in the world. When my son's class went on a field trip to see some exhibits, they fell in love with *Dot Nation*. The entry by Brian Delozier was a 2-D pointillism mural made one dot at a time, using 7.3 million dots altogether.[3] When Brian was a teenager he was paralyzed from the neck down in a skiing accident. He has regained some mobility and now walks with forearm crutches.

When the fourth graders visited the exhibit, they saw a video clip of Brian and how he created the art piece. The art teacher learned that the artist was in Grand Rapids for ArtPrize and invited him to visit the fourth graders at our school. He graciously agreed to come, and the kids received him like a genuine rock star. They cheered, hugged him, and told him how much he had inspired them. I'm pretty sure being in proximity to him has changed their lives forever. They will not view disability the same again.

Understanding the Issue
Disabilities occur in three different forms: cognitive, emotional, and physical. Throughout a lifetime, illness, injury, or aging can lead to disability, or a disability can occur before or during birth. Disabilities take on various

forms. They can be long- or short-term, invisible or visible to others, and static, episodic, or degenerative. We build empathy for those who experience disability by understanding the challenges they face and the adaptations they make in their daily lives. The high monetary cost and time constraints those adaptations require also help us look at disability through a different lens. Disability requires additional costs to achieve an equal standard of living. Discrimination against those with disabilities often means reduced participation and access to community.

Help your children imagine having a physical disability and managing everyday tasks. How do you climb stairs with leg and arm braces? What about navigating a wheelchair through the slushy mess of melting snow? School lunchrooms burst with competing voices; imagine trying to listen to your friends when you have a hearing impairment. How do you navigate the world with impaired sight? Can you imagine visiting the school nurse four times a day for blood sugar checks and insulin adjustments? What about having to stop and use your inhaler during your favorite game in gym class?

When people have physical disabilities, they often need adaptive equipment to assist them. They might need a wheelchair, a leg or arm brace, a ramp, prosthetic limbs, or a soft shell helmet. Homes and buildings are adapted with automatic door openers, elevators, or ramps. With the right adaptive equipment, people with wheelchairs can even drive vehicles. When children learn about adaptive equipment, they better understand how important it is to the people who use it.

Many individuals who are deaf use sign language to communicate. They might attend a school specifically for children with hearing impairments. They could use a vibrating alarm clock or watch to be alerted to critical times of the day. A smoke detector in the home of someone who is hard of hearing might feature a flashing light along with sound when it goes off. They may use closed captioning on television programs.

We should treat others with love, not make them feel uncomfortable or unwanted. We should treat everybody equally.
—Rebecca, age 13

People with visual impairments might use books or games in Braille, magnifiers to see a computer screen, or voice recognition.

If you look at public signs, you will often spot a line of Braille beneath the printed words.

Cognitive disabilities encompass challenges people have with mental tasks of varying complexity. Classmates with dyslexia have difficulty reading and interpreting letters. Speaking with clarity is difficult for those with speech impediments. Paying attention and controlling responses is challenging for kids with attention deficit disorder. Individuals with autism may have difficulty communicating and forming relationships. Kids with Asperger's have challenges similar to those with autism but differ in that they usually have a higher IQ and greater speech ability. People with Down syndrome have extra genetic material that typically causes growth delays, characteristic facial features, and mild to moderate intellectual disability.

> I care about making sure my friends don't get teased.
> —Abigail, age 11

Mental health disabilities are harder to detect, can be irregular, easier to hide, and often carry stigma. Kids with depression can feel very sad for a period of time or all the time. Anxiety can make someone feel uncomfortable and they do not even know why. Kids with obsessive-compulsive disorder feel the need to do certain things over and over again, like washing their hands. Anorexia causes people to control their weight by not eating. People with bulimia eat a lot of food and then throw up to control their weight. Kids who self-harm do so believing it will release bad feelings. Understanding various physical, cognitive, and mental health disabilities helps children engage others with empathy.

Global Concerns

Disability challenges in the developing world are made even more difficult due to misinformation. In India, the BBC World Service Trust and two Indian broadcasting networks developed a sixteen-month campaign to teach viewers and listeners that leprosy is not caused by bad deeds in a previous life nor spread by touch. In Uganda, Action on Disability and Development International works to destigmatize albinism. The myth that people born with albinism are demons or are cursed makes living with the condition challenging. People who live with a disability can end up in isolation due to stigma. Children with a disability can be institutionalized, never to leave.

When children grow up in poverty and experience malnutrition and poor health, they are at risk of developing a disability. People in poverty may also work in environments that are unhealthy or high risk, resulting in disability. Being disabled makes it hard to break free from poverty. Not only is employment harder to obtain but the cost of living is higher when you need expensive medical care. The World Health Organization's Global Disability Action Plan for 2014–2021 states, "Disability is a development priority because of its higher prevalence in lower-income countries and because disability and poverty reinforce and perpetuate one another."[4]

Nations and cities in conflict prove difficult for people with disabilities, as they cannot always access the care they need. The insecurity and lack of protection they experience can lead to long-term mental health needs. Depression is a common secondary condition of people with disabilities and often a primary condition for those who have experienced trauma. Human Rights Watch reports a staff member of Médecins Sans Frontières (Doctors Without Borders) in Greece saying, "There is a lack of resources, time, and expertise dedicated to the identification of vulnerable people."[5] When people with disability are forgotten, gaining access to care and resources becomes increasingly difficult. When natural disasters and quick evacuations occur, if plans are not in place for the disabled, their lives become further endangered.

Globally there is a lack of access to rehabilitation centers and assistive technology devices that would raise the standard of living for people with disabilities. Public transportation can also make a huge difference in the life of the disabled, but many areas worldwide lack this option of mobility. And public transportation is not the only need. Infrastructure such as ramps, smooth sidewalks, and curb cuts to support adaptive equipment also makes a positive difference. Access makes all the difference for helping people with disabilities experience a full life.

Next-Door Concerns

In the United States, an area of improvement for children with disabilities is in the classroom. "In public schools today, children with disabilities are far

I feel that no matter if you are different, we could still be friends.
—Dalton, age 13

more likely than their classmates to be disciplined, removed from the classroom, suspended, or even expelled."[6] Schools that focus on positive behavior interventions, tiered assistance, and multilevel support better meet the needs of children with disabilities. When teachers, administrators, students, and parents are educated on particular disabilities and their impacts, that understanding leads to demonstrably stronger outcomes for children.

Parents can help children realize that having a disability or having a family member with a disability can be isolating. Children with disabilities might not always receive a birthday party invitation or a playdate offer. As a family, take time to be inviting. It may take an extra phone call to double-check how you can be the most accommodating, but that little effort makes such a difference. Everyone has a need to feel like they belong and have caring friendships. Family members who are primary caregivers to someone with a disability can experience fatigue. Consider offering respite through babysitting, doing household chores, or running errands.

Providing accessibility can be expensive for families. Imagine changing your home to accommodate a wheelchair, and think of the costs related to each of those changes. On a larger scale, imagine those changes needing to take place in a bigger infrastructure like a school or an office building. In developing countries, those resources might not be easily accessible. Think about how much children and families enjoy playgrounds. Are the playgrounds in your area accessible to those with disabilities? Mayor Thomas M. Menino Park in Charlestown, Massachusetts, was envisioned after the Boston Marathon bombing. If you visit the park, you will find horizontal bars at all heights, a roller table for those with autism, sensory-rich activities, and full support swings.[7] Something as small as being thoughtful and intentional about the needs of the disabled in your communities makes a huge difference.

Everyone is different and you can't be nervous around everyone. Even siblings are different from each other.
—Harris, age 13

Hope

Move through the pages of history to find contributions those with disabilities have made not only to the fabric of our culture but also to inspire others to overcome barriers. Did you know Wolfgang Amadeus Mozart and Albert Einstein are thought to have been on the autism spectrum? Mystery novelist Agatha Christie and magic maker Walt Disney had dyslexia and struggled with reading. Former Prime Minister of England Winston Churchill and President Theodore Roosevelt both had speech impairments. Artist Claude Monet and civil rights activist Harriet Tubman were visually impaired. Scientist Isaac Newton, author Virginia Woolf, and artist Vincent van Gogh all struggled with depression.

Meet August Pullman in *Wonder*, Melody in *Out of My Mind*, and Ally in *Fish in a Tree*, characters in literature being read in classrooms all over the country. Students find themselves invited into the hearts of young people with a facial deformity, a learning disability, and a physical disability. The empathy that develops shapes our perspective. Young people see the commonalities between themselves and children with disabilities. They understand that there is a deeper resilience, hope, and strength in those who struggle. Bullying or making fun of someone with a disability loses its attraction when you understand all that has been experienced and felt. The reader is left in wonder of what those with disabilities accomplish, overcome, and offer.

Organizations that work to provide hope and access for those with disabilities focus on accessibility, affordability, availability, and quality. Another way to make a difference is to meet the needs of caregivers with respite services. Nonprofits that ask people with disabilities to be a part of their development process find they have unique insight into problem solving. Action on Disability and Development International's work in western Uganda has developed four rainbow drama groups using actors from diverse ethnic backgrounds and those with a disability to promote living in peace with one another. People living with disability often have unique perspectives on how to best meet their needs. They often offer excellent responses as to how they can give back as well.

What would be more delightful to a child than a single balloon tied to a wrist or even a bouquet of balloons? How about a thousand, like Carl Fredricksen tied to his home in the movie *Up*? A balloon filled with helium lifts upward. Drawing near to those with disability gives us hope that is higher than if we were only standing alone. Being in proximity to, and being exposed to, disability makes our own lives deeper. Disability Services of the Reformed and Christian Reformed Church states, "Everybody belongs, everybody serves."[8]

INNOVATION TO EXPLORE

- *Using Technology and Design*: At Tikkun Olam Makers (also known as TOM Global), a person with a disability and an unmet need are matched with an expert in a Makeathon. The expert then works to create a solution. Technology opens up new doors for those with disabilities.
- *Using Technology*: An article by Scientific American describes a tablet-size, renewable Braille display using a new technology called piezo-electric ceramic actuators.[9] Talk about the promise of technological advances!
- *Using Robotics*: The DEKA arm is a "mind-controlled" robotic prosthetic that can move multiple joints.[10]
- *Building Community*: At Western Seminary in Holland, Michigan, the Friendship House is an apartment complex where groups of students are paired with young adults with cognitive impairments to live in community.
- *Building Community*: Also in Holland, Michigan, Benjamin's Hope is a place where adults with intellectual and developmental differences live together in an intentional community of work, worship, and play. Members of the community worship with residents on Sunday evenings.

Appreciate Special Olympics

In July 2018, Special Olympics celebrated fifty years of inclusion. They support 5.7 million athletes in 172 countries. Learn more about the history of the Special Olympics at specialolympics.org/50th.aspx.

TALK JUSTICE

Ages 3–6

What is something special about you? Do you think kids who act and look different from you have something special about them too?

_____

_____

Have you ever seen a service dog? What did you think about the job it does?

_____

_____

Do you know someone who uses a wheelchair, walker, or cane? What challenges might they face?

_____

_____

Have you ever seen someone communicate with sign language? We all use hand signs sometimes. What signs do you use?

_____

_____

Does your school or church have more than one floor? Do they offer an elevator? Why are elevators important?

_____

_____

Ages 7–11

How could you adapt games on the playground for kids with disabilities?

_____

_____

When someone you know has a disability, how does that make you feel?

_____

_____

How would you feel if everyone only called you the "brown-haired kid"? Is that the only thing that defines you? Do labels describe a whole person?

_____

_____

_____

How could you demonstrate acceptance to someone with a disability?

_____

_____

_____

In what ways could you be a friend to someone in your life with a disability?

_____

_____

_____

Ages 12+

Do we all learn differently? What subjects do you find most challenging?

_____

_____

What are the obstacles someone with a hidden disability might face?

_____

_____

What might someone with a physical disability need at school or at church to adapt to the environment?

_____

_____

Describe what happens when people with disabilities are accepted for who they are—individuals who were wonderfully and beautifully made in the image of God.

_____

_____

Given unlimited resources, how would you make life easier for those with disabilities?

_____

_____

STUDY GOD'S WORD

1 Corinthians 12:12
Just as a body, though one, has many parts, but all its many parts form one body, so it is with Christ.

What are the individual parts of your body? You have arms, hands, legs, feet, ears, a nose, mouth, and eyes, to name a few. Each of these parts of your body has a specific job to do. Think about just one of those body parts. The human anatomy of an eye has twenty individual parts, such as its cornea, optic nerve, and a medial rectus muscle. All those tiny parts work together for the eye to function with the rest of your body. And that's just one part of your body!

God's body is made up of each one of us. Every believer is part of the body of Christ. He designed us all to love others in this world. No one could do the work he has specifically set apart for you. We are all exceptionally unique and special, people with differing abilities. We live in a vast and beautiful world designed for all of us to have a role and a unique part to play. Have you thought about the role God might have for you?

Extend Study of God's Word
Talk to God about 1 Corinthians 12:12. Then rewrite the verse in your own words.

_____

_____

_____

_____

_____

_____

When you attend church, how could you help everyone feel like they belong, despite whether anyone has visible and invisible disabilities?

_____

_____

_____

What gifts has God given you that you could use to love others?

_____

_____

_____

How are the gifts God has given people with disabilities the same or different from people without disabilities?

_____

_____

_____

Choose an organization that supports individuals with disabilities that your family or group can pray for:

_____

_____

Choose a specific community of individuals with disabilities that your family or group can pray for:

_____

_____

God, thank you for the gifts we all bring to the world. Please be near to those with disabilities and their caregivers. Help us know how to be the body of Christ by celebrating our strengths and holding each other in our weaknesses. Teach us to slow down enough to be welcoming and make space for those with disabilities. Show us how to widen access to those with disabilities in our lives. Help us to live in community with each other. Amen.

EXPLORE JUSTICE

Ages 3–6

Read: *The Black Book of Colors* by Menena Cottin

Using raised lines and descriptive imagery, readers are invited to imagine living life without sight.

Connection—Students experience the world as a person with a visual impairment might.

Read: *Wilma Unlimited: How Wilma Rudolph Became the World's Fastest Woman* by Kathleen Krull

At age five, polio left Wilma Rudolph with a paralyzed leg. She was told she would never walk again. But Wilma went on to win four Olympic medals in track and field—and three of them were gold!

Connection—Students are encouraged by the story of someone with a disability who persevered and accomplished a great dream.

Read: *Emmanuel's Dream: The True Story of Emmanuel Ofosu Yeboah* by Laurie Ann Thompson

Born with a deformed leg, Emmanuel overcame his disability and eventually rode four hundred miles across Ghana as a cyclist. His message: disability is not inability.

Connection—Readers learn about someone who overcame disability and continues to advocate on behalf of the disabled.

Read: *We're All Wonders* by R. J. Palacio

Along with his dog, Daisy, Auggie Pullman, a boy with a facial deformity, embraces who he is as a person—in picture-book form.

Connection—Readers are encouraged to embrace their own uniqueness and the wonder of others' differences.

Explore: Braille

Gather supplies: Provide children with various items someone who is blind might use, like a Braille book, a Braille ruler, Braille playing cards, Braille dice, a soccer ball with bells inside, Braille measuring spoon set, tactile chess set, or a letter-writing guide.

• Allow children space to explore and try out the items.

Connection—Children experience what it feels like to use products specifically designed for those who cannot see.

Ages 7–11

Read: *Thank You, Mr. Falker* by Patricia Polacco

Mr. Falker, a thoughtful and perceptive teacher, helps Trisha with her dyslexia. This story is based on author Patricia Polacco's childhood.

Connection—Students learn to be sensitive to those with reading disabilities and the specific challenges they face in a school environment.

You can view all of Dorothea Lange's Great Depression photography at historyplace.com /unitedstates/lange.

Read: *Dorothea's Eyes: Dorothea Lange Photographs the Truth* by Barb Rosenstock

Dorothea Lange, left with a limp after having polio as a child, wished for nothing more than to slip into the background and observe others. She went on to become a famous documentary photographer of the Great Depression.

Connection—Students learn that a disability can give people a different outlook on life and make a difference for others.

Read: *El Deafo* by Cece Bell

This graphic novel chronicles the journey of Cece trying to fit in at school while wearing her bulky Phonic Ear to correct hearing loss.

Connection—Students build empathy for those who experience hearing loss.

Read: *My Brother Charlie* by Holly Robinson Peete and Ryan Elizabeth Peete
Callie navigates life with her brother Charlie, who has autism.

Connection—Loving insights from a sibling's point of view on disability.

Read: *Rules* by Cynthia Lord
Catherine wants a normal life, but it's difficult when her family's world revolves around her brother, who has autism.

Connection—Readers learn to ask the question, What is "normal"?

Read: *Six Dots: A Story of Young Louis Braille* by Jen Bryant
A picture-book biography of Louis Braille, the teen who invented the Braille alphabet system that is still used today by the blind community.

Connection—Readers experience the gifts those with disabilities offer and how those gifts can sometimes be uniquely attuned to what others need for a better life.

Try writing part of Rose's story from the perspective of another character, like her dad or Rain.

Read: *Rain Reign* by Ann M. Martin
Rose, who has OCD and Asperger's, must navigate finding her lost dog, Rain, and a tumultuous relationship with her father.

Connection—Rose's voice will draw you into what it means to have a disability and show you a unique perspective of the world.

Read: *The War That Saved My Life* by Kimberly Brubaker Bradley
Ada spent the first ten years of her life hidden away because of a twisted foot. When she evacuates from London with her brother during World War II, she has much to overcome.

Connection—Readers identify with a character who has a disability yet is not defined by that challenge alone.

Create: Writing
Gather supplies: paper, pens and pencils.

- Prompt: A disability can be a strength when . . .

Connection—Writers think about the strengths people with disabilities possess.

Play: LEGO Challenge
Gather supplies: bin of LEGOs, blindfolds.

- Provide students with a bin of LEGOs.
- Encourage them to build a tower with a blindfold on.

Find LEGO challenges for other topics at lisavanengen .com.

Connection—Builders use senses other than sight. What was difficult about building without sight? What was easier than you imagined?

Play: Painting Challenge
Gather supplies: canvases, paints, smocks, cups of water, "challenge" items such as blindfolds, mittens, or illegible directions.

- Supply students with canvas, paints, smocks, and water.
- Encourage them to paint a picture, but before you begin, give each student a challenge. Examples might be using no arms, painting blindfolded, wearing mittens, or being given written directions they cannot read.
- After giving them time to paint with their challenge, have them come together to share their work.
- Talk about their experiences.

Connection—Students create art with a simulated physical or cognitive impairment. Encourage them to think about what it might be like to be blind, cognitively impaired, or without limbs.

Play: Board Games in Silence
Gather supplies: various board games.

- Pick a board game to play with a group.
- Explain to the students that when you play, no one is allowed to talk, only to use hand gestures.
- At the conclusion of the game, discuss what felt harder and easier about not having a voice.

Connection—Remind students that those with disabilities often feel that their voice is not heard. In what ways could we help magnify their voices?

Ages 12+

Read: *Wonder* by R. J. Palacio
August Pullman is entering school for the first time as a fifth grader. Being the new kid is hard, but being a new kid with a facial deformity is even harder.

Read additional Wonder books: *Auggie and Me: Three Wonder Stories* **and** *365 Days of Wonder: Mr. Browne's Precepts.*

Connection—Helps children understand disability from multiple perspectives: a child with a disability, his family, friends, classmates, and even the school bully.

Read: *Fish in a Tree* by Lynda Mullaly Hunt
Ally, who has dyslexia, learns that everyone is more than a label . . . including herself.

Connection—Readers learn about the power of friendship, the influence of teachers, and the perspective of someone with a learning disability.

Read: *Out of My Mind* by Sharon M. Draper
Because she can't walk, talk, or write, everyone assumes eleven-year-old Melody is mentally challenged—but she's determined to make the truth known.

Connection—Readers are challenged to think about life with a disability, encouraged to know how alike all people are, and shown how powerful friendship can be.

Read: *Soul Surfer* by Bethany Hamilton
Internationally ranked surfer Bethany Hamilton lost her arm in a shark attack. This is the true story of her courage and faith after the accident.

Connection—Readers can see how people with disabilities defy expectations, adapt, and conquer dreams.

Read: *Paperboy* by Vince Vawter
A Newbery Honor book that follows the story of Little Man, who throws a mean fastball but whose stutter makes speaking a whole different ballgame.

Connection—Readers will build empathy for those with speech impairments.

Create: Writing
Gather supplies: paper, pens and pencils.
- Prompt: I can choose to be kind at home, at school, in my neighborhood, at practice, at church, by . . .

Connection—Encourage students to think about how they would choose kindness wherever they may be.

Create: YouTube Video
Gather supplies: phone or camera for video recording.
- Gather a group of friends and create a short video for YouTube that encourages peers to "Choose Kind." (The idea of "Choose Kind" is taught in R. J. Palacio's book *Wonder*.) Use visual images, stories, and music to pull the message together.

Connection—Students define what "Choose Kind" means to them and practice making their message clear to viewers.

Gather: Outdoor Movie Screening
Gather supplies: outdoor movie screen; equipment to play the movie *Soul Surfer*; beach-theme decorations such as beach blankets, surf boards, beach

balls; beach-themed snacks such as surfboard cupcakes and pool-noodle licorice.

- Decorate for your beach-themed party.
- Gather friends for an outdoor movie screening featuring the movie *Soul Surfer* and some yummy snacks.

Connection—After the movie, discuss how Bethany overcame challenges after her accident.

Gather: Blood Drive

Gather supplies: download a Blood Drive Coordinator Toolkit from the Red Cross (redcrossblood.org).

- Host a Red Cross blood drive at your school or church. Work with the Red Cross to support your community.

Connection—Students gain skills in organizing an event that strengthens health care in their community. Donors contribute lifesaving blood for those in need.

CHALLENGE AND EXTEND AWARENESS AT HOME

- Read "30 Mealtime Facts about Disabilities," found at lisavanengen.com.
- Practice "30 Days of Prayer for Disabilities," found at lisavanengen.com.
- Sign the #ChooseKind Pledge on Tumblr (choosekind.tumblr.com).
- Watch disability clips from Sesame Street together at autism.sesame street.org/videos/kids.
- Schedule a playdate for your child to meet with a friend who has a disability.
- Learn about the work of Paws with a Cause (pawswithacause.org) and what working dogs do.
- Go to YouTube and watch Plan International's "Listen Up! Children with Disabilities Speak Out," a video about global disability.
- Learn about adapted sports and people who compete in them from Disabled Sports USA (disabledsportsusa.org).

- On Vimeo, watch the video "Voices of Children ISL AD" from UNICEF Disability Unit.
- Share the Sibling Support Project with siblings who have disabled brothers and sisters (siblingsupport.org).

I am different, not less.

—TEMPLE GRANDIN, PROFESSOR OF ANIMAL SCIENCE AND AUTISM SPECIALIST

MAKING A DIFFERENCE

- Support PACER's National Bullying Prevention Center (pacer.org).
- Support the Children's Craniofacial Association (ccakids.org).
- Support your local chapter of Special Olympics.
- Access a disability checklist for your church from the Americans with Disabilities Act at adachecklist.org.
- Support global children with disabilities through World Vision (donate .worldvision.org).
- Support Solar Ear, Vision Spring, or Wheelchairs of Hope, providing affordable devices to children in the developing world.
- Get involved in planning an Easterseals Walk with Me event to support families with disabilities in your community (easterseals.com).
- Familiarize yourself with the helpful resources from the Center for Parent Information and Resources (parentcenterhub.org).
- Read about the What If Challenge from Google Impact Challenge. What ideas do you have?
- Check out the inspiring artwork of Brian Delozier at Brian's Dots (briansdots.com).

For direct links to any of these resources plus additional materials, go to lisavanengen.com and click the And Social Justice for All tab.

Local Ideas

- _____
- _____
- _____
- _____
- _____

Education: Summoning the Best of Us

I raise up my voice—not so that I can shout, but so that those without a voice can be heard.

—MALALA YOUSAFZAI, NOBEL PEACE PRIZE LAUREATE

Raise Awareness

January—National Mentoring Month
March 2—Read Across America
May (first full week)—Teacher Appreciation Week
June 6—National Higher Education Day
August 9—National Book Lovers Day
September 8—International Literacy Day
October (first Wednesday)—National Walk to School Day
October 5—World Teachers' Day
October 11—International Day of the Girl
November (third Thursday)—National Parental Involvement Day

A popular destination for young children at preschool is the play dough table. They love to shape and mold the dough into creatures, cookies, and anything silly. Vivid colors remain temporary as they mix the dough into blended creations. Just like children form play dough, education has the power to shape lives. An education offers children hope for their future. Schools promote peace by teaching vital skills in communication within our local and global communities. Education builds on children's strengths and allows their natural gifts and aptitudes to grow and their hearts to be encouraged.

I first read Jonathan Kozol's book *Savage Inequalities* while in college. Kozol gathered data from 1988 through 1990 to show the sharp contrast in resources between poor school districts and their wealthy neighbors. The inequality, as the title suggests, can be described as savage, especially when considering the physical proximity between the schools. What Kozol documented was profound, and that data only covered school districts in the United States. Education shows even greater gaps globally. Though *Savage Inequalities* was written decades ago, inequality and lack of access to education still exist today.

Understanding the Issue

Opportunities for early education greatly benefit young children. "To fight poverty, preschool must provide an enormous early boost that changes the academic trajectory of a child forever."[1] Early childhood education provides resources and time for children who might not otherwise receive a strong educational beginning. Children who receive primary and secondary educations reduce their chances of experiencing poverty in adulthood. Education also improves communities, fosters peace, and helps children live healthier lives. Opportunities for young people to further their education in technical, vocational, college, and postgraduate work increasingly raise income levels.

According to UNESCO, 750 million adults and youth globally cannot read or write.[2] Adults who are functionally illiterate cannot read above a fourth-grade level.[3] These individuals struggle to find and keep employment, help their children with schoolwork, and perform lifesaving tasks like reading a medicine bottle. Illiteracy and crime are also closely related. The Literacy Project Foundation found that in the criminal justice system, three out of five adults are illiterate, while up to 85 percent of juveniles cannot read.[4] Disproportionate numbers of people in the criminal justice system are functionally illiterate compared to the general population.

Global Concerns

The 2013 documentary film *Girl Rising* cites that 62 million girls do not attend school. Globally, girls are not given equal access to educational opportunities. The year the film released, I hosted a sold-out screening of *Girl Rising* at our local theater. The film shares the story of nine girls and their journey to receive an education. Wadley from Haiti stands on the edge of an outdoor classroom that her family can't afford and states, "I will come back every day until I can stay." Most children know the name Malala Yousafzai, 2014 winner of the Nobel Peace Prize. Malala was an Afghan student who fought for her right to an education and survived being shot in the head by the Taliban, who object to girls being educated.

> Everyone deserves to become who they want to be.
> —Vismitha, age 12

What stands out about their remarkable stories is that the girls often had someone championing them and pushing against societal norms. If you read Malala's story, her father was a tireless advocate for her right to schooling. In *Girl Rising*, Azmera of Ethiopia was protected from early marriage by an older brother, who also encouraged her in her education. In Elizabeth Suneby's story *Razia's Ray of Hope*, Razia's grandfather, Baba gi, intervenes for her education. Voices that speak out against injustice make a difference. When you educate girls and women, you educate caregivers who, in turn, educate and inspire the next generation.

In the book *The Way to School* by Rosemary McCarney, Samuel is pushed in a homemade wheelchair, Jackson passes wild animals on the savannah, Zahira hikes through the Atlas Mountains, and Carito takes a ninety-minute horseback ride. As students travel to school in unique ways, their classrooms differ as well. Classrooms are set up in open-air rooms and refugee tents. Students sit at individual desks, in groups at tables, and on cracked earth. Some classrooms are filled with books and technology,

> You need math to cook.
> —Micah, age 8

and others have bare walls and limited supplies. Looking at photographs of classrooms around the world, you witness the common theme that schools anchor communities. Educational spaces may not all look the same, but they provide hope, care, and upward mobility to each student.

After children inhabit classrooms, the next task is providing quality education. Communities require infrastructure for buildings, sanitation, safe water, and feeding programs. They need resources to purchase lab equipment, technology, books, and curriculum. Proper student-to-teacher ratios, teacher training, and the ability to focus on inclusion make schools stronger. "In Malawi, for example, there are 130 children per classroom in grade 1 on average."[5] When schools are able to eliminate fees or offset costs to families, enrollment increases.

One huge draw globally for prioritizing education is feeding programs. When students are fed at school, a huge burden is lifted from parents. Studies show malnutrition stunts brain development. For classrooms in the developing world, this might look like a bowl of rice over an open fire for a daily meal. No matter how great a school is, education does not work unless students are properly fed. Meals open up access for a larger number of students.

Ongoing conflict in an area makes attending school difficult for students. Children in conflict areas experience gaps in education. Refugee children experience similar breaks in schooling. Their chances for schooling become sporadic and dependent on what a refugee camp is able to provide. Language barriers and cultural assimilation of refugee and immigrant students make learning challenging, especially if support services are not in place. Global education is greatly affected by conflict, disaster, health epidemics, and flight from persecution.

Boys and girls should go to school so they can be teachers.
—Lily, age 4

Poverty also hinders children's opportunity for education. Areas of poverty might lack access to a nearby school, transportation, or resources to pay school fees. Children who live in poverty may also move frequently and not find stability in their education. The trauma of tumultuous homes brings hunger, exposure to violence, and drug abuse, making learning difficult for students. Students who live in rural poverty find access to education even harder due to the amount of time and travel distance necessary to attend school. Disability hinders children globally from attending school in some areas because they lack resources specific to their needs. Child labor forces children to take on jobs to support their families rather than attend school. Any one or more of these factors makes access to education challenging.

Next-Door Concerns

In a landmark Supreme Court case in 1954, *Brown v. Board of Education of Topeka*, racial segregation of children in public schools was deemed to violate the Fourteenth Amendment. If you look closely at the current American school systems, you will still find pockets of schools with unequal resources. As the choices for schooling expand, unequal opportunity remains. Today families in the United States can choose to homeschool; attend classes virtually; go to private, public, or charter schools; or even curate hybrids of these options. Often the students left behind are those in public schooling. Districts that have higher property values have more economic capital, which provides more revenue to fund schools.

In his book *The Shame of a Nation*, Jonathan Kozol interviews civil rights leader and congressman John Lewis. "'Sometimes,' [Lewis] said, 'you have to ask for something that you know you may not get. And still you have to ask for it. It's still worth fighting for and, even if you don't believe that you will see it in your lifetime, you have got to hold it up so that the generation that comes next will take it from your hands and, in their own time, see it as a goal worth fighting for again.'"[6] The United States needs to continue the effort to find an educational model that provides access for students of all socioeconomic and racial backgrounds.

Microscopes help us discover what we cannot see with the naked eye. Place any child under a microscope and you would see an unquestionable curiosity and thirst for learning. An educator becomes a sacred part of a child's life. At school, children discover who they are and who they want to become. Some kids arrive at school significantly impacted by stress and poverty at home. Ongoing trauma and nutritional deficiencies affect brain development. Erratic schedules, worry, and uncertainties at home cause weariness. These children's ability to learn is hindered before they step inside the school door.

All kids should have equal opportunities so they can achieve their dreams.
—Mila, age 13

These same children often thrive within the walls of a school. They flourish with structure, warm meals, information, friendship, and the love of staff who refuse to give up on them. Studies consistently show that early education is imperative to ending cycles of poverty. Many schools offer free and reduced lunch and sometimes breakfast. An early childhood center in Michigan serves breakfast midmorning and lunch around 2:30 right before students go home, hoping to bridge the gap if there is no dinner at home.

Hope

How many of us can remember a special teacher? There are teachers who give us positions of leadership. They speak into little spaces that summon the very best of us. They tell us we are strong and don't let us give up. Teachers are some of the most dedicated professionals I know. I have worked in education for close to a decade, and I see teachers sacrifice themselves day after day. Why do they teach? Their answer will always be the brilliant children in their care.

You will make new friends.
—Nayeli, age 8

The amount of money teachers spend out of their own pockets is significant. Their emotional investment is immeasurable. I have witnessed the hours they invest above and beyond what is required, the changing standards they adjust to, the continuing education they obtain, the creativity they employ to meet a classroom of children with vastly different needs. Teachers invest a great deal of themselves into the future, year after year. Supporting education means supporting those who commit their lives to teaching.

If you are a reader, do you remember when you fell in love with reading? My windows were open to a soft breeze one summer night, and I was immersed in Laura Ingalls Wilder's *The Long Winter*. I must have been around eight years old. I remember thinking how full my heart felt as I lay there, immersed in a different time period.

Literacy opens up the world to children. A big part of placing myself in proximity to justice has been through books. I've never physically left the borders of the United States, but I have traveled internationally a thousand times within the pages of books. Through books we are invited into others' lives. We get to experience their world and what is important to their hearts. One of the most compelling ways to talk about justice with kids is through a big stack of books. Cuddle up and read together and then talk about what you read. Check out publishers that promote diversity, like Lee & Low Books and CitizenKid. Read about children in different countries and cultures. Join campaigns like #WeNeedDiverseBooks. Your worldview unfolds and expands when you read.

> I like to help people read.
> —Nora, age 10

What if schools continued to dream big? Imagine if, instead of standardized tests as markers, global citizenship and social-emotional learning were stressed in curriculum. Around the world, young mothers are often forced to drop out of school to obtain jobs or care for their young children. What if childcare centers were offered on-site? What if classrooms were opened up to the outdoors, where exploratory learning could take place and green technology was used for its infrastructure?

Globally, educators have found teaching "soft skills" has a huge return on investment. Incorporating communication skills, collaboration, creativity, life skills, extracurriculars, and leadership training help form a well-rounded education and better prepare young people for the workforce. "All around the world, there are many great schools, wonderful teachers, and inspiring leaders who are working creatively to provide students with the kinds of personalized, compassionate, and community-oriented education they need."[7]

> Even if you just go to primary school, you learn skills that will help you in life forever.
> —Caleb, age 13

The nonprofit group KaBOOM! encourages play and play spaces, especially in low-income areas. In play, children learn life skills such as problem solving, creativity, and collaboration. Brain development occurs during unstructured, open-ended playtime. Children need access to education and play. We can fight for them to climb playground structures, put on plays, debate respectfully, engage history, explore books, create art, learn foreign languages, make music, experiment, and write stories. *All children* deserve a chance to be their brilliant and creative selves.

INNOVATION TO EXPLORE

- *Using Community Development*: Schools have experimented with being housed adjacent to a community center offering health care, child-care, dental care, mental health services, meals, and other support systems. Check out The Primary School, an integrated health and educational model in the East Palo Alto and Belle Haven communities in California.
- *Investing in Girls*: Studies also found that educating girls provides a huge return on investment and betters communities. In developing, low-income countries, every additional year of education can increase a person's future income by an average of 10 percent.[8] Education strengthens households, communities, and entire nations.
- *Building Community*: A study from California State University at Sacramento found that teacher home visits improved the performance of students in the classroom as well as forged a connection with parents that increased their involvement and positive attitudes.[9]
- *Using Education*: Schools around the world are meeting students in areas of need—for example, Makoko Floating School in Lagos, Nigeria, a coastal region.
- *Using Technology*: Hewlett-Packard's Future Classroom in India provides access to technology inside refurbished shipping containers.

Appreciate True Life Stories

Follow the work of Girl Rising (girlrising.org) and see firsthand the difference education makes. And meet the nine girls, writers, and artists from the film *Girl Rising* at girlrising.org/meet-the-girls/. Their powerful stories inspire us to make education accessible to all children.

TALK JUSTICE

Ages 3–6

What should kids learn at school?

_____

_____

What do you think parents should teach their kids?

_____

_____

What does a schoolteacher do?

_____

_____

What is your favorite subject to learn about?

_____

_____

What do you think school was like for your grandparents and parents?

_____

_____

Ages 7–11
Why do you feel school is important?

_____

_____

_____

Why would it be important for both boys and girls to attend school?

_____

_____

_____

What would it be like to be in a school with no books? What if there was only one teacher for ninety students?

_____

_____

_____

How many years of schooling did your parents have?

_____

Who has been your favorite teacher in school? Why?

_____

_____

Ages 12+
How has education changed over time?

_____

_____

If you could design your own school, what would it be like?

_____

_____

Do you think play is an important part of learning? Why?

_____

_____

Should higher education be accessible to more students worldwide and in the United States?

_____

_____

If you could travel into the past, what would you do to change education?

_____

_____

STUDY GOD'S WORD

Proverbs 31:8–9
Speak up for those who cannot speak for themselves, for the rights of all who are destitute. Speak up and judge fairly; defend the rights of the poor and needy.

Believers are called to fight for the rights of our brothers and sisters in Christ. *Defend* means to protect others from harm. Coming to one's defense can also take the form of speaking or writing in favor of an idea. Having the freedom to obtain an education is life changing for not only individuals but also communities. We can use our voices to speak out for equal access to education for all. God encourages us to speak up. We can declare that access to education is important for everyone.

The words of Proverbs 31:8–9 can become a prayer in our hearts. We can pray for the courage to speak for those who cannot speak for themselves or help them access a platform to share their perspective. We can share from our hearts that we hope all children will have the same chance to learn, be loved by educators, play, and create.

Extend Study of God's Word

Rewrite Proverbs 31:8–9 using "I can" statements. (Example: "I can speak up for those who cannot speak for themselves.")

_____

_____

_____

How does education fit into God's call to defend people's rights?

_____

_____

How can you seek guidance from God to speak up for others?

_____

_____

_____

How could you join in God's work of defending the rights of the poor and needy?

_____

_____

Choose an organization that supports access to education that your family or group can pray for:

_____

_____

Choose a specific place or community in need of access to education that your family or group can pray for:

_____

> *Thank you, God, for the chance to attend school, to grow, and to learn. Please be near kids all over the world who can't attend school. Help them have the opportunity to learn too. Be close to educators as they love young people and make a difference every day. We pray that children from every part of the globe, girls and boys alike, would have a safe space to learn in. Amen.*

EXPLORE JUSTICE

Ages 3–6
Read: *Miss Dorothy and her Bookmobile* by Gloria Houston
Dorothy Thomas operates a traveling bookmobile in the Blue Ridge Mountains. Based on a true story.

Connection—Children learn not everyone has the same access to education or even books.

Read: *Ruby's Wish* by Shirin Yim Bridges
No wedding dreams for Ruby. Ruby longs to attend university in China when she grows up, just like her brothers. But will she be able to?

Connection—Readers learn about following their dreams and gender inequality in education.

Read: *Malala's Magic Pencil* by Malala Yousafzai
In a story from her childhood in Pakistan, Malala wishes for a magic pencil that could make everything right in her world.

Connection—Readers witness Malala's extraordinary hope even in times of difficulty.

Connect: Field Trip

Gather a group and schedule a visit for a behind-the-scenes look at your local library.

- Ask questions like, How many books are available to borrow in the library? How many people use the library in a year? What things besides books does the library offer people?

Connection—Students see the work that goes into operating a library and the many resources that libraries provide to the public.

Play: Parachute

Gather supplies: play parachute (a bedsheet would work too).

- Gather a play parachute and students outdoors. Play one or all of the following parachute games and relate them to education.

1. Popcorn

- Gather additional supplies: alphabet-letter beanbags.
- Place alphabet-letter beanbags in the center of the parachute and let the kids move the parachute up and down for the beanbags to "pop" up and down like popcorn.

Why do kids need to learn the alphabet? Can you learn to read without the alphabet?

2. Making Waves

- Have the kids move the parachute like a wave.
- Call out different ways for them to experiment with large, medium, and small waves.

What we learn at school can help us change the world. We can take our knowledge and make big waves to help others.

3. Merry-Go-Round

- Have the kids circle clockwise with the parachute.
- Try different ways of circling like walking, jogging, skipping, hopping, and reversing direction.

When we are a part of a classroom, it is important that we work together.

What would happen if you all went a different way with the parachute and didn't listen to each other?

Connection—Students think about education through play and teamwork.

Ages 7–11

Read: *Off to Class: Incredible and Unusual Schools Around the World* by Susan Hughes

Features twenty-four classrooms around the world that have met challenges with innovation to provide education to students.

Connection—Students learn about the importance of education, how creativity can solve challenges, and about global differences and similarities.

Read: *The Girl Who Buried Her Dreams in a Can: A True Story* by Dr. Tererai Trent

As a young girl in Rhodesia, where girls are rarely educated, all Tererai wanted was to learn. This story tells of her journey all the way to obtaining a PhD and building a foundation to improve the lives of children in rural Africa.

Connection—Readers learn about the privilege of education, following their dreams, and giving back.

Read: *Razia's Ray of Hope: One Girl's Dream of an Education* by Elizabeth Suneby

A young Afghani girl named Razia fights for her right to attend school in a village where girls haven't been allowed to attend school for years. But Razia doesn't have to fight alone.

Connection—Children learn that going to school is difficult for girls in many countries.

Read: *School Days Around the World* by Margriet Ruurs

Schoolchildren from thirteen countries share their school experiences.

Connection—Students can see the differences and similarities of their own schools in comparison to schools around the world.

Create: Design Bookmarks
Gather supplies: sturdy cardstock, scissors, art supplies.

Design a bookmark around any of the social justice topics.

- Encourage each student to design a bookmark that promotes global education opportunities.

Connection—Students explore why education is important by creating bookmarks to share.

Observe: Study Art
Study the Syrian Refugee Art Initiative with Joel Artista.

Connection—Families and students join together to bring color, life, and hope to a refugee camp. Do you think it is important for students to have access to expressing themselves through art in an educational setting?

Connect: Little Free Library
Start a Little Free Library in your neighborhood or an area in your community where there is a need for access to books. Visit the Little Free Library's website (littlefreelibrary.org) for an insider's guide to getting your library started.

Connection—Be a part of providing access to books in your area.

Create: Acrostic Poem
Write an acrostic poem using the word *education*. Each line of the poem starts with a letter of the word *education*. Share or display your work.

Give an acrostic poem a try with any of the social justice topics.

Connection—Participants think about what words and phrases best describe access to education.

Ages 12+

Gather: *Girl Rising*

Plan a party or sleepover featuring the film *Girl Rising*. The film features nine girls living in the developing world and highlights their fight for access to an education. Curriculum and response activities for discussion are found at girlrising.org/educatortools.

Connection—Girls learn the importance of global education and have an opportunity to respond.

Consider beginning a mom-and-daughter book club. *I Am Malala* would be a great book to start with.

Read: *I Am Malala: The Girl Who Stood Up for Education and Was Shot by the Taliban* by Malala Yousafzai

Malala almost lost her life fighting for education. She survived with the bravery of her family, who championed her work and heart's desire.

Connection—Readers understand the privilege of obtaining an education.

Create: Writing

Gather supplies: paper, pens and pencils.

• Prompt: I want to be . . .

Connection—Writers share their greatest dreams and how education might play a role in reaching those dreams.

Gather: Global Classroom Simulation

Gather supplies: paper, pens and pencils, desks for only Group 3, laptop, an expert in the field of your choice.

• Break students up into three groups:

   Group 1: No paper, writing utensils, or desks.

   Group 2: Basic supplies, but only boys can speak for the group.

   Group 3: Access to all supplies, technology, and an expert in the field.

- Give the three groups the same assignment. (Possible assignment might be to present evidence as to why education is important to communities.) Have each group present their findings. What was it like to have no resources or limited resources? Abundant resources? Did the groups feel their situations were fair or unfair? Why?

Connection—Students learn and work with limited resources, just like many children globally.

Create: Photo Booth

Gather supplies: backdrop for the photo booth, poster board, markers.
- Using your chosen backdrop, create a photo booth where students can take pictures.
- Encourage students to create signs to hold up for photographs. Some ideas—#girlrising, #globaleducation, #literacy, #educolor, #withmalala, #ActiveforEducation.
- Encourage young people to share their photo booth pictures on social media.

Connection—Raise awareness for global education through advocacy.

Create: Pinterest Awareness Board

Gather supplies: internet access, Pinterest account.
- Compile a Pinterest board with the theme of access to education. Include infographics and resources from educational nonprofits. Always cite your sources.
- Share your board with others to raise awareness.

Connection—Students learn to curate applicable information to teach others about global education.

Gather: Prayer Walk

Gather a small group and walk by a school and its surrounding neighborhood in your community. As you walk, pray for specific needs you notice, for those who attend the school, and for the educators who work there.

Connection—Students intercede for access to education right in their own neighborhood.

CHALLENGE AND EXTEND AWARENESS AT HOME

- Read "30 Mealtime Facts for Education," found at lisavanengen.com.
- Practice "30 Days of Prayer for Education," found at lisavanengen.com.
- Donate a new book to Project Night Night (projectnightnight.org), providing comfort bags to homeless children.
- Go online to learn about Reach Out and Read, then ask your pediatric health-care provider if they participate (reachoutandread.org).
- Try the Day Without Reading Challenge from Room to Read (room toread.org).
- Look at the photo gallery of Afghanistan at Razia's Ray of Hope Foundation (raziasrayofhope.org).
- Thank your teachers and education staff for their time and monetary investments, for their caring approach to teaching, and any other amazing things you catch them doing.
- Learn about why educating girls is so important at camfed.org.
- Sponsor a School-in-a-Box from UNICEF, which is used after natural disasters (market.unicefusa.org).
- Cuddle up with your family and read one of the book suggestions from this chapter.

Let us become the first generation that decides to be the last that sees empty classrooms, lost childhoods, and wasted potentials.

—MALALA YOUSAFZAI, NOBEL PEACE PRIZE LAUREATE

MAKING A DIFFERENCE

- World Vision offers bicycles for girls to have access to a safe education (donate.worldvision.org).
- Support the Malala Fund, which advocates for a girl's right to an education.
- Give to KaBOOM! to help communities provide balanced, active play to all children (kaboom.org).
- Sponsor a girl's education through Razia's Ray of Hope Foundation (raziasrayofhope.org).
- Plan a Friendiversary fund-raiser with a kit from First Book to provide Elephant and Piggie early reader books to classrooms (support.first book.org).
- Secondary school scholarships can be sponsored through CARE (gifts .care.org).
- Support a classroom through Donors Choose (donorschoose.org).
- Support a teacher through Pencils of Promise (pencilsofpromise.org).
- Pick a project to sponsor through Adopt a Classroom (adoptaclass room.org).
- Create a school kit through Lutheran World Relief (lwr.org).

**For direct links to any of these resources plus additional
materials, go to lisavanengen.com and click the
And Social Justice for All tab.**

Local Ideas

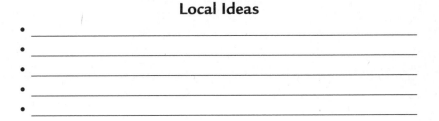

Fair Trade: Giving Beyond Our Means

When one tugs at a single thing in nature, he finds it attached to the rest of the world.

—JOHN MUIR, NATURALIST AND ENVIRONMENTAL PHILOSOPHER

Raise Awareness

March (last week)—National Farmworker Awareness Week
May (second Saturday)—World Fair Trade Day
June 16—International Domestic Workers' Day

People are consumers due to need and, in developed nations, also due to want. How often do we slow down to consider what we buy? Where it originated? How it was made? Do we ever think about the faces and families behind the products we use and the conditions they work in? In many societies, farmers and farm workers earn barely enough to survive. But when they band together, they can demand better—fairer—prices for their products. Fair trade is a principle that aims to pay producers in developing countries a fair price for their products, the goals being to reduce poverty, promote ethical treatment of farmers and workers, and implement sustainable practices.

Selfishness isn't
acceptable.
—Charlie, age 15

Though buying fair trade involves a little extra label reading and research on our part initially, we can build these habits into our lives and buy accordingly. For a bit higher out-of-pocket cost, we can stand in the gap and support efforts to equitable trade. We can slow down and be conscious of what we consume, seeking to replace often-used items with those we know are traded fairly. When we learn about where our food and products actually come from, we are able to connect with other cultures. We build partnerships between the people who grow food and those who consume the food. Practicing fair trade shows our gratitude for what we have received and also for those who have a part in getting it to us.

Thinking about the actual process of how our food and drinks are made changes how we see them. We are not as tempted to take what we have for granted. When taking the time to be conscious of where the goods you purchase come from, you might be surprised. Did you know Serbia is one of the world's largest exporters of raspberries?[1] Most of the bananas you eat come from within twenty degrees of the equator. That is quite a distance from the United States. Cote d'Ivoire produces 40 percent of cocoa in the world.[2] Sixty percent of shoes and 70 percent of mobile phones are made in China.[3]

Understanding the Issue

When we buy fair-trade products, a chain reaction of life-giving space is opened. When artisans, farmers, and laborers receive a fair payment for

A fair trade
would be to
trade dresses
if you don't fit
them and the
other person
does.
—Bayleigh, age 8

their hard work, that money can be invested back into their businesses, families, and communities. They experience safe working conditions. The salary they earn can be invested back into their communities. Laborers have a voice, and child labor is not used. Fair trade protects the environment by limiting carbon emission and the use of chemicals and GMOs, and it encourages crop rotation. A primary goal of fair trade is sustainability to ensure we do not deplete resources with growing demand.

Fair-trade products have changed communities by providing a living wage to workers. When employers receive fair-trade income for their products, they are better able to provide their workers with health insurance, free vaccinations, subsidized meals, continuing education, and improvement of the infrastructure of their communities. Some communities set up cooperatives to share costs of marketing, provide credit, offer health insurance, and ensure maternity leave. Community centers in fair-trade communities offer night classes for continuing education, and workers are able to pay for children's school fees. Quality of life expands when workers receive a fair wage for their work.

Remember Julie Andrews in *The Sound of Music* singing with the Von Trapp children "My Favorite Things"? Many of our favorite things are readily available as fair-trade items. A significant percent of the US population navigates their day with coffee or tea in hand. We wear clothing every day. Shopping for fashion and rotating wardrobes is a pastime for many. Most people will not turn down their favorite chocolate bar. Sugar finds its way into much of what we eat. Bananas are often a staple of babies and young children. All these items occupy the top of the fair-trade list.

According to the National Coffee Association, if you purchase three coffees a week, in one year your total bill would exceed one thousand dollars. "Coffee is the second most valuable commodity exported from developing countries,"[4] bested only by petroleum. We often don't think of coffee beginning as a seed that grows into a tree. Coffee trees grow best in the bean belt located around the equator in developing nations. Coffee beans are harvested by hand or machines. An average picker might be able to gather twenty to forty pounds of coffee in a day. The wet method uses a pulp machine to process the beans; the dry method uses the sun. Afterward, the beans are hulled, polished, graded, and sorted. The beans are then exported and travel to your kitchen counter or local coffee shop to be roasted, ground, and brewed. The whole process is much more complicated than just standing in line at your local coffee shop.

> A fair trade would be to give someone a toy.
> —Olivia, age 6

Chocolate comes from cacao trees that grow cacao pods. Long poles with cutting edges cut down the football-size pods. Cracked open by a machete, the pods reveal cacao beans. The beans are fermented and then dried in the sun. At the processing plant, beans are cleaned, roasted, and winnowed. They are then ground into a paste and added to other ingredients. Finally, the chocolate is tempered and molded, packaged, and delivered.

Every day we put on clothes. We wear clothing all day long and toss it in the hamper at bedtime. Have you ever thought about the process of getting clothing into the form you can slip onto your body? Harvested cotton is fed into gin machines to remove seeds and trash. The cotton is spun into yarn, then knit into fabric rolls that must be cleaned, stabilized, and softened. The fabric is cut, sewn, printed, and dyed. When finished, the clothing still has to be packaged and transported to find its way to the department store and into your possession. Consider your family's favorite things and research how they come to be, from their beginning to their arrival in your home.

Global Concerns

The work of the garment industry is labor-intensive and measured per piece. Bangladesh garment workers are among the lowest paid laborers. In 2013, at the Rana Plaza Complex in Bangladesh, young women were working more than twelve hours a day. Though the owners were notified of large and dangerous cracks in the exterior of the structure, the fabric workers were still forced to enter and work. On April 24, less than an hour into their work shift, the factory collapsed and more than a thousand women were killed. Globally, factory workers daily face conditions such as poor ventilation, cramped workspaces, low lighting, and exposure to toxic chemicals. The price we pay for our goods may come at a cost for others. Do we turn a blind eye, or do we try to be intentional with our purchases?

The Human Thread Campaign found its beginning in Catholic teachings. After the Rana Plaza garment factory fire, the campaign sought to bring awareness between consumers and producers. A common thread of humanity connects us. A CNN article reports that "98% of clothes sold in the United States are made overseas."[5] If we take Colossians 3:12 seriously—"As God's chosen people, holy and dearly loved, clothe yourselves with compassion"—we know that we can act compassionately by thinking beyond our purchases to the people behind them. Often fair trade can be used as a justice tool to look deeply at exploitative systems where wages and trade are not equitable.

Another way fair trade fights injustice is that companies often employ people who have been rescued from human trafficking and have found freedom. They also hire women who might have turned to prostitution for income without a fair-trade work opportunity. These women make pajamas, jewelry, bags, cards, and blankets. Their income benefits not only their family but also the larger community. Fair-trade organizations like Starfish Project go a step further and train their workers in marketable skills like computer certification and Photoshop.

Next-Door Concerns

In the United States and globally, we see a widening gap between minimum wage and a living wage. A living wage should rise in proportion to yearly cost-of-living estimates. A wage that is adequate should account for housing, food, transportation, childcare, health care, taxes, and other living expenses. The pay gap forces many to work multiple minimum wage jobs and still not earn enough to live comfortably.

> A fair trade is giving away something you don't need.
> —Liam, age 6

When workers are not compensated fairly, their families remain locked in cycles of poverty. Poverty puts people at risk for hunger, lack of health care, and unequal access to education. Those working in substandard conditions are often immigrants and refugees, further perpetuating their vulnerable status.

In the United States, Student Action with Farmworkers estimates 85 percent of the fresh fruits and vegetables we eat are picked by hand.[6] Migratory farm workers often leave their families behind to work in the United States. They face further isolation due to illegal documentation and fear of deportation. According to the Southern Poverty Law Center, about six out of ten farmworkers in the United States have undocumented status.[7]

Hope

When we buy fair-trade items, the market for those goods expands. Julius Ethang'atha, a tea producer from Kenya, shares, "When a consumer pays more for Fairtrade tea, this extra money goes to the farmer and improves lives."[8] Members of the UC-CPC de Djidian cooperative, cotton farmers in Mali, used their fair-trade earnings to build a school, a maternity center, a new road, and a food storage facility. Tea farmers from the Sukambizi Association Trust opened up community access by building bridges and purchasing an ambulance, among other community-strengthening projects.[9] Fair-trade wages continue to be invested back into families and communities.

According to Fair Trade USA, more than one million farmers and farm workers in fifty-eight developing countries across Africa, Asia, and Latin America benefit from fair trade.[10] That is encouraging news. A World Bank report titled *Poverty and Shared Prosperity 2016: Taking on Inequality* shows that in 2013, 767 million people lived on less than $1.90 a day.[11] Work continues so more communities can benefit from fair trade. Irish playwright George Bernard Shaw said, "I am of the opinion that my life belongs to the whole community and as long as I live it is my privilege to do for it whatever I can."[12] Justice multiplies. When we treat others fairly, we give them the dignity to do the same to others. The expansiveness of that giving should move us.

INNOVATION TO EXPLORE

- *Using the Influence of Companies*: Grocery company Kroger expands the fair-trade offerings of their in-house brand Simple Truth. As of 2018, they carry nearly three hundred fair trade–certified products across sixty brands.[13]
- *Using Business Partnerships*: GoodWeave focuses on the carpet and rug industry. When rugs are GoodWeave-certified, it means they are produced under documented working conditions, and without child labor and forced labor. Partnering with more than 350 companies worldwide, GoodWeave helps provide freedom and education for children who would normally be laboring (goodweave.org).
- *Using Social Media and History*: Join with athletes, thought leaders, and corporations like Patagonia and Athleta in remembering the Rana Plaza factory collapse with the digital photo campaign "We Wear Fair Trade." Use #wewearfairtrade.

- *Using Agriculture and Fair Trade*: The first US fair-trade farm in Amado, Arizona, is the Wholesum Harvest's tomato farm. The farm provides basic health care for their workers and transportation to school.
- *Using Community*: Fair Trade USA helps towns, universities, congregations, and schools become leaders in the fair-trade movement.

Appreciate Community

In preparing to write this chapter, I read through the blog of Fair Trade USA. As a part of a Nicaraguan coffee company's fair-trade certification, the company formed a workers' committee. Together the committee decided what to do with money set aside for community projects. They chose to build new latrines and bring three new doctors to the community. The last project they chose was to deliver hot meals to impoverished elderly people in the community who had no families.[14] The committee developed projects generous to those most in need, even though they did not have much themselves.

TALK JUSTICE

Ages 3–6

What do you think would be a fair trade?

_____

_____

What do you need to survive?

_____

_____

What do you want to buy?

_____

_____

Why do people have jobs and go to work?

_____

_____

Have you ever handpicked fruits or vegetables? What was it like?

_____

_____

Ages 7–11
Look at the labels of your clothing. Where were your clothes made?

_____

_____

Look at the labels of your fruits, vegetables, and other whole foods. Where did they come from?

_____

_____

What kind of journey do you think your food and clothing take? What kind of transportation is used to get them to you?

_____

_____

_____

What kind of labor is used to harvest your food or make your clothing?

_____

_____

_____

What do you think it means to trade fairly?

_____

_____

_____

Ages 12+
Would you be willing to pay more for products to ensure their makers were being paid fairly in return?

_____

_____

Would you still buy products if you knew children were unfairly used to make them?

_____

_____

Do you like coffee drinks? What coffee shops do you go to most? Do they use fair-trade products?

_____

_____

Why do we need to trade?

_____

_____

Do you buy anything locally? What could you buy locally?

_____

_____

STUDY GOD'S WORD

2 Corinthians 8:3–4

For I testify that they gave as much as they were able, and even beyond their ability. Entirely on their own, they urgently pleaded with us for the privilege of sharing in this service to the Lord's people.

Small groups that attend the Boys and Girls Club of Holland, Michigan, participated in the social justice survey for this book. I received a large stack of their answers. As I read, I was struck by the way many children answered the question, What would be a fair trade? About a dozen students said a fair trade would be giving someone a toy. Not trading a toy with someone else, but straight-out giving someone a toy who needed one. Not just one student but many answered this way.

Those answers were a living example of 2 Corinthians 8:3. In this Bible passage, the people gave what they could afford to give, and then they gave what they couldn't afford as well. They gave beyond. They did it voluntarily.

No one forced them. They didn't feel guilt. They did not pretend it was a heavy obligation. They gave what they had and then went even further. Fair trade models this sentiment. Through fair trade, we have the opportunity to give what is fair, and sometimes even beyond that.

Extend Study of God's Word

Work on memorizing 2 Corinthians 8:3–4 with your family.

What are three things you could give to others? Do you know anyone who could use these gifts?

_____

_____

_____

What does it mean to you to have a willing heart?

_____

_____

What would it mean for you to give beyond what is expected?

_____

_____

_____

Choose an organization that supports fair trade that your family or group can pray for:

_____

_____

Choose a specific place or community that could benefit from fair trading practices that your family or group can pray for:

_____

_____

God, help us think about the things we buy. Help us slow down and consider all the people who make the products we use. Show

us how to incorporate fair-trade products into our everyday lives.
We pray for fair working conditions for workers around the world.
Change our hearts to think about not only what is fair but what is
even beyond fair. Teach us how to live with open and willing hearts.
Amen.

EXPLORE JUSTICE

Ages 3–6

Read: *Juliana's Bananas: Where Do Your Bananas Come From?* by Ruth Walton

Two children from a family of banana farmers on the Windward Islands share their story of how fair trade affects their lives. Readers learn about bananas from growth to arrival in the supermarket.

Connection—Children learn what it means for others when we practice fair trade.

Read: *Roses for Isabella* by Diana Cohn

Isabella's life changes when her family finds work at a fair-trade rose farm in Ecuador.

Connection—Children learn how the quality of life increases for families whose employers and customers support fair-trade practices.

Play: Market

Gather supplies: various fair-trade items, such as pretend chocolate bars, toy bananas, clothing, baskets, sealed bags of coffee beans, artificial flowers, sealed containers of honey, tightly sealed spices, boxes of tea.

- Set up a play market with fair-trade items. Encourage the kids to make trades such as a bunch of bananas for a bouquet of flowers.

Connection—Children have a hands-on play opportunity to explore trade with common fair-trade items.

Play: Homemade Chocolate Play Dough

Gather supplies: measuring cups, measuring spoons, spoon for mixing, large bowl, stove or microwave, candy forms, cookie cutters, cupcake liners, ingredients for recipe.

Recipe: 2 cups all-purpose flour, ½ cup table salt, ½ cup cocoa, 3 tablespoons vegetable oil, ½ teaspoon vanilla, 1 ½ cups boiling water.

- To make the play dough, first stir together the flour, salt, and cocoa. Next, add the vegetable oil and vanilla. The last step is to mix in the boiling water. If the play dough seems sticky, add small amounts of flour until it reaches the right consistency.
- Use candy forms, cookie cutters, and cupcake liners for creative play.

Connection—Children think about chocolate through play. Talk about how chocolate is acquired and the labor that goes into getting it in our markets.

Ages 7–11

Read: *Think Fair Trade First!* by Ingrid Hess

Aunt Mabel helps Stella and Henry pick the perfect birthday gift for their mom. As they do so, they learn that the way they shop can help people around the world.

Connection—Readers learn that kids can make a difference with their purchasing choices.

Read: *Bring Me Some Apples and I'll Make You a Pie: A Story About Edna Lewis* by Robbin Gourley

Read the story of Edna Lewis, one of the first female and African American chefs in New York, and a champion of farm-to-table food long before it became popular.

Connection—Readers learn about the origins of food, using fresh ingredients and southern recipes.

Observe: Study Art

Study *The Fourth Estate* by Giuseppe Pellizza da Volpedo.

Connection—Students study a painting of striking workers at the turn of the century in Italy.

Create: Play
Write, act, and perform a play that encourages families to use goods that are fairly traded. Use costumes and props to make your ideas come alive.

Connection—Students share the message of fair trade through drama.

Create: Wanted Poster
Gather supplies: poster board, markers, and so on.
- Encourage each student to make a wanted poster for fair trade. Examples might include "Wanted: fair pay and safe working conditions" or "Wanted: protection for children from child labor."

Connection—Students learn to display important fair-trade concepts through the form of a wanted poster.

Ages 12+
Read: *Fair Trade: A Human Journey* by Éric St-Pierre
Portraits and stories from around the globe tell the story of fair trade.

Connection—Readers will not only learn about fair trade but also gain visual images of fair trade at work.

Read: *The Omnivore's Dilemma: Young Readers Edition* by Michael Pollan
Michael Pollan shares facts on where our food really comes from and thoughts on the personal and global impact of our food choices.

Connection—Readers are encouraged to think about their food choices and how they affect the greater world.

Connect: Nursing Home Visit
- Contact the activities director ahead of planning your event.
- Organize a time for a group of students to visit the nursing home.

- Pair students up with nursing home residents for them to trade skills. Nursing home residents share a story from their childhood. Students teach residents a skill they might need to understand, like text messaging, video chatting, or emailing.

Connection—Students and nursing home residents participate in a reciprocal relationship that encourages trading fairly.

Create: Coffee Timeline

Gather supplies: computer and internet access.

- Encourage students to create a timeline on a computer program like Excel, an infographic template, or off-line on poster board.
- Research the time span of making coffee from bean to market.
- Make points in a chronological sequence.
- Add text, photos, and miles traveled from cacao tree to market.

Connection—Students track a fair-trade product from its beginning to its purchase and arrival in a home.

CHALLENGE AND EXTEND AWARENESS AT HOME

- Read "30 Mealtime Facts About Fair Trade," found at lisavanengen .com.
- Practice "30 Days of Prayer for Fair Trade," found at lisavanengen.com.
- Try out a fair-trade recipe from Fair Trade Certified (fairtradecertified .org).
- Learn how to find fair-trade products at the store. Use a shopping guide from Fair Trade Certified.
- On YouTube, watch "My Fairtrade Adventure" from the Fairtrade Foundation.
- Print out and work through the *Fair Trade Chocolate Activity Book* from Global Exchange (scribd.com/document/30719462/).
- Watch "Playing Fair: The Story of Fairtrade Footballs" together (schools .fairtrade.org.uk).
- Shop through Global Goods Partners (globalgoodspartners.org).

- Check out the interactive Living Wage Calculator for your state at living wage.mit.edu.
- Explore a global map from the International Center for Tropical Agriculture to see where different crops originate (blog.ciat.cgiar.org).

There is no worse material poverty . . . than that which does not allow people to earn their daily bread and deprives them of the dignity of work.

—POPE FRANCIS, 266TH POPE

MAKING A DIFFERENCE

- Consider making your church a Fair Trade Congregation (fairtrade campaigns.org).
- Doing a fund-raiser? Consider working with Equal Exchange (equal exchange.coop).
- Check out these teaching resources through Traidcraft for Schools (traidcraftschools.co.uk).
- Use the free *Get It* curriculum from Heifer International about consumers affecting the global marketplace (heifer.org).
- Explore lesson plans from Fairtrade Schools Resources (schools.fair trade.org.uk).
- Order the DVD and watch *A Thousand Fibers* from Partners for Just Trade (partnersforjusttrade.org).
- Watch the TED Talk "Bandi Mbubi: Demand a Fair Trade Cell Phone."
- Use classroom resources from Global Footprint Network (footprint network.org).
- Track where your T-shirt came from at Where Your Clothing (where yourclothing.com).
- Host a screening of the movie *The True Cost* (rated PG-13 for thematic elements).

**For direct links to any of these resources plus additional
materials, go to lisavanengen.com and click the
And Social Justice for All tab.**

Local Ideas

- _____
- _____
- _____
- _____
- _____

Families: Those We Love

*The biggest problem in the world today is that we
draw the circle of our family too small—we need to draw
it larger every day.*

—MOTHER TERESA, NUN AND MISSIONARY

Raise Awareness

January 1—Global Family Day
March 21—National Single Parent Day
April 10—National Siblings Day
May—National Foster Care Month
June 1—Global Day of Parents
September (first Sunday)—National Grandparents Day
October—Pregnancy and Infant Loss Awareness Month
November—National Adoption Awareness Month
November (Saturday before Thanksgiving)—National Adoption Day

Growing up, I loved the Berenstain Bears books. Maybe it was because Mama Bear, Papa Bear, Sister, and Brother reflected my own family composition. That 1950s vibe of a nuclear family of four who live in a little house with a white picket fence does not echo most households today. But no matter how families are structured, the family plays a defining role in each child's life and development. Globally, many families live in the same household with extended family members such as grandparents, aunts, uncles, or cousins. Divorce shapes families into a blended family. There are single-parent households or homes headed by same-sex couples. Families also grow through adoption and foster care. Many families speak more than one language in their home. Immigrant families adapt to a new culture while maintaining their own traditions. Adult children care for aging parents. Kinship care occurs when someone from the extended family becomes a child's caregiver. Around 1.3 million children in America under age eighteen live with their grandparents.[1]

In the 2006 film *Little Miss Sunshine*, the Hoover family, made up of a grandfather, father, mother, uncle, and two children, Dwayne and Olive, all travel cross-country to the Little Miss Sunshine Pageant. At one point in the movie Richard, the father, says, "Everyone, just . . . pretend to be normal." We can all pretend, but complex people shaped into a family unit are a recipe for challenge. Yes, sharing breathing room is almost intolerable sometimes. Jealousy wriggles its way into our dreams and ambitions. We unclog toilets together and clean up vomit in the dark night. No one knows our idiosyncrasies better, or which buttons to push that send us over the edge. We are forever connected, and that changes everything. If you have a family, you have hope, life, and a chance to overcome any obstacle. Protecting and standing up for family no matter what that looks like is so important.

Understanding the Issue

In the study of human behavior, family systems theory looks at families as an emotional unit that is understood in connection with each family member, not in isolation. We are interconnected to our family on various levels, and those connections shape who we are and how we live. Every justice issue is inevitably tied to families, because we experience life together. Strengthening family systems helps families develop the tools they need in order to overcome injustice with resiliency and support.

Family-centered practices allow families to find strength by expanding beyond the immediate family. Parental resilience deepens when extended family, friends, neighbors, teachers, and churches build social connections for children. Supportive neighborhoods and communities offer concrete support. "Family is the most fundamental factor influencing the lives and outcomes of children. Aside from a child's physical needs, such as food and clothing, children need an emotionally healthy home environment and stable and reliable relationships with adults and caregivers."[2] When we extend the circle of our families we find strength, resources, and community to stabilize and expand well-being.

Global Concerns

One of my favorite literary families is the Weasleys of the Harry Potter series. Arthur and Molly have seven red-haired children: Charlie, Bill, Percy, Fred, George, Ron, and Ginny. They live in a five-story home called The Burrow, and though their economic situation is lacking, they make up for it in warmth, love, and hideously knit sweaters. Economically, not all families look the same. By no means is a bank account a true measurement of their love or happiness. Families can live in poverty but still provide their children with a loving, strong childhood.

While what constitutes poverty varies widely depending on culture and where we live in the world, poverty puts stress on the family unit. Job loss, hunger, parents' inability to provide, homelessness, and lack of health care press against a family's stability. So many families living in poverty make difficult decisions, with parents often putting their children first, in order to survive. Some families must separate while a breadwinner works transnationally. To share housing costs and childcare, many families cohabitate. Sometimes these families are related, but often they are not. While these relationships can be mutually beneficial, tight quarters and the merging of different households can add to family tension.

In the early years of life, children experience huge amounts of brain development. From birth to eight years, important neural pathways are connected in children's brains. These connections develop properly with good nutrition, secure attachment, caring interactions, and stimulation. But more and more research shows early stress adversely affects children. Adverse childhood experiences involve abuse, neglect, domestic violence, divorce, substance abuse, mental illness, incarceration, and economic hardship. A research brief found that one in ten children in the United States experience three or more adverse childhood experiences. With that data we see a "need for increased attention to the early detection and treatment of children affected by trauma, as well as to the conditions in families and communities that contribute to adverse development."[3]

Not one of the topics in this book is experienced in isolation but in familial units. Families are affected by hunger and lack of clean water. Health-care costs impact an entire family. Refugees and immigrants move as a family unit. Race affects families. When goods are not fairly traded, families are affected. Parents in the developing world have to make heart-wrenching decisions to provide for and save their children, especially in times of conflict. Human trafficking tears apart families. Children who enter the foster care system have a higher likelihood of later entering the criminal justice system. And the effects of adverse childhood experiences impact children around the world.

Next-Door Concerns

According to Safe Horizons, every year more than three million children witness domestic violence in their homes. In the United States, 437,465 children are in foster care at any given time.[4] Of these children, 117,794 are eligible for adoption, but nearly 28 percent will wait more than three years in foster care before being adopted. In 2016, there were 20,532 youths who aged out of the US foster care system without the emotional and financial support necessary to succeed. Children are removed from homes for abuse and neglect and often suffer trauma as a result of their experiences. Foster care is their safety net.

Refugee children face separation from their families during conflict and flight from their homeland, and many become orphans in the process. When these children receive refugee status and resettle in their new countries, they become unaccompanied minors in need of refugee foster care. Their foster families face unique challenges such as language

> I am different because my parents are white and I am black. My hair is more curly than my brother's even though he is black, like me. I have some special needs like cerebral palsy and a math learning disability.
> —Samuel, age 14

and cultural barriers, as well as the trauma their refugee foster children have experienced and witnessed.

Families that provide foster care offer their homes as a safe haven for these children to regroup, find shelter, and experience love. Foster parents provide children with a family exactly when they need it most, and letting go for reunification or adoption is often an emotional experience.

> If I meet someone different than me, I want to know everything about them.
> —Zac, age 15

A young student I once worked with sat slumped at her desk. Skye was an island. She met encouragement and direction with an unaffected eye roll. She scratched her answers carelessly and walked the perimeter of the playground alone. Her behavior clip hovered on red. She glared at the world through her fringe of messy bangs. One day I walked alongside her in the hallway and she reached up her hand and took mine.

No words, just a gesture that her tough exterior was actually paper-thin armor. The next morning, her desk was empty. She would travel to another foster home, another school. Skye is not an isolated example; there are so many children like her.

Child welfare caseworkers move families toward reunification through family permanency. Permanency builds on family strengths and addresses concerns using a multidisciplinary approach. Families receive home visits, family-centered services, and parent education. When permanency planning does not work, parental rights are terminated and children become eligible for adoption through foster care. Babies can also be adopted at birth when parental rights are terminated. According to the National Council for Adoption, around 110,373 children are adopted internationally and domestically each year.[5] Adoptions occur domestically and globally. In 2014 the highest number of children adopted by Americans came from China, followed by Ethiopia, Ukraine, Haiti, and the Democratic Republic of Congo.

In college I was assigned the book *Hard Living on Clay Street*. The author, Joseph T. Howell, moved to Clay Street, a white, working-class neighborhood in Washington, DC, to document the lives of two families. The look into their lives took place in the early 1970s, but its message transcends

Adults should
know how to
love each other.
—Miles, age 5

time. The Shacklefords and the Mosebys are the same as our present-day, blue-collar, lower-middle-class families who feel unheard and uncared for. Undoubtedly there are things that hurt such families—devastating behaviors such as domestic violence, child abuse, and parental neglect, and subtler, hidden actions such as drug abuse, excessive drinking, and pornography. Hard living can lead to family instability perpetuated by changing boyfriends and girlfriends, constant moving, and changing schools often. "Most family violence occurs behind closed doors. It is often hidden, unnoticed, and ignored."[6] We hurt each other, and sometimes it's hard to find forgiveness. Strong community support and places of faith are of such importance to families that need healing.

A relatively new struggle for families is technology. The daily use of electronic devices, when left unchecked, severely contributes to our inability to effectively communicate with one another. While technology is positive in allowing us to connect with family across states and countries, it can also draw us away from one another. "Media also impacts in person family contact, hindering face-to-face interactions and social involvement."[7] When we think of family stability and strength, technology will continue to play a role.

Hope

The importance of family cannot be overstressed: the safety, the sense of belonging, the love. Research shows that family mealtime discussion boosts literacy rates in children.[8] Children who eat meals with their family eat more nutritiously.[9] The frequency of family meals correlates with a decrease of adolescent high-risk behaviors.[10] Taking time out of our fast-paced schedules to eat and connect makes a huge difference in the strength of families.

I think of an after-school program in our community called ACTS that meets with our Talk Justice Playgroups. Jaime Blom and her tight-knit neighborhood crew make up an untraditional yet deeply loving family. They eat, play, create, and care for one another during their neighborhood after-school program. They experience life together even though they are not biologically related. If you ask any member of ACTS, they would say that they belong to one another. They will always be there for each other. Families are sometimes drawn outside the lines, and it is a beautiful thing to witness and be a part of.

When we invest in systems that support families, families become stronger. Families build resilience with concrete support services. Increasing emotional competence helps all members of a family resolve problems peacefully. Community development that offers free family activities and resources gives families opportunities to spend time together without using their own funds. Any organization that considers families contributes to justice.

> **Maybe their mom and dad have different skin colors and they're mixed— fine.**
> —Rakiyah, age 8

INNOVATION TO EXPLORE

- *Using Nonprofits*: Since 2015, Hope Pkgs, based in Holland, Michigan, has received donations for more than seven hundred first-night bags for children entering foster care.[11] So many foster children enter care without any belongings or just a few things tucked into a trash bag.
- *Using the Church*: Safe Families provides families in distress with a safe space for their children to stay, working through a network of churches. Churches have hosted more than 35,000 children since 2003.
- *Building Community*: The Family Dinner Project encourages families to make dinners together a priority.
- *Using Engineering*: KaBOOM! is a national nonprofit committed to creating structures and spaces that encourage play in low-income areas.
- *Using Community Development*: Older adults support foster care adoptive families in the Hope Meadows Neighborhood model. For subsidized rent, elderly neighbors volunteer hours to be spent with adoptive children to give adoptive parents respite.

Appreciate a Biblical Example

Read Acts 2:44–47. How can you apply the teaching of the fellowship of the believers to your family? What concepts of a healthy community of believers can we apply to make our own family stronger?

TALK JUSTICE

Ages 3–6
Who is in your family?

_____

_____

What are your favorite things to do with your family?

_____

_____

_____

Why are grandparents, aunts, uncles, and cousins important to a family?

_____

_____

How can you show your family love?

_____

_____

What do you think is important for all families to have?

_____

_____

_____

Ages 7–11
What makes your family special?

_____

_____

_____

What family traditions do you have that you feel are important?

_____

_____

_____

Think about your family and two other families you know. How are your families the same and how are they different?

_____

_____

What do you think it means to be a part of a family?

_____

_____

How could you improve your family's communication?

_____

_____

Ages 12+
What makes a family a family?

_____

_____

What challenges do families face?

_____

_____

How could you help strengthen your own family?

_____

_____

How could you help strengthen families in your community?

_____

_____

_____

How could you improve your family's communication?

_____

_____

_____

STUDY GOD'S WORD

Psalm 68:5–6

A father to the fatherless, a defender of widows, is God in his holy dwelling. God sets the lonely in families.

One of my grandma's favorite books growing up was *The Runaway Bunny* by Margaret Wise Brown. She gave me a copy when I had my daughter. In the story, a little bunny keeps running away from his mother. "If you run away," said his mother, "I will run after you. For you are my little bunny."[12] The little bunny's running away and his mother's sweet love is a little game they play together.

What is home to you? Maybe more than a place or objects, home is the people who love us steadfastly, who will run after us and love us no matter what.

The Bible describes God as one who defends those who are alone. God hopes for a home for all of us, a place to be cared for and loved. When loneliness sets in, God's gift to us is a family to belong to. He marks the defenseless as his own. Everyone matters to him—particularly the most vulnerable. Psalm 68:5 talks about God being in his holy dwelling. God resides in a sacred space. He is great and mighty but also loving and kind. If he remembers the most vulnerable, how much more should we seek to remember them too? He knows we need to feel his great love on earth, and we can experience that through the warmth of families, friends, and communities that truly care.

Extend Study of God's Word

Write a letter to God thanking him for your family.

How can you love the family God has given you?

_____

_____

How has God shown you love through your family?

_____

_____

_____

What does it mean to you to be a part of the family of God?

_____

_____

Choose an organization that supports families that your family or group can pray for:

_____

_____

Choose someone who could use the support of a family whom your family or group can pray for:

_____

_____

> *God, thank you for families. Thank you for showing us love through families. We pray that those who do not have a family might be placed in one. Help us love the people you have given to us as a family. Teach us to recognize the challenges families face. Show us how to help families in need. Show us how to support justice issues that strengthen families. Amen.*

EXPLORE JUSTICE

Ages 3–6
Read: *Global Babies* by The Global Fund for Children
Global Babies is a sweet full-color board book with photographs of babies from around the world.

Connection—Kids see images of babies from all different cultures.

Also in the board book series: *Global Baby Girls, Global Baby Boys, Global Baby Bedtimes,* **and** *Carry Me.*

Read: *Our Grandparents: A Global Album* by Maya Ajmera
A photographic album featuring the relationships between children and grandparents around the world.

Connection—Kids learn that grandparents are very important parts of families.

Read: *We Belong Together* by Todd Parr
We Belong Together features colorful pictures of adoption and families.

Connection—Families can talk about adoption and the special families it makes.

Read: *The Invisible String* by Patrice Karst
Twins Liza and Jeremy learn that love is an invisible string connecting us all.

Connection—Readers are reassured that even when they're facing difficult situations, like separation from loved ones, families are still connected by the love we have for one another.

Read: *Mom and Dad Glue* by Kes Gray
The topic of parental separation is introduced to readers.

Connection—This gentle story helps children understand that even though parents sometimes separate, they still love their children very much.

Create: Drawing
Gather supplies: drawing paper, art supplies.
  • Prompt: Encourage kids to draw a picture of their family.

Connection—Children think and talk about the special people who make up their family.

Play: Celebration Play Dough
Gather supplies: play dough, confetti, glitter.

- Make celebration play dough by adding confetti and glitter to regular play dough. Have fun creating with one another.

Connection—Families are something to celebrate!

Create: Family Thanksgiving Tree
Gather supplies: large jar, twigs, colorful cut-out leaves, strings, markers.
- Arrange the twigs in the jar.
- Set out the cut-out leaves for family members to write or draw what they are thankful for.
- Tie the leaves with string to the twig branches.
- Display your tree during the Thanksgiving season.

Adapt the family Thanksgiving tree as a classroom or youth group Thanksgiving tree.

Connection—Families share what they have to be thankful for and build gratitude.

Ages 7–11
Read: *Tell Me Again About the Night I Was Born* by Jamie Lee Curtis
Remembering the night of a child's birth through the lens of adoption.

Read Psalm 139:13–18 together and talk about how God knew us before we were born and how much he loves us.

Connection—Children feel the enormous love parents have for their adoptive children.

Read: *Mixed Me!* by Taye Diggs
A little boy named Mike navigates being biracial.

Connection—Children understand that not all families are the same skin color or culture.

Read: *The Case for Loving: The Fight for Interracial Marriage* by Selina Alko
The Loving family fights for interracial marriage all the way to the Supreme Court.

Connection—Readers learn that before 1967, Americans of different races were not allowed to be married. Students learn about the historic case that changed that law.

Read: *Families Around the World* by Margriet Ruurs
Vividly illustrated two-page spreads tell the stories of fourteen children and their families from around the world.

Connection—Children can compare similarities and differences of their own families to families from around the world.

Read: *Homecoming* (book one in The Tillerman Cycle) by Cynthia Voigt
Four abandoned siblings make their way to their great aunt's house, hoping to find someone to trust, someone to love them . . . hoping to find home.

Homecoming is the first book in a series of seven.

Connection—Students learn from Dicey Tillerman the experience of abandonment and the importance of home and family.

Create: Family Prayer Bucket
Gather supplies: small bucket, label for or photo of each immediate and extended family member, glue or tape, craft sticks.

You could add to the bucket or make another one for people in your life who are part of the family of God, such as neighbors, friends, classmates, and church members.

• On each craft stick, place a label or affix a photograph of an immediate or extended family member.
• Place sticks in the bucket.
• During mealtime pull out a stick and pray for that family member.

Connection—Families pray together and remember family members in their prayers. When you pull a stick out of the bucket, talk about specific ways you can pray for that person.

Observe: Study Art
Study *The Family* by Diego Rivera.

Connection—Study an indigenous Mexican family of a mother and two children.

Create: Self-Stick Note Collaborative Art
Gather supplies: self-stick notes, supplies for drawing, one large poster or foam board.
- Give each student a self-stick note and art supplies.
- Encourage students to draw a picture of their family.
- Put the finished notes together to create a collaborative art piece.
- Display the art piece in a location where others can view the work.

Connection—Students share their family and get to see different kinds of families.

Ages 12+

Read: *One for the Murphys* by Lynda Mullaly Hunt
When Carley becomes a foster child, she has to decide whether to trust the Murphys and allow them to really love her. Then her mom wants Carley back. Where will Carley choose to live?

Connection—Readers understand the complexities of being in foster care and finding a place of belonging within it.

Read: *Kids Cook the World* by Sean Mendez
A cookbook full of healthy choices using food from around the world.

Connection—Families cook recipes from different cultures. Talk about what you liked and disliked. Ask, Would you make this recipe again?

Read: *Counting by 7s* by Holly Goldberg Sloan
When twelve-year-old Willow loses her adoptive parents, she finds hope and a multicultural surrogate family.

Connection—Readers grasp that sometimes the circle of family widens to include those not related biologically.

Read: *Kira-Kira* by Cynthia Kadohata
Katie and her family are anchored to hope by her sister, Lynn, when they move from a Japanese community in Iowa to Georgia. When Lynn becomes sick, it's Katie's turn to hold her family together.

Connection—Students are reminded of the strong bond of family.

Read: *Half a World Away* by Cynthia Kadohata
Jaden journeys with his own adopted family to Kazakhstan to adopt again. A story about overseas adoption, hope, and second chances.

Connection—Readers learn about overseas adoption and some of the struggles that many adopted children face.

Read: *Secret Survivors: Real-Life Stories to Give You Hope for Healing* by Jen Howver and Megan Hutchinson
Real teens share their stories of surviving painful secrets, such as an eating disorder, addiction, rape, and abortion. In this book written by veteran youth ministry leaders, readers learn about the healing that can come from sharing your story. Includes a chapter on how to write your survivor story.

Connection—Readers better understand life events that can change the stories of a family, and they build empathy through stories of survival, healing, and hope.

Create: Writing
Gather supplies: paper, pens and pencils.
  • Prompt: What makes a family?

Connection—Writers think about the components that make up a family and how these building blocks are not always biological.

Gather: Plan a Family Date Night
Young people plan a surprise outing for their family like bowling, hiking, road tripping to a location no one has visited before, miniature golfing, or going out for ice cream. Take care of all the details.

Connection—Young people experience doing something special for their families and offer the gift of spending time together.

Gather: Coffee Shop Poetry Slam
Gather supplies: venue, five judges, score sheets, chairs, sound system (if needed).

- Poetry slams are spoken word competitions. Hold your slam at a local coffee shop, with their permission, or create your own coffee shop atmosphere. You'll need to advertise for poets in advance.

  Try a poetry slam with any *And Social Justice for All* topic as the theme.

- Set up the venue with chairs for the audience, five chairs for judges, and performance space for poets with sound system (if needed).
- Each participant has three minutes to perform their original poem based on the theme of family.
- Have the five judges score poets based on content and performance. They typically score 1–10 points. The highest and lowest scores are dropped and the middle three added together.

Connection—Students have the opportunity to share their perspective of family publicly in a unique art form.

CHALLENGE AND EXTEND AWARENESS AT HOME

- Read "30 Mealtime Facts About Families," found at lisavanengen.com.
- Practice "30 Days of Prayer for Families," found at lisavanengen.com.
- Start a family giving bank to collect coins. Choose what cause you would like to support with its contents.
- Slow down and spend time with your family.

- Support community events, your local library, and parks that benefit families in your community.
- Watch or bring the documentary *Screenagers* to your community.
- Grant the wish of a child in foster care through One Simple Wish (onesimplewish.org).
- Host a bake sale fund-raiser for No Kid Hungry with your family (bake sale.nokidhungry.org).
- Visit the Family Dinner Project to bring food, fun, and conversation to your family gatherings at the table (thefamilydinnerproject.org).
- Look at the Alphabet of Illiteracy from Project Literacy (projectliteracy .com). (Parents, please review the site first, as some illustrations may not be appropriate for small children.)

Dear friends, since God so loved us, we also ought to love one another. No one has ever seen God; but if we love one another, God lives in us and his love is made complete in us.

—1 JOHN 4:11–12

MAKING A DIFFERENCE

- Make a card for military spouses and children through Support Military Spouses (supportmilitaryspouses.org).
- Participate in Free a Family from World Renew (worldrenew.net).
- Give the Gift of a Healthy Home from Heifer International (heifer .org).
- Provide a family kit for survivors of natural disasters through CARE (gifts.care.org).
- The Wello WaterWheel provides an innovative way for families to transport clean water (wellowater.org).
- Support a family through Trees for the Future to plant life-giving trees (trees.org).

- Support a community or family garden through CWS (cwsglobal.org).
- Donate a bag, bike, or scholarship for a child in foster care through Together We Rise (togetherwerise.org).
- Donate a family-size water filter through World Renew (worldrenew .net).
- Support the work of Caring Bridge that keeps families up-to-date during difficult times (caringbridge.org).

For direct links to any of these resources plus additional materials, go to lisavanengen.com and click the And Social Justice for All tab.

Local Ideas

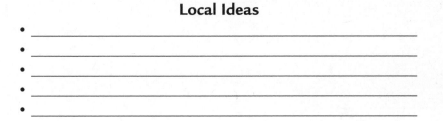

7

Health Care: To Touch the Hem of His Robe

Of all the forms of inequality, injustice in health care is the
most shocking and inhumane.
—MARTIN LUTHER KING JR., BAPTIST MINISTER AND CIVIL RIGHTS ACTIVIST

Raise Awareness

February—National Children's Dental Health Month
February (last day)—Rare Disease Day
February 4—World Cancer Day
February 14—National Donor Day
March 24—World Tuberculosis Day
April (first week)—World Health Workers Week
April 2—World Autism Awareness Day
May—Lyme Disease Awareness Month
May—National Mental Health Month
May (first week)—National Children's Mental Health Awareness Week
June 14—World Blood Donor Day
August—National Immunization Awareness Month
September—Childhood Cancer Awareness Month

September (second Friday)—Stand Up to Cancer Day
September 10—World Suicide Prevention Day
October 10—World Mental Health Day
November (third Thursday)—Children's Grief Awareness Day
December 1—World AIDS Day

While the developing world suffers the most from lack of health care, developed nations also struggle with equal access due to rising health-care costs and insurance coverage. Annually, close to 100 million people fall into poverty due to out-of-pocket health-care expenses.[1] According to Doctors Without Borders, one-third of the world lacks access to essential medicines.[2] Not feeling well can be a miserable experience, but not having access to medical care makes the situation excruciating and even life threatening. Being in that space is not what we wish for ourselves, our loved ones, or any of God's people.

> I care about finding a cure for rare diseases. Me and my siblings have a rare disease called dysautonomia and finding a cure would change our lives.
> —Aliya, age 16

Kids and adults alike enjoy watching contestants conquer Ninja Warrior courses. The grit, agility, and stamina of the players are admirable; even so, not many contestants find themselves at the finish line. Health care in many ways provides equally challenging obstacles. Whether it's being able to obtain access, carry insurance, or wade through forms, those who are the most vulnerable are affected the most.

Understanding the Issue

About one in five children will experience the death of someone close to them by age eighteen.[3] Talking about death and gently preparing children help them when actual death occurs. I remember the first time my mom read me Tomie dePaola's *Nana Upstairs and Nana Downstairs*. The story of Tommy, who lost a great grandma and a grandma, was gentle and offered the hope that sweet memories provide to grieving hearts. According to the National Child Traumatic Stress Network, across one's life span, complex trauma is linked to a wide range of problems, including addiction, chronic physical conditions, depression and anxiety, self-harming behaviors, and other psychiatric disorders.[4] After the death of close family members or friends, some children benefit greatly from grief counseling and care.

> To survive, people need care.
> —Maci, age 7

Minimizing loss and suffering is a justice issue. Health care disproportionately affects those in poverty. While health-care access has become troublesome for most socioeconomic classes, those in poverty experience the deepest disparities. "We [found] that living in disadvantaged neighborhoods reduces the likelihood of having the usual source of care and of obtaining recommended preventative services, while it increases the likelihood of having unmet medical need."[5] When the Bible calls believers to care for the "least of these," health care is a pressing justice issue (Matt. 25:40).

Global Concerns

Globally, health-care concerns include shortages of health-care workers and inadequate infrastructure to support the health of communities. Services that focus on trauma-informed care, human trafficking, vaccines, HIV prevention, and maternal and infant care strengthen health care. Other concerns about health care include preparedness for outbreaks, natural disasters, and emergencies. The more medical personnel, supplies, and transportation that respond to crisis situations, the more lives are saved. Communities need resources to prepare their responses to crises. Research, education, and collaboration allow nations to work together to respond globally.

Survivors of war and conflict, soldiers, civilians, and refugees often experience trauma. Trauma-informed care improves outcomes and cost to health care, but policymakers and practitioners need to invest in making it a priority. Traumatic experiences occur in war, abuse and neglect, natural disasters, and emotionally abusive situations. Treating patients through the lens of trauma-informed care, when needed, improves mental health and post-traumatic stress. Being able to provide those services as soon as possible makes positive outcomes in people's lives more likely.

Victims of human trafficking might be unable or fearful to access the health care they need. When they are afforded access, "health care providers should be prepared to identify, treat, and assist victims of trafficking as part of their regular clinical practice."[6] With the right training and screening tools, health-care providers are in the unique position of identifying victims, providing care, and taking steps for the victim's rescue. Investing in health-care workers who can meet those needs saves lives and lowers health-care costs in the long run.

As unclean water and poor sanitation contribute to the spread of disease and health-care costs, so does air pollution. Countries with high populations and growing pollution have poor levels of air quality; China and India suffer the most. Air pollution contributes to heart disease, stroke, lung cancer, premature births, and asthma. Severe smog forces citizens to wear masks when outdoors or stay inside, sometimes suspending school on high-pollutant days. Indoor air filters help, but their prices can be prohibitive to many.

Global health care only becomes stronger with improved training programs and funding for research. As superbugs and drug-resistant bacteria emerge, there is a need for the development of new vaccines. According to the World Health Organization, antibiotic resistance is one of the largest threats to global health.[7] Less potent antibiotics can lead to longer hospitalizations and greater stress on health-care systems. Experiencing a drug-resistant infection increases a person's chances for an extended hospital stay, long-term disability, or death. An Ebola virus outbreak occurred in West Africa between 2014 and 2016, and more than eleven thousand people died from the virus. Chronic poverty and civil war made West Africa particularly susceptible to the deadly outbreak. With unstable infrastructure, poor sanitation, limited health-care workers, and poor access to care, infectious diseases spread quickly and easily.

According to the World Health Organization, "the world will be short 12.9 million health-care workers by 2035; today, that figure stands at 7.2 million."[8] Health-care workers are not just doctors and nurses, but also social workers, midwives, community health workers, educators, and pharmacists. Growing global population, fewer people entering the profession, and migration of health workers all contribute to regional shortages. Shortages of health-care workers disproportionately affect the rural poor. The first week in April is World Health Workers Week; the week seeks to bring awareness to their impact and also to the need to support training and access to supplies.

Nearly 36.7 million people globally are living with HIV/AIDS.[9] AIDS has orphaned an estimated 17.8 million children.[10] HIV is often associated with behaviors that are seen as moral failure. Not only do people live with this disease, but they also must contend with stigma and discrimination. Access to testing, counseling, and antiretroviral drugs increase the life expectancy of people living with HIV.

An estimated 1.5 million children die annually from diseases that are preventable by vaccination. According to UNICEF, immunizations save up to three million children a year.[11] One of our summer playgroups supported Shot@Life, a United Nations organization that supports lifesaving vaccines for the developing world. The kids who attended brought along a favorite stuffed animal. They visited the vaccination tables, where their animals received a toy shot from nurses and a bandage. Participating in the stuffed animal clinic helped them tangibly see how we can protect the people we love with vaccinations. In the developing world, disease can spread quickly through inadequate sanitation facilities and unclean water supplies; there, vaccinations find even greater importance in stopping the spread of disease.

> I help people who are sick.
> —Molly, age 6

Focusing on maternal and infant health care saves lives globally. "Every day about 800 women die from preventable causes related to pregnancy and childbirth."[12] Imagine being a refugee and giving birth in a strange place without familiar resources. Prenatal care and postnatal care, including nutrition, save many lives. Access to health care, including the use of midwives, increases women's and babies' chances of survival. Even simple actions like promoting kangaroo mother care—placing infants skin to skin with their mothers or caregivers—saves lives. The Embrace Infant Warmer, essentially a high-tech sleeping bag with a warming pouch that does not require electricity, evolved from a Stanford University design course. The warmer costs 1 percent of the price of an incubator for low weight, preterm babies.[13] When we give babies and their mothers a strong start, their future becomes brighter.

Next-Door Concerns

The Unites States faces unique health-care concerns like health-care coverage, an aging population, antibiotic resistant infections, the stress of balancing work and life, and obesity. Health-care coverage allows patients to gain entry into the health-care system. Delayed entry might result in a patient being diagnosed later or dying prematurely. Having a primary care provider that a patient trusts and can communicate with makes a huge difference to health over time. Paying for acute health-care needs often takes all of a family's resources, and preventative care becomes something only wished for. Developmental well-checks, immunizations, and lead, hearing, and vision screenings make a huge difference in giving children a strong start. Adults who receive blood pressure, mental health, and cancer screenings that help monitor changes in health stay healthier long-term. Often these preventative measures are outside of insurance coverage and one's ability to pay out of pocket.

> **Kids don't need cavities or to get sick.**
> —Liam, age 6

I have stood in line at the pharmacy and watched the elderly, people in poverty, and people from the middle class being told their medications are not covered by insurance. They are forced to decide what to purchase and what to leave behind. I wonder whether they will be able to come back days later to buy the medicine they need or will face a period of time without it. Will the choice they make move them into a place where their health grows even more precarious?

We can give thought to the strain of extended illness on families. Navigating insurance, appointments, new and quickly changing information, travel, and extended hospital stays all consume great quantities of time and monetary resources. Maybe even more exhausting is the emotional toll of navigating illness. Nothing wrings out a heart like seeing a loved one suffer. All the unknown and fear weighs heavily on caregivers. Often family members must continue working through illness to maintain health-care insurance and care for other siblings. We can make a difference by meeting the needs of families in the midst of illness.

> **People need medicine to survive.**
> —Jaeyiah, age 8

According to the American Heart Association, 78 million adults and 13 million children deal with the effects of obesity daily in the United States.[14] Although many factors come into play, the rise of obesity aligns with increased screen time, fewer physical demands in our work, and fewer options for affordable healthy food choices. Obesity puts a strain on the health-care system because it leads to health problems like heart disease, type 2 diabetes, high blood pressure, certain cancers, asthma, and sleep apnea. For children who are obese, bullying can play a formative role in their growing-up years, creating a need for mental health care.

In the United States particularly, adults struggle to balance work and life stress. The US Travel Association estimates American workers fail to use five vacation days per year.[15] Most say their work culture makes it difficult to catch up or be absent. The rise of social media and easy access to technology make truly separating work and home life a challenge. Failing to exercise a healthy balance results in a weakened immune system, isolation, mental health struggles, and poor diet and sleep. All these factors contribute to poor health and put strain on our health-care system.

By the year 2030, the baby boomer generation will number 61 million in the age bracket of sixty-six to eighty-four.[16] The United States will need to strengthen access to long-term insurance options for this population, apply advances in technology to ensure optimal health in the elderly, and meet what will be a growing demand for health-care careers. Accessible community services will also help meet the needs of the growing elderly population.

Hope

Hope emerges when justice in health care is put into action. The Coalition for Epidemic Preparedness Action was created by global and interdisciplinary organizations for preventing infectious diseases from becoming epidemics. Twelve countries approved a vaccination for dengue fever, a mosquito-borne illness without a previously developed vaccination. The Global Burden of Disease study found that the death rates for HIV/AIDS, malaria, and diarrhea have decreased globally in the last two decades.[17] While great gains continue to be made, we need to remember that the unifying factor of them all is access. If people have access to health care, lives are saved.

The children's game Kerplunk requires players to place marbles on strategically placed horizontal sticks in a translucent tube. The goal is to extract the sticks in a way that prevents the marbles from falling. If we experiment and think of the sticks as the safety net of health care and the marbles as people, our goal would be to construct something that would not allow any marbles to fall. Justice applied to health care would mean developing systems where no one falls through the cracks.

INNOVATION TO EXPLORE

- *Using Medicine*: In more than sixty countries, Médecins Sans Frontières (Doctors Without Borders) provides medical aid to places in the world where it is most needed. The doctors work neutrally and impartially.
- *Using Medicine*: Through Shot@Life, if someone receives a flu shot at Walgreens, another lifesaving vaccine is provided to someone in the developing world.
- *Using Athletics*: Every sixty seconds, a child dies from malaria. Malaria is spread through disease-carrying mosquitoes. Sometimes the difference between life and death can be as simple as a bed net. The culture of sports dominates family life in the United States. The organization Nothing But Nets allows teams to connect sporting events to sending mosquito nets to save lives.
- *Using Hospitality*: Ronald McDonald House Charities operates homes away from home so that families can stay together during long medical treatments or prolonged illnesses. Homes include playrooms for siblings, home-cooked meals, and private rooms at little to no cost. Some hospitals have Ronald McDonald Family Rooms with quiet space, play areas, showers, sleeping areas, and laundry and kitchen space.
- *Using Medicine*: Ronald McDonald Care Mobile services takes pediatric health care on the road to provide immunizations, dental care, prenatal care, and asthma education in areas where there is limited access to these services.

Appreciate the Depth of Technology

The IBM World Community Grid allows volunteers to download a toolkit in the health-care research area of your choice. When your computer sits idle, it donates spare computing power to do research calculations. What might take scientists years can be calculated in months with the help of the World Community Grid. Currently, the grid powers research for cancer, Zika, TB, Ebola, and AIDS.

TALK JUSTICE

Ages 3–6
What can you do to stay healthy?

_____

_____

_____

How could you get outdoors and move more often?

_____

_____

Have you ever been sick? What made you feel better?

_____

_____

Do you go to the doctor sometimes? In what ways does a doctor help you?

_____

_____

Why is it important for people to have care when they are sick?

_____

_____

Ages 7–11
Do you know anyone who has an illness? In what ways could you show them care?

_____

_____

_____

How would your body feel if you never could see a doctor or a dentist?

_____

_____

How much sleep do you get at night? Why is sleep important?

_____

_____

What healthy habits do you have in your life?

_____

_____

What would a family need in order to make a hospital stay easier?

_____

_____

Ages 12+

Is there a free health clinic in your area? How could you support their efforts?

_____

_____

How would you define having access to health care?

_____

_____

What role does health care play in your family's life?

_____

_____

How does nutrition relate to health care?

_____

_____

How do you practice self-care? Why is self-care important for mental health?

_____

_____

STUDY GOD'S WORD

Luke 8:46–48

But Jesus said, "Someone touched me." . . . In the presence of all the people, [the woman] told why she had touched him and how she had been instantly healed. Then he said to her, "Daughter, your faith has healed you. Go in peace."

The woman, whose story is told in Luke 8:42–48, had a condition that caused her to bleed for twelve years. Twelve years is a long time to be ill and suffer. That entire time she had been considered unclean and isolated. She probably felt unworthy and hid in the crowd. While hiding, she reached out to touch the very edge of Jesus's robe. She had faith that Jesus could heal her, but she did not want to be discovered.

Despite people pressing against Jesus on all sides, Jesus sensed her touch, and he stopped. He stopped for her. Her touch could have made people consider him unclean too, but he was not ashamed to be touched by her. He called her out into the public eye. He spoke to her. He cared. In Hebrews 4:15 we are reminded that "we do not have a high priest who is unable to empathize with our weaknesses." Even in a crowd, Jesus was sensitive to the needs of this individual. He left her with the words, "Go in peace." He responded to the simple touch of the hem of his cloak. And when we reach out to Jesus, he responds to us too.

Extend Study of God's Word

Reread Luke 8:42–48 and highlight words and phrases that stand out to you. Think about how to apply to your life the things you highlighted, so they become more than just knowledge.

Who do you know that needs care? Write out a prayer for that person.

_____

_____

_____

_____

_____

_____

_____

Jesus slowed down to help the woman. Who might you slow down for in order to help?

_____

_____

_____

Like the woman in the Bible passage, what could you ask God for in faith?

_____

_____

Choose an organization that supports access to health care your family or group can pray for:

_____

_____

Choose a specific place or community in need of health-care access your family or group can pray for:

_____

_____

> *God, we pray for others to have a chance to receive medical care and to visit a doctor when needed. Please be with families that are facing illnesses and disease. Hold close families that have faced the death of a loved one. We pray that we could help bring access to more and more people locally and globally to receive the health care they need. Amen.*

EXPLORE JUSTICE

Ages 3–6

Read: *Bear Feels Sick* by Karma Wilson

Bear feels sick and is cared for by his forest friends.

Connection—Children are gently introduced to the concept of sickness and learn what things might bring comfort to others.

Read: *A Sick Day for Amos McGee* by Philip C. Stead
When Amos, an elderly man who works at the zoo, is too sick to visit his friends at the zoo, they visit him at home instead.

Connection—Children learn how important support and friendship are during illness.

Read: *Ida, Always* by Caron Levis
Inspired by the true story of iconic polar bears Gus and Ida, who resided in the New York City's Central Park Zoo. When Ida passes away, Gus realizes she will always be with him in his memories.

Connection—Children think about what makes a relationship special and how those things remain even after death.

Play: Stuffed Animal Vaccination Clinic
Gather supplies: toy shots from children's toy doctor kits, sign-in sheet and pens, bandages, small suckers, health-care volunteers, older children volunteers.
  • Invite children to bring their favorite stuffed animals.
  • Older kids make great helpers by signing in the stuffed animals.
  • Set up health-care volunteers to administer "vaccinations" with toy shots from children's toy doctor kits.
  • After the vaccination, give each child a bandage for the animal and a small sucker for the child.

Connection—Children are introduced to vaccines and their importance by helping their stuffed animals receive lifesaving medications.

Play: Teeth Cleaning
Gather supplies: yellow construction paper, marker, white water-based acrylic paint, toothbrushes.
  • Using the marker, outline a tooth on each piece of construction paper.
  • Provide each student a "tooth," toothbrush, and white paint within reach.

- Students then paint the tooth using the toothbrush and white paint, making it clean and white.

Connection—Kids learn that dental care is important for your health.

Play: Healthy Choice Red Light, Green Light
Gather supplies: start and finish lines.
- Line up the children at the start line.
- The game leader stands at the finish line.
- Typically, "green light" means go (the children run toward the finish line), and "red light" means stop (the children stop instantly and stand very still). Any student who keeps going when they are supposed to stop returns to the starting line. In this version of the game, students go when a healthy food choice is called and stop when an unhealthy food choice is called (see below for healthy and unhealthy food suggestions).
- The winner is the child who crosses the finish line first.
    Healthy Choices: carrots, apples, blueberries, whole-grain bread, broccoli, milk, grapes, brown rice, bananas, tomatoes, and potatoes.
    Unhealthy Choices: cake, hot dogs, french fries, cookies, bacon, candy bars, soda, chips, pizza, and cupcakes.

Connection—Kids think about what healthy food choices are and why they are the best option for people who experience hunger.

Ages 7–11
Read: *Mimi's Village: And How Basic Health Care Transformed It* by Katie Smith Milway

On a map, look up the places in the world where the stories you read take place.

Basic health care and clean water transform Mimi's family and her entire village in Kenya.

Connection—Children learn about what makes a healthy community and are encouraged to make a difference, just like Mimi.

Read: *Wilfrid Gordon McDonald Partridge* by Mem Fox
Wilfrid goes on a quest to help Miss Nancy, a resident of his next-door nursing home, find her memory.

Connection—Children learn about dementia and the value of intergenerational friendships.

Read: *The Lemonade Club* by Patricia Polacco
Best friends Traci and Marilyn face a challenge when Marilyn is diagnosed with leukemia and their entire fifth-grade class finds a way to support Marilyn.

Connection—Readers learn the power of friendship and witness the difference the support of others makes in times of illness.

Read: *My Abuela Is Sick* by Jennifer Bisignano
An eight-year-old girl's grandmother battles cancer. Written in both Spanish and English, this book includes a page on how to talk to children about cancer.

Connection—Readers are introduced to cancer and the emotional battle of seeing someone you love endure sickness.

Read: *The Princess and the Fog* by Lloyd Jones
The Princess and the Fog introduces childhood depression and offers hope that things can get better with a little help—all in fairy-tale form. Includes an essential guide for anyone supporting a child affected by depression.

Connection—This story can serve as a starting point for talking about depression and sadness.

Read 1 John 5:14: "This is the confidence we have in approaching God: that if we ask anything according to his will, he hears us."

Connect: Prayer Braid
Gather supplies: three strips of cloth (suggested

dimension: two inches wide by three feet long) for each student, clothesline, notecards, pens.

- Hang a clothesline.
- Encourage participants to take three strips of cloth and think of three people they know who need prayer for good health and healing.
- Help students tie the end of the strips to the line and braid them.
- As they braid, encourage them to pray for the people they thought of.
- Using the notecards and pens, have each student write a note to let their three individuals know that they were lifted up in prayer.

Connection—Students think about the importance of praying for those who are sick.

Call ahead of time and check to see what items the nonprofit would be able to give to their clients.

Create: First Aid Kits
Gather simple items to make a basic first aid kit (bandages, antiseptic wipes, instant cold pack, pain reliever, and so on). Put together a kit or more than one kit. Donate them to your local food bank or other nonprofit.

Connection—Kids learn that even simple health-care items can be hard to access for many people.

Ages 12+

Read: *The Heaven Shop* by Deborah Ellis
The Heaven Shop follows the arduous journey of three siblings, Junie, Kwasi, and Binti, who are orphaned because of AIDS and must face a dramatically different future than they might have otherwise.

Connection—Helps students understand what the reality of HIV/AIDS can look like for some global families.

Read: *Sadako and the Thousand Paper Cranes* by Eleanor Coerr
Based on the true story of Sadako, a young Japanese woman who contracts leukemia through atom bomb sickness. According to legend, if Sadako

creates a thousand paper cranes, she will be healed. After her death, her classmates complete enough cranes to reach her goal of one thousand.

Connection—Readers learn about terminal illness and the power of hope.

Create: Self-Care Kit
Create a self-care kit for yourself or someone else. Gather supplies. Examples include: fidget toy, notebook, pen, sketchbook, coloring book, crayons, earbuds, tissues, lotion, small stuffed animal, bubble bath. Consider adding an encouraging note if you are making one for a friend.

Race for a cause: many nonprofits and organizations allow you to run, walk, and bike in races to raise money for their cause.

Connection—Students think about what self-care items might be useful to themselves and others.

Gather: Relay for Life
Gather a group of friends to volunteer or walk in a Relay for Life fundraising event supporting the American Cancer Society.

Connection—Young people give back to their community and get involved in taking action against cancer.

Create: Infographic
Research facts about global health and access to health care. Create a shareable infographic using a free template from Piktochart. Remember to cite your sources.

Try making an infographic for other justice issues.

Connection—Students learn to gather factual information and present it in a relatable and visually appealing way.

CHALLENGE AND EXTEND AWARENESS AT HOME

- Read "30 Mealtime Facts for Health Care," found at lisavanengen.com.
- Practice "30 Prayers for Health Care," found at lisavanengen.com.

- Color a picture together from the Kid's Corner at Alex's Lemonade Stand (alexslemonade.org).
- Follow the journey of a bed net from Nothing But Nets in the fight against malaria (nothingbutnets.net).
- Listen to Jane Chen's talk "A Warm Embrace That Saves Lives" about the work at Embrace Global, which is helping newborns in developing countries (ted.com).
- Buy a toothbrush from Smile Squared and help a child in a developing country receive one too (smilesquared.com).
- Learn about the Hawa Abdi Hospital in Somalia, where health-care workers treat refugees. Save money to give to their work (dhaf.org).
- Fill out paperwork to be an organ donor, and talk about it with your kids.
- Make chemo care kits using a great guide found at Pennies of Time (penniesoftime.com).
- Send a monetary gift to global lifesaving mobile medical clinics through Project HOPE (projecthope.org).

Humanitarian action is more than simple generosity, simple charity. It aims to build spaces of normalcy in the midst of what is abnormal . . . to enable individuals to regain their rights and dignity as human beings.

—DR. JAMES ORBINSKI, NOBEL PEACE PRIZE LAUREATE

MAKING A DIFFERENCE

- Organize a dance marathon for the Elizabeth Glaser Pediatric AIDS Foundation (up4thefight.org).
- Bring Pennies for Patients to your school through the Leukemia and Lymphoma Society (studentseries.org).
- Host a blood drive through the American Red Cross at your school or church (redcrossblood.org).

- Support a Ronald McDonald House pop can tab collection (rmhc.org).
- Support Shot@Life, providing lifesaving vaccines where they are most needed (shotatlife.org).
- Support UNICEFs initiatives for prevention, treatment, protection, care, and support for children and teens most at risk for the HIV/AIDS epidemic (unicefusa.org).
- Purchase an HIV test kit (to go to people in Nigeria) through the World Renew gift catalog (worldrenew.net/gifts).
- Support Alex's Lemonade Stand (alexslemonade.org).
- Support Nothing But Nets to fight malaria (nothingbutnets.net).
- Shop the Operation Smile gift catalog to support children with a cleft lip or cleft palate (operationsmile.org).

For direct links to any of these resources plus additional materials, go to lisavanengen.com and click the And Social Justice for All tab.

Local Ideas

- _____
- _____
- _____
- _____
- _____

8

Human Trafficking: Modern-Day Abolitionists

Any time, any time while I was a slave, if one minute's freedom had been offered to me, and I had been told I must die at the end of that minute, I would have taken it—just to stand one minute on God's [earth] a free woman—I would.

—ELIZABETH FREEMAN, FIRST ENSLAVED AFRICAN AMERICAN TO WIN A FREEDOM SUIT IN MASSACHUSETTS

Raise Awareness

January—National Slavery and Human Trafficking Prevention Month

February 1—National Freedom Day

April—National Child Abuse Prevention Month

June 12—World Day Against Child Labor

July 30—World Day Against Trafficking in Persons

November 25—International Day for the Elimination of Violence Against Women

December 2—International Day for the Abolition of Slavery

December 10—Human Rights Day

I n New Delhi, India, a fifteen-year-old named Rajan sells roasted corn to support his six younger siblings.[1] A photograph taken at twilight features a twelve-year-old boy in Mumbai with a makeshift stick. At nighttime he is employed full time as a rat killer.[2] A young girl in a purple sari sits at a sparse sewing machine in Bangladesh; stacked far above her head lie piles of blue jeans.[3] Since age two, Enso has been a *restavek* (a domestic servant) in Haiti. Now ten years old and in charge of all the chores for a household of six, he is photographed sitting beside a five-gallon bucket with dirty knees.[4]

Of all the social justice topics discussed in this book, human trafficking might be the most difficult to broach with children. The concept in itself is scary and terribly unjust. The *And Social Justice for All* project began during a conversation with my friend and author Amy Sullivan. She told me about a human trafficking project her daughter's middle school class had done. We discussed with our kids the importance of talking about issues that affect others, even when the topics are hard. Over time the project grew. Every family will have a different timeline for sharing sensitive information with children. We are encouraged that whenever sharing occurs, opening our hearts to what others face deepens our empathy.

Understanding the Issue

In Exodus, Moses led the Israelites out of slavery and into the promised land. He was an unlikely leader, acutely aware of his own limitations and quick to pass responsibility to another, yet God used him, just as he uses modern-day abolitionists. In Exodus 3:7 God says, "I have indeed seen the misery of my people. . . . I have heard them crying . . . and I am concerned about their suffering." God called Moses, and he calls abolitionists today because God is acutely aware of the enslaved.

Article 4 of The Universal Declaration of Human Rights (1948) states, "No one shall be held in slavery or servitude; slavery and the slave trade shall be prohibited in all their forms."[5] Human trafficking today is a multibillion-dollar industry. The International Labor Organization estimates that 20.9 million people of all ages are "trapped in jobs into which they were coerced or deceived and which they cannot leave." Five and a half million of them are children. In the industries of agriculture, construction, domestic work, and manufacturing, an estimated 14.2 million people are trapped in forced labor.[6]

Travel backward, not so far in time, and find slavery in the United States. When my daughter was in fifth grade, her class learned about slavery. To reenact the conditions of a slave ship, her classmates laid down on the floor shoulder to shoulder. They imagined traveling over the ocean with their bodies closely compacted, a long journey to enslavement.

Upon arrival in the States, slaves were sold and enslaved for life on plantations, enduring injustice all their days. Read the picture book *Henry's Freedom Box* to young children. Desperate to be free, a man traveled in a box to reach that freedom, shipping himself like a package. Kids will tell you the Flat Stanley series of books, about a boy flat enough to mail himself in an envelope, are fantasy. But Henry Brown, a very real man, actually did mail himself because he longed not to be owned by another.

> To survive mentally and emotionally, I think people need loving peers and help from anyone willing to help them.
> —Regan, age 15

When our children grow older, we can introduce the concept of child laborers. Child labor often entails long hours that deprive children of regular developmental activities and is harmful mentally and physically. About 215 million children worldwide are considered child laborers.[7] These children are forced to work up to eighteen hours a day. They are often not given adequate nutrition, living conditions, or education. In developing countries, it was estimated that in 2016, there were 115 million children ages five through fourteen who were coerced to work.[8] Poverty forces parents to make such terrible decisions as selling children into domestic servitude. Parents reason that at least their children might have a chance of survival in servitude.

Help children imagine going to work every single day, early morning to late at night, no more recess and gym class, no more lunchtime and laughter. Paint realistic pictures of a hot field on a summer day, doing the backbreaking work of picking crops; scrubbing floors in a home; caring for children not much older than themselves; scavenging in a dump and selling the scraps. The weekend does not exist anymore. When child laborers do get time off, they fall asleep in exhaustion.

The last component of human trafficking to talk about is sex trafficking. This type of trafficking occurs by force, fraud, or coercion and includes the recruiting, housing, transporting, or providing of people for the purpose of commercial sex. Writer Flannery O'Connor once wrote in a letter to a friend, "The truth does not change according to our ability to stomach it emotionally."[9] We might wish to always shield our children from the horror of sex trafficking, but their safety as they age is also important. I once thought this kind of trafficking only happened in red-light and impoverished districts across the globe; this could not be further from the truth. Sex trafficking occurs all over the world, including the town you live in.

Global Concerns

Globally, young people are promised jobs, which they desperately need to support their families. They travel on a promise and end up disoriented, stripped of their passport, and enslaved. They are forced to pay off debts of shelter and food, and they realize that repayment is impossible. Other victims are offered advertised modeling jobs, marriage, or education only to be sex trafficked instead. When victims have the courage or opportunity to escape, they face trauma from what they have experienced. Rescued victims need legal support, rehabilitation, and reintegration into safe homes and communities.

I wish there was a way to make people see how our actions and choices have impacted this world.
—Hayden, age 15

There are 15 million people in debt bondage, the highest numbers in India, Nepal, Pakistan, and Bangladesh.[10] Debt bondage occurs when children or adults are forced to work to pay off debt. Often the salary given to the worker is not enough to sustain their family and pay off the debt, pushing them into a life where they are forever stuck in bonded labor. Migratory workers are vulnerable to being enslaved through debt bondage. Human trafficking yields profits of roughly $150 billion a year.[11] Modern-day slavery looks different than in history. Today, slaves are disposable; their purchase cost is low, but their profits are high.[12]

In areas of poverty, traffickers might promise desperate parents a better life for their child, only to sell the child into slavery. Traffickers also prey on orphaned and runaway children. In the book *The Locust Effect*, Gary Haugen of International Justice Mission talks about an invasion of locusts in the Midwest United States during the year 1875. The locusts ruined emerging crops and, with them, the progress of the settlers. He compared that destruction to the way violence and trafficking destroy the growth of those rising out of poverty.[13] Those who are the most vulnerable and live in poverty are at the greatest risk to be trafficked or to lose their children to trafficking.

Next-Door Concerns

Homeless young people in the United States are at the greatest risk of being sex trafficked. We must acknowledge the disproportionate amount of US runaways identified as lesbian, gay, bisexual, and transgender (LGBT) youth. Around 20 percent of homeless youth identify as LGBT, yet 58.7 percent are exploited through sex trafficking.[14] Those statistics do not match up. We need to ask why this population of young people runs away frequently and falls into trafficking. As the church, can we prevent these young people from finding themselves in such a vulnerable space? What could we be doing differently?

In July 2017, a semitrailer with around forty people inside was found in a Walmart parking lot in sweltering Texas heat. Ten people died and thirty were hospitalized because of heat asphyxiation.[15] These migrants were smuggled into the United States by human traffickers looking to profit off their vulnerability. The migrants hoped to gain access into the United States, the smugglers sought to make the most money possible, and in doing so, they endangered and ended lives. This type of trafficking occurs every day in the United States and globally across international borders.

Hope

The critically acclaimed 1906 novel *The Jungle* by Upton Sinclair follows a Lithuanian immigrant who works at a slaughterhouse in Chicago. Sinclair writes,

> The great packing machine ground on remorselessly, without thinking of green fields; and the men and women and children who were part of it never saw any green thing, not even a flower. Four or five

miles to the east of them lay the blue waters of Lake Michigan; but for all the good it did them it might have been as far away as the Pacific Ocean. They had only Sundays, and then they were too tired to walk. They were tied to the great packing machine, and tied to it for life.[16]

Trafficking strips human beings not only of basic needs but also of hope. There are no mornings at the park, afternoons at the beach, or evenings under the stars. A beautiful life of promise withers under the power of bondage.

There is a need for modern-day abolitionists, people willing to fight slavery in their time. That is all of us. In 1850, the Fugitive Slave Act was passed by the US Congress to stop abolitionists. The law allowed slaves, when found, to be returned to their owners, along with harsh punishments to those who aided escape. Abolitionists, then and today, put themselves in danger to help those in slavery. Trafficking is a huge criminal industry, and many individuals would not like to see it end. Would we be so brave as to say no anyway? Isaiah 61:1 says, "The Spirit of the Sovereign LORD is on me, because the LORD has anointed me to proclaim good news to the poor. He has sent me to bind up the brokenhearted, to proclaim freedom for the captives and release from darkness for the prisoners."

In Eleanor Coerr's story *Sadako and the Thousand Paper Cranes*, twelve-year-old Sadako was diagnosed with leukemia after exposure to the atom bomb dropped in Hiroshima. She threw herself into the Japanese tradition that says folding a thousand paper cranes will bring healing. Hundreds hung over her hospital bed, and when she passed away, her classmates finished the rest. Imagine lying on the floor, looking up at one thousand colorful paper cranes floating. Unhindered flight brings freedom. What the birds of the air experience, so should children and the most vulnerable of the world.

INNOVATION TO EXPLORE

- *Using Craftsmanship*: Many fair-trade artisans are survivors of human trafficking. When you purchase fair-trade items, you often support survivors.

- *Using Nonprofits*: Love146 offers rapid-response backpacks to children suspected of being exploited, including a cell phone set to call 911, care items, and a teddy bear.[17]
- *Using Technology*: The Global Modern Slavery Directory is a searchable map that shows organizations all over the world that address human trafficking. This partnership ensures that help can be found quickly in the closest location to the victim.
- *Using Technology and Leadership Development*: The organization Annie-Cannons partners with shelters to train survivors of human trafficking in digital fluency and software programming. Their approach is collaborative and trauma informed, creating a platform for survivors to thrive in the job market.
- *Using Journalism*: The CNN Freedom Project uses journalism to amplify the voices of survivors and end modern-day slavery.

Appreciate Symbolism

The Blue Heart Campaign represents the sadness of those who are trafficked. The campaign raises awareness and builds political support for fighting human trafficking.

TALK JUSTICE

Ages 3–6

What do you think it means to be free?

_____

_____

Do you think kids have a right to attend school and to play?

_____

_____

What things do children need so they can grow up healthy and strong?

_____

_____

_____

Ages 7–11

What would it be like if you went to school all day and never got a lunch, recess, or bathroom break?

_____

_____

What do you think it would be like to work an adult job each day instead of attending school?

_____

_____

Would you be able to pick crops in 100-degree heat every day?

_____

_____

Would you have risked helping people through the Underground Railroad (a network of safe houses and allies helping slaves escape to freedom in the northern states)?

_____

_____

Would you have had the courage to escape through the Underground Railroad?

_____

_____

Ages 12+

What would it feel like to *not* be free?

_____

_____

What questions do you have about human trafficking?

_____

_____

_____

Should we support companies that use child labor to make their products?

_____

_____

_____

How might refugees or those in poverty be at greater risk for being trafficked?

_____

_____

_____

Thinking about the topic of human trafficking, what are some smart safety tips for young people to practice online?

_____

_____

_____

STUDY GOD'S WORD

Isaiah 58:6

Is not this the kind of fasting I have chosen: to loose the chains of injustice and untie the cords of the yoke, to set the oppressed free and break every yoke?

Have you ever ridden your bike to a location and then locked it up? Bike chains are thick and secure so that no one can take your bicycle. Children caught up in human trafficking are held tightly too, as if they are a possession instead of a human being. This is wrong and inhumane, yet it happens even in the country where you live.

What is fasting? In Scripture, fasting is almost always linked to going without food for a period of time in order to grow closer to God. But this Scripture writer isn't giving up food; he's choosing to fast in a different way. He is fasting from injustice and oppression. He doesn't want this awful treatment of humanity to happen in his world.

We can give up something special to us for a time—TV, video games, chocolate—and ask God to show us injustice and oppression near us so we can join in to help erase it from our world.

Extend Study of God's Word

Gather colorful markers and poster board and explore this passage further by writing the text of Isaiah 58:6 in poster form.

Are their things in your life that keep you in bondage and far from God?

_____

_____

How could God use you to loose the bonds of injustice in the world?

_____

_____

_____

What does freedom in Jesus look like? Describe what it means to have freedom in Jesus.

_____

_____

_____

Choose an organization that fights human trafficking that your family or group can pray for:

_____

_____

Choose a specific place or community that is vulnerable to human trafficking that your family or group can pray for:

_____

_____

God, we pray for those vulnerable to being trafficked. Help them find freedom. We pray that they could feel safe. Give us courage to be modern-day abolitionists. Help us loosen the burden of others. Give us the ability to see those around us who are enslaved and oppressed, so we can offer help. Let us not forget those in the shadows seeking freedom. Amen.

EXPLORE JUSTICE

Ages 3–6

Read: *Dave the Potter: Artist, Poet, Slave* by Laban Carrick Hill
Dave, a slave living in rural South Carolina in the 1800s, creates art, and through that art he also creates hope and lasting beauty.

Connection—Readers see the beauty that people, both free and enslaved, bring to the world.

Create: Foil Sculptures
Gather supplies: roll of aluminum foil.
- Tear the foil into various sizes.
- Set the foil pieces on a table.
- Invite the kids to take a piece of foil and shape it into a bird sculpture.
- Encourage them to share their creations.

Connection—Talk about the freedom birds have to fly wherever they would like to go. Should all people have freedom to try new things and make choices?

Create: Feather Collaborative Art
Gather supplies: neutral-colored construction paper, scissors, art supplies, black-colored backdrop.
- Prior to the art session, cut a large feather out of each sheet of construction paper (one feather per child).
- Allow children to decorate their feather using the art supplies.
- Combine and display the feathers as two large wings.
- Display the wings on the black-colored backdrop.
- The collaborative art piece can become a photo opportunity as well.

Connection—Artists think about wings and the concept of freedom.

Play: Go Fish with Keys
Gather supplies: dowels, string, magnets, paper clips, metal keys, a "fishing pond" made of construction paper, a blanket or plastic tablecloth.

- Use the dowels as fishing poles and tie string to the end (hot glue or Gorilla Glue the tied string to the dowel). Fishing poles can be made ahead of time for participants.
- Tie a paper clip or attach a magnet to the end of the string as "bait."
- Create a "fishing pond" out of construction paper, a blanket, or a plastic tablecloth. Lay the metal keys out on the pond. (Participants could help set up the pond.)
- Allow the kids time to go fishing for keys.

Connection—Children learn about the concept of freedom through keys. Talk to kids about what keys are used for. Ask them why keys are important and why we need them. Talk about being free and not being locked up.

Create: I Spy Bottle
Gather supplies: uncooked rice, used keys, acrylic paint, clear bottle or jar with lid.
- Before children arrive, prepare the I Spy bottles.
- Paint the keys various colors. Let them dry completely.
- Fill the bottles with the rice and keys, leaving a gap so the items can move around.
- Make sure the bottle tops are secured tightly.
- Allow the kids to play with the bottles and see what keys they can spy.

Connection—Children play with a sensory toy while thinking about the purpose of keys and what locking and unlocking means.

Ages 7–11
Gather: Movie Party
Gather supplies: *The Prince of Egypt* movie, food, craft supplies, baby doll.
Host a *Prince of Egypt* movie party.
- Share parts of Moses's story in the book of Exodus, like Moses being saved as a baby (2:1–10) or the parting of the Red Sea (13:17–15:21).
- Serve flatbreads, candy kabobs, or cake with frosting shaped like the parting waves of the Red Sea.
- Create hieroglyphic posters.

- Play Hide Baby Moses. Have one person be Miriam and hide a baby doll, and have the other participants work together to find him.

Connection—Children learn about the concept of slavery and God's rescue through a child-friendly movie.

Read: *We Are All Born Free: The Universal Declaration of Human Rights in Pictures* by Amnesty International
The Universal Declaration of Human Rights states the rights and freedoms that all human beings should experience in their lives. These rights are depicted in picture-book form.

Connection—Children learn what human rights are and their importance to people around the world.

Read: *This Child, Every Child: A Book About the World's Children* by David J. Smith
A beautifully illustrated book that draws children into the lives of fellow children around the world.

Connection—Children learn that all kids have the right to live safe and healthy lives.

Read: *Henry's Freedom Box: A True Story from the Underground Railroad* by Ellen Levine
The unbelievable true story of Henry, a man who escaped slavery by mailing himself to freedom.

Connection—Children connect with a man named Henry and his experience in slavery.

Read: *Moses: When Harriet Tubman Led Her People to Freedom* by Carole Boston Weatherford
A fictional story based on the spiritual journey of Harriet Tubman, a well-known conductor on the Underground Railroad.

Connection—Readers witness Tubman's bravery and learn about the Underground Railroad.

Read: *Unspoken: A Story from the Underground Railroad* by Henry Cole
A young girl helps a runaway slave. Told entirely through illustrations in this wordless book.

Connection—Readers are challenged to think about how ordinary people can fight injustice.

Observe: Study Art
Study a community mural project in India, *Together We Can End Human Trafficking*, led by Joel Artista.

Connection—Students study different forms of trafficking depicted on the dress of a woman pictured in the mural.

Create: Writing
Gather supplies: paper, pens and pencils.
  • Prompt: We were all born free to . . .

Connection—Writers express their thoughts about the things we are free to do and dream in our lives.

Create: Key Wind Chime
Gather supplies: old keys, stick (approximately 1–2 feet long), colorful yarn, string, colorful acrylic paints, paintbrushes.
  • Direct students to paint the keys various bright colors. Let them dry completely.
  • Decorate the stick by repeatedly wrapping the entire length of the stick with colorful yarn. Use as many colors as you wish.
  • Tie one length of yarn to the stick for each key you wish to hang from the stick.
  • Tie one key to each dangling thread. You can hang all keys the same length or varying lengths—crafter's choice.

Connection—Kids create a symbol of freedom. Ask participants what they use keys for and what they represent.

Ages 12+

Connect: Slideshow Viewing
Scroll through a Love146 slideshow about slavery (love146.org/slavery/). (Suggested for ages 14+.)

Connection—Students see a comprehensive primer on human slavery, building background knowledge of the issue.

Read: *Sold* by Patricia McCormick
The story of thirteen-year-old Lakshmi, sold by her stepfather into prostitution in India. Written in free verse. (Suggested for ages 14+.)

Connection—Readers are exposed to the reality of a life that has been sold.

Read: *Copper Sun* by Sharon M. Draper
Amari journeys from slave trade to plantation life and eventual escape to a free Spanish colony.

Connection—Readers gain greater understanding of slavery and the roles that friendship and sanctuary play for those seeking freedom.

Read: *Be the Change: Your Guide to Freeing Slaves and Changing the World* by Zach Hunter
Zach founded Loose Change to Loosen Chains as a twelve-year-old and continues on his mission to prove that one person can make a difference.

Connection—Students see a real-life example of a young person who made a difference in human trafficking.

Read: Freedom Series by Kathi Macias
A Christian trilogy that tackles the topic of human trafficking: *Deliver Me from Evil, Special Delivery,* and *The Deliverer.*

Connection—Human trafficking revealed through the perspective of fictional characters.

Create: Editorial to Newspaper
Give students these instructions:
- Find a local newspaper and look at their submission guidelines for an editorial.
- Write an editorial about how your community can fight against modern-day slavery.
- Use a strong thesis statement.
- Build your argument with statistics, real-world examples, and quotations.
- Offer ideas for readers to respond and find solutions.
- Find someone to edit your work before you submit it to the newspaper.

Write an editorial on any of the topics in *And Social Justice for All*.

Connection—Students refine their thoughts on human trafficking through editorial writing and have the opportunity to share their work with the public.

Gather: *Break the Chain*
Host a screening of the movie *Break the Chain*. This documentary looks at the issue of human trafficking in the United States and how it often goes unnoticed in our own communities. The movie features more than twenty interviews with survivors and experts in the field.

Connection—The film encourages those who watch to consider how we are all connected and how we can work together to break the chain of human trafficking.

CHALLENGE AND EXTEND AWARENESS AT HOME

- Read "30 Mealtime Facts About Human Trafficking," found at lisa vanengen.com.
- Practice "30 Prayers for Human Trafficking," found at lisavanengen .com.

- Sign up your family to be an International Justice Mission prayer partner (ijm.org).
- Watch "End Slavery in Ghana Fundraiser" from jlaw321 on YouTube and learn about supporting the International Justice Mission.
- As a family, take the Slavery Footprint survey that looks at your consumption and how it relates to child labor (slaveryfootprint.org).
- Work through the website of Sue Scheff, parent advocate and internet safety expert (suescheff.com). Many children become vulnerable to human trafficking through the internet.
- Know the National Human Trafficking Hotline: 1-888-373-7888.
- Advocate for the END IT Movement as a family (enditmovement .com).
- Send an e-card for various holidays, with a donation benefiting Love146 made in the name of the recipient (love146.org).

Few human rights abuses are so widely condemned, yet so widely practiced. Let us make [child labor] a priority because a child in danger is a child that cannot wait.

—KOFI ANNAN, FORMER SECRETARY-GENERAL OF THE UNITED NATIONS

MAKING A DIFFERENCE

- Donate items for rapid-response backpacks through Love146 (love146 .org).
- Watch a short Vimeo video to learn about the mining of mica (for cosmetics) through child labor in India from Made in a Free World (vimeo.com).
- Consider hosting a screening of the documentary *Not My Life*, a film about slavery in our time.
- Watch *Stand with Sanju*, a child labor cartoon from GoodWeave (good weave.org).

- Look through the Faces of Freedom gallery (facesoffreedom.goodweave .org).
- Bring "Speak Truth to Power: The Curriculum" to your school (blogs .nysut.org).
- Invest in a future free of slavery through Not For Sale (notforsale campaign.org).
- Raise funds for International Justice Mission (ijm.org).
- Participate in Loose Change to Loosen Chains, a student-led campaign for students of all ages through International Justice Mission (ijm.ca).
- Monetary donations provide transitional care to survivors through Exodus Road (theexodusroad.com).

For direct links to any of these resources plus additional materials, go to lisavanengen.com and click the And Social Justice for All tab.

Local Ideas

- _____
- _____
- _____
- _____
- _____

9

Hunger: Gleaning the Edges

Surely there is enough for everyone within this country. It is a tragedy that these good things are not more widely shared.

—JONATHAN KOZOL, *SAVAGE INEQUALITIES*

Raise Awareness

June—National Fresh Fruit and Vegetable Month
August—National Breastfeeding Month
August (first full week)—National Farmers Market Week
September—Hunger Awareness Month
October—National Farm to School Month
October 16—World Food Day

Families experience food insecurity when they lack the resources for enough affordable, quality food. Food insecurity affects a child's ability to develop and learn. Sleep comes slowly with a hungry tummy. Growth becomes stunted, and development slows. Hunger negatively hinders social interactions, mood, and behavior. Families living in poverty deal daily with food insecurity, and it becomes a major stressor. According to Feeding America, one in six kids in America do not always have enough food.[1] Globally, 795 million people in the world do not have enough food to lead a healthy and active life.[2] Three out of four teachers see hungry students in their classrooms, according to data collected by the national organization No Kid Hungry.[3]

A hunger season occurs in the period between when crop stockpiles run out and the next harvest occurs. Most of us might experience hunger for a few hours at most, but imagine an entire season of hunger, months long. It is not as easy for those of us in the developed world to understand hunger seasons. Even when fruits and vegetables are out of season, we are able to access them at the supermarket, where they have been transported from other places in the world.

> Donate extra food you have lying around the house. To some people a few snacks are a whole feast.
> —Levi, age 10

The truth is that while most of us do not experience a hunger season, too many families still do. One day at school I was meeting with a reading group. We were reading a story about soup and pretending to make our own. While we made our soup, I asked the students what their favorite food was to eat for dinner. One little boy, age six, who had been in and out of foster care, answered in his gravelly voice, "We make our own dinner. Ramen noodles. My baby brother just bites them off like this." He imitated his brother ripping off a chunk of uncooked noodles. Hunger hurts.

Understanding the Issue

Currently we produce more than one and a half times enough food to feed the nearly seven billion people on our planet.[4] The Food and Agricultural Organization of the United Nations estimates one-third of all food produced is wasted. That waste would be enough food to feed three billion people.[5] In the United States, 40 percent of all food is thrown away, enough to feed 25 million Americans.[6]

When thinking about hunger, there are different degrees to which it is experienced. If people experience hunger, they are not getting enough nutrition. Malnutrition presents as an extreme form of hunger where people lack essential nutrients, which in turn impairs health. People who experience undernutrition do not have access to food with enough protein, calories, and nutrients to be healthy. Food insecurity occurs when people cannot be confident they will have food each day.

Global Concerns

"Hunger is the worst in Asia at 520 million people, Sub-Saharan Africa at 243 million, and Latin America/Caribbean with 42 million."[7] Hunger occurs in every nation and disproportionally affects vulnerable people groups like women and children, aging populations, and refugees.

In the book *What the World Eats*, photographer Peter Menzel documents what families around the world eat in a day. The contrasts are deeply affecting. As a family, church, community, and school, we could examine our consumption and food waste. This is a simple place to start in our own families to fight the injustice of hunger. Look at what food you purchase each week. Is there an item you could forgo, instead donating it to your local food pantry? Or could you use the money saved to contribute to an organization that fights hunger? Look at what food you throw away each week in your home. Can you make smaller portions? Can you use leftovers in a more strategic way? Involve kids. They love using their problem-solving skills. Help them get into detective mode and brainstorm how to fight food waste.

> Quit being greedy and selfish, and try not to waste food.
> —Marissa, age 17

One solution to global hunger is creating sustainable farming practices for small-scale farmers. Providing access to land and resources like seeds, tools, credit, and markets to sell allows rural farmers food sources and capital. Sustainable practices often use renewable energy sources. Organizations teach farmers how to have healthy soil by rotating crops and using natural pest management. Water management allows farmers to use the scarce water resources they may have access to. Enhancing local farms gives communities access to food that does not need extra transportation and storage, thus cutting the costs to the consumer while still providing income to farmers.

> To help hunger we could make sure that each country has good, productive farms and make food easy to get to.
> —Megan, age 13

Hunger occurs disproportionately during emergencies, drought, and conflict. Countries and communities with a safety net and backup plan in place fare better when these situations occur. Relief agencies that focus on such action plans help address hunger during crisis. During crisis, more food goes to the hungry when nongovernmental organizations are willing to work together. Instead of transporting food from other nations, purchasing food in the country affected or in a neighboring country "speeds up delivery, reduces transaction costs, better respects cultural eating habits, and supports local and regional markets."[8] The World Food Programme piloted a program to provide electronic vouchers via text message for Iraqi refugees in the Syrian Arab Republic. Refugees can choose the quantities and types of products from a nearby shop rather than traveling long distances for a two-month ration.[9] Using innovation and group problem solving allows more food to reach those in need while supporting local economies.

Next-Door Concerns

In the United States, the front lines of fighting hunger are often found within education. National School Lunch and School Breakfast programs serve meals to eligible students. In the summer, many school-age children receive lunch at local parks through Summer Food Service Program. Schools in developing countries find greater attendance when they serve a meal. Sometimes the meal is as simple as a bowl of rice, but warm nourishment in a hungry tummy means life.

Food deserts exist in areas where there are no healthy food options, typically inner cities and low-income rural areas. Without access to grocery stores or farmers markets, many families turn to what is in walking distance, such as fast-food restaurants and gas stations, to meet their food needs. These places provide less nutritious choices and charge more for food, not allowing families frugal choices for their food dollars. Families in food deserts end up spending more money for unhealthy food.

> If you had too much food, you could give other people some of your food.
> —Asher, age 7

The United States government provides food assistance through two programs: Supplemental Nutrition Assistance Program (SNAP) and Women,

Infants, and Children (WIC). SNAP provides food support to families in times of need in the United States. The program serves about 42.6 million people.[10] Families typically use this safety net from one month to three years. More than half of those who use benefits are children, the elderly, and the disabled. Undocumented immigrants cannot and have never been able to access SNAP benefits. Most recipients are employed in some capacity while using benefits or were employed before needing assistance, and many find employment after using SNAP.

Children who suffer malnutrition in the one-thousand-day window after birth face lifelong challenges. They experience health problems, difficulty learning, and have a harder time gaining employment and later raising their own healthy families. WIC provides healthy food and nutritional education to at-risk low-income women, infants, and children.

> We could order or prepare what we know our bodies can take. That way we do not waste food and are able to give to others.
> —Ashley, age 14

A 2014 Feeding America Study found that families used a variety of coping strategies to be wise with their food dollars. They might purchase unhealthy but inexpensive food, take help from friends, water down food or drinks, sell or pawn items, garden, brush without toothpaste, delay payments, cut back on medical expenses, or skip laundry. "More than 25 million employed individuals earn less than $11.50 per hour, wages that leave many of them in, or at the edge of, poverty."[11] Though they are working families, they still do not have the income to meet basic food needs.

A population we do not automatically equate with hunger is the elderly: "81% of older adult households are food insecure."[12] Feeding America estimates around 13 million adults age fifty and older receive assistance from their network each year.[13] Senior citizens are likelier to experience hunger if they are disabled, live in the South, are divorced, or live with grandchildren. The elderly often do not seek assistance due to lack of mobility, lack of technology education, and fear of stigma. Older adults with food insecurity are more likely to skip medications and experience depression. When organizations emphasize screening and referral, it helps identify senior citizens experiencing hunger so they receive the help they need.

Hope

I love reading *The Very Hungry Caterpillar* by Eric Carle to children and listening to them giggle. To grow and transform into a beautiful butterfly, the caterpillar needed to fill his stomach with food. The same is true for every child in the world. To grow up healthy, build their minds, and strengthen their immunity, children need to eat healthy food.

I help by cooking food.
—Naylin, age 5

According to FoodLab Detroit, as of 2015, there were 1,500 community market and school gardens.[14] This becomes a beautiful picture of hope when you think of these urban gardens in light of the desolation the city of Detroit has faced. In those abandoned lots and struggling schools, new life has thrived. In the desolate space of hunger, we can bring hope too.

Animal microloans provide income and a source of food to global families. Many organizations offer gift catalogs of various options. Gathering monetary donations in your home, classroom, or group allows young people to pursue a shared goal. Providing bees, cows, pigs, goats, llamas, and other animals to global families deepens understanding of hunger and solutions.

Get a lot of food for yourself, but split it and give it to people who need it.
—Xander, age 9

In a roundtable discussion led by Feeding America, teens gave solutions and strategies for alleviating hunger.[15] Some of their ideas included incorporating food into programming and services (discretely, to reduce stigma), creating programs where teens volunteered and then received food, establishing community farms, and bringing people and stores closer together. Looking at these solutions, I am encouraged by young people's sensitivity, their awareness of collaboration, and their ownership of being involved.

We need more community gardens.
—Navaeh, age 15

On the shore of the Sea of Galilee, Jesus sat with his disciples facing an approaching crowd that would take a half year's wages to feed (John 6). Jesus went to a boy with a basket of five loaves of bread and two fish. He gave thanks, and that offering was multiplied to feed more than five thousand people, with some food left over. The small offering of a child was used to feed many and grew in size and scope. This story in the Bible reminds adults that God makes a difference through children. We, as adults, are integral in helping them learn to see the needs around them and meet those needs by giving from their own resources.

INNOVATION TO EXPLORE

- *Building Community*: Community Action House, a food bank in Holland, Michigan, operates a community garden from March through October. Volunteers plant, care for, and harvest fresh fruits and vegetables for families in need.
- *Using Urban Farming*: Windy Harvest Farmers in Chicago farm atop the McCormick Center on 20,000 square feet. They are one of 359 rooftop farms operating in Chicago.[16]
- *Using Food Recovery*: Two hundred and thirty college chapters in forty-four states participate in Food Recovery Network. Students recover food waste from their campuses to feed the hungry. Learn more at foodrecoverynetwork.org.
- *Using Policy Development*: The United States Department of Agriculture has partnered with the Farmers Market Coalition to accept SNAP benefits at local farmers markets, giving access to fresh, locally grown food to those who need it most.
- *Using Culinary Arts*: No Kid Hungry offers a Cooking Matters program that helps families increase their knowledge of how to stretch food dollars with healthy meals. Their farm-to-school movement connects local farms with schools for farm field trips, cooking classes, and school gardens.

Appreciate a Gift

Leanne Brown recognized the need for people on SNAP to stretch their food dollars for nutritious meals. She compiled a cookbook of recipes that could be made on a budget of $4.00 a day (the average individual allocation for SNAP). The cookbook, *Good and Cheap*, is available free online (leannebrown.com). The book has been downloaded more than one million times.

TALK JUSTICE

Ages 3–6
What is your favorite food to eat?

_____

_____

When do you know that you feel hungry?

_____

_____

How many meals and snacks do you eat in a day?

_____

_____

Do you think food is important for your body and brain to learn and grow?

_____

_____

What do you think is a good meal to share with others?

_____

_____

Ages 7–11
How often do you throw away food?

_____

_____

Where does your food come from?

_____

_____

How would you feel if there was no food on your plate at dinner?

_____

_____

What if the whole town you lived in did not have enough food?

_____

_____

What ideas do you have to get healthy food to hungry people?

_____

_____

_____

Ages 12+

If you had to grow all your own food, how would your eating habits change?

_____

_____

_____

If you were hungry, in what ways would it be hard to keep up with school, sports, and other activities?

_____

_____

Do you think teenagers who experience hunger are likely to tell others? Why or why not?

_____

_____

_____

What groups of people do you think might be especially susceptible to hunger?

_____

_____

_____

What ideas do you have to get healthy food to hungry families?

_____

_____

STUDY GOD'S WORD

Leviticus 19:9–10

When you reap the harvest of your land, do not reap to the very edges of your field or gather the gleanings of your harvest. Do not go over your vineyard a second time or pick up the grapes that have fallen. Leave them for the poor and the foreigner. I am the LORD your God.

In this Leviticus passage, we witness God instructing landowners to leave a margin space for those who need provision. God's people are asked to harvest their fields but not take every last bit for themselves. If their fields produced a second crop, they were to leave it for those in need. They were to leave the edges unpicked and only harvest one time. If they dropped some of the crop during harvesting, they were to leave it for someone else to gather.

The poor and the alien do not have access to their own land to grow crops and their own food. God remembers them and provides for their needs. God is asking his people to give of their land and their harvest. He is asking that we don't keep taking until there is nothing left. He asks us to take what we need and leave the remainder for others. In our present world marked by consumption and individualism, we can learn much from these instructions about leaving a margin for others. He is the Lord our God, and he is commanding us to be holy—set apart—to do things that look different from the rest of the world. God instructs us to have a broad margin in our lives, not for our own comfort, but to make space for other people who have little.

Extend Study of God's Word

Read the Leviticus passage five times, emphasizing different words each time you read it.

What in our lives could we leave or save for others?

_____

_____

_____

What are we holding on to that God could help us let go of?

_____

_____

Where in our lives can we leave a margin space to provide for the needs of our brothers and sisters in Christ?

_____

_____

_____

Choose an organization that fights hunger that your family or group can pray for:

_____

_____

Choose a specific place or community that experiences hunger that your family or group can pray for:

_____

_____

> *Thank you, God, for the food we have to eat. We pray for those who do not have enough to eat. Help those who are hungry have enough food to eat—healthy food with the vitamins and minerals their bodies need to grow strong. Help us remember immigrants, refugees, and those trapped in conflict areas who do not have access to enough food.*
> *Amen.*

EXPLORE JUSTICE

Ages 3–6
Read: *Community Soup* by Alma Fullerton

Kioni has some little goats that followed her to school . . . and are trying to eat the community garden the Kenyan children tend! Teamwork creates a clever resolution and some tasty vegetable soup.

Connection—Kids learn about working together to provide access to fresh food for everyone in their community.

Make soup with your family and deliver it to someone who would be encouraged by it.

Read: *Stone Soup* by Heather Forest
Two travelers are in need of food. When no one in the village they are passing through shares with them, they decide to make magical soup . . . from stones. A story about sharing, generosity, and vegetables.

Connection—Readers learn the message that when people work together to fight hunger, no one has to go without.

Create: Birdseed Pine Cone
Gather supplies: pine cones, dull knife, peanut butter, birdseed, string.
- Go on a hunt for at least one pine cone per student, or provide each student with a pine cone.
- Tie string on the pine cone if you want to hang the finished product.
- Cover the pine cone with peanut butter and sprinkle with birdseed.
- Hang the pine cone in a tree or lay it on the ground to feed birds in the winter season.
- Observe what kinds of birds eat from it.

Connection—Kids learn that all living things need food.

Create: Place Mats
Gather supplies: construction paper, colorful markers or crayons, lamination sheets.
- Design place mats for your local Meals on Wheels that deliver meals to the elderly in your community.
- Rectangular place mats are typically 12" x 18".
- If you are able to laminate the place mats, recipients can use them longer.
- Add encouraging messages to the mats.

Connection—Kids contribute encouragement to the elderly in their community who face hunger.

Play: Garden-Themed Play Area
Gather supplies: ideas could include empty seed packets, gardening tools, toy fruits and vegetables, baskets, empty watering cans, gardening gloves, wheelbarrow, and so on.
- Set up a "garden" and allow children to play freely.

Connection—Hands-on playtime helps children think about food, how it's grown, and our need for it.

Play: Relay Race
Gather supplies: multiple sets of toy food from various food groups, four baskets, posters, markers.
- Divide kids into four teams, with each team making one poster representing a food group: dairy, grain, fruit/vegetable, meat.
- While the kids are creating the posters, talk about what foods are in each group and why every group is important.
- In an open space appropriate for a running game, set one poster next to each basket.
- Give each team toy food from various food groups.
- Kids then take turns racing to put the food into the correct food group basket.

Connection—Kids learn about healthy foods through active play.

Ages 7–11
Read: *Maddi's Fridge* by Lois Brandt
Sofia and Maddi are the best of friends, but Sofia's refrigerator is full while Maddi's is empty. Sofia struggles with how to help Maddi, resulting in a thoughtful story of empathy and sensitivity.

In *Maddi's Fridge*, Sofia's mom is able to help because Sofia talked to her about Maddi. Encourage the kids in your life to ask questions and tell you what they are noticing.

Connection—Not all children have enough food to eat every day. This book encourages children to look at childhood hunger and how they might make a difference.

Take photographs of what your family eats in a week. How does it compare to the photographs in the book?

Read: *What the World Eats* by Faith D'Aluisio
The author and a photographer visited families in twenty-one different countries to observe and photograph what each family ate during one week. Beautiful, full-color photographs are included throughout.

Connection—Powerful visual learning about the differences in the food families eat and the differences in what we eat to stay healthy. What pictures made the most impact on you? What did you notice about the amounts each family had?

Read: *One Hen: How One Small Loan Made a Big Difference* by Katie Smith Milway
Kojo, a boy from Ghana, receives a small amount of money. With it he buys a hen and begins raising his own flock. Soon his farm is the largest in his area. Based on a true story.

Connection—The gift of a single baby chick changes the lives of many families.

Read: *The Good Garden: How One Family Went from Hunger to Having Enough* by Katie Smith Milway
On their farm in Honduras, eleven-year-old Maria Luz and her family struggle with hunger. Then Maria learns about new sustainable farming methods to help her family move from food insecurity to having enough to thrive.

Connection—Children learn how simple changes can make a difference and how a little girl led her family.

Gather: Field Trip
Meet up with a group and take a tour of your local community garden, farmers market, or food pantry.

> *Connection—Young people get real-world, hands-on experience with places that provide food for families in their communities. Think about how you could help hungry people in your community better access these resources.*

Create: Writing
Gather supplies: paper, pens and pencils.
- Prompt: If I could only eat one food for a week, I would feel . . .

> *Connection—Writers contemplate what it would feel like if their food access was limited.*

Observe: Study a Photograph
Study *Waiting for Work on Edge of the Pea Field* by Dorothea Lange.

> *Connection—Study artwork that depicts the farm workers who harvest the food we eat.*

Create: Stop-Motion Film
Gather supplies: digital camera, editing software.
- Create a stop-motion film around the theme of fighting hunger.
- For every second of the short film, you could shoot up to ten photographs.
- Shoot your animation, download your photographs to your computer, upload them to a program like iMovie, fill in the timeline of your film, and add music. You can also use an app like iStopMotion, Stop Motion Studio, or iMotion.
- Share your stop-motion film with others.

Try making a stop-motion film for any of the social justice topics in this book.

> *Connection—Through technology and innovation, students share a message about the importance of fighting hunger.*

Ages 12+
Gather: Food Pantry Collection Contest
- Talk to local food pantries and compile a list of the most-needed items.
- Challenge another school or youth group to a collection contest.
- Set start and end dates, and begin collecting.
- Set a date to celebrate the success of the collection contest with all the groups involved, and deliver the food to the local food pantry.

Connection—Help students contemplate the most-needed items in their community. Talk about why they think those items are needed.

Gather: *MasterChef* Contest
Gather supplies: three staple foods per student group (for example, chicken, rice, sweet potatoes), pantry basics (for example, butter, garlic, honey, milk, salt, olive oil, herbs, spices, soy sauce), pots and pans, utensils for cooking, one oven per group.
- Organize a *MasterChef* contest for students.
- Students enter the competition in groups of two.
- Create a panel of three or four judges. Consider inviting chefs from area restaurants to volunteer their time as judges.
- Give each group the three staple foods they will use in their creation.
- Give each group access to pots, pans, utensils, pantry basics, and an oven.
- Allow each group ample time to plan and make their dish.

Connection—Students learn to cook creatively with limited resources while bringing awareness to the justice issue of hunger.

Create: Scene Writing
Gather supplies: plate, dried rice, paper, pens and pencils.
- Set out a single plate with a teaspoon-size circle of rice in the center.
- Using the scene as a writing prompt, give kids ten minutes to free write.

Connection—Students write from a scene representing hunger. Encourage writers to share what they wrote with one another.

Create: Public Service Announcement

Gather supplies: recording equipment, editing software.

- Write an informative ad about hunger using persuasive text and inviting visual elements. Consider ending your announcement with a call to action.
- Typically, public service announcements are around thirty seconds (about 60–75 words).
- Groups define their audience, research, write a script, storyboard, film, and edit their own announcement.
- Share the announcement with your classroom or group. Consider submitting your announcement to a local radio station, television station, or nonprofit.

Try a public service announcement for any of the *And Social Justice for All* topics.

Connection—Create a focused message educating your viewers about hunger.

CHALLENGE AND EXTEND AWARENESS AT HOME

- Read "30 Mealtime Facts for Hunger," found at lisavanengen.com.
- Practice "30 Prayers for Hunger," found at lisavanengen.com.
- Bring a meal to a family in need, a single parent, or the elderly.
- Sharpen your vocabulary skills by playing freerice.com. Every correct answer donates ten grains of rice through the World Food Programme. Play together—grains add up fast!
- Onehen.org offers more than one hundred curriculum ideas for all grades and subjects, including math, English language arts, and social studies. The website also offers four games that give back.
- *The Good Garden* has a companion curriculum with activities and extensions (citizenkidcentral.com).
- Map the Meal Gap lets you look at hunger statistics for your county (feedingamerica.org).
- Know where your town's food pantry is located and what you can contribute there.

- View the "10 Faces of Food Assistance in 2014" slideshow from the World Food Programme (wfp.org).
- Talk with your family about food waste. Brainstorm ways your family can curb waste with careful planning.
- Visit cookingmatters.org, where you can access more than ninety recipes and learn to stretch your food budget while cooking healthy meals.

We know a peaceful world cannot long exist one-third rich and two-thirds hungry.

—JIMMY CARTER, 39TH PRESIDENT OF THE UNITED STATES

MAKING A DIFFERENCE

- Have each kid bring a small donation to combine in order to support an organization that offers microloans to purchase animals that contribute to food security.
- Organize your community using resources from Bread for the World (bread.org).
- Encourage kids to bring a small donation to contribute to Edesia Nutrition projects hosted at GlobalGiving (globalgiving.org).
- Hold a bake sale and donate proceeds to an organization that fights hunger.
- Become a Hunger Free Community with The Alliance to End Hunger (alliancetoendhunger.org).
- Find a local Feeding America location to serve at (feedingamerica.org).
- Bring Heifer International's Read to Feed to your school (heifer.org).
- Choose a category to support through the Feeding America gift catalog (feedingamerica.org).
- Organize a screening of the film *A Place at the Table* (takepart.com /place-at-the-table).
- Read the stories of smallholding farmers at oneacrefund.org/blog.

For direct links to any of these resources plus additional materials, go to lisavanengen.com and click the And Social Justice for All tab.

Local Ideas

- _____
- _____
- _____
- _____
- _____

Immigrants and Refugees: The Gift We Received

Since you cannot do good to all, you are to pay special attention to those who, by the accidents of time, or place, or circumstance, are brought into closer connection with you.

—AUGUSTINE OF HIPPO, BISHOP AND THEOLOGIAN

Raise Awareness

March 31—Cesar Chavez Day
May 1—World Day for Cultural Diversity
June 20—World Refugee Day

In the city where I live, Holland, Michigan, on the shore of Lake Macatawa, in Kollen Park, stands a bronze statue of seven figures with traveling bags. The statue is called *The Immigrants* and represents the heritage of the city.

The following history I found in the depths of a public museum library, in a dark basement room lined with file drawers. Everything lay in one thin folder—no placards or bronze statues to mark what was before the traveling figures.

In the spring of 1847, a group of immigrants journeyed from Rotterdam,

Netherlands, to New York City's Ellis Island. The Atlantic passage took forty-seven days. They sought to settle in a new land because of religious and economic oppression. Eventually, they settled in West Michigan. There the Ottawa Native Americans lived on the shore of Lake Macatawa, then called Black Lake. The Ottawa Native Americans had cleared fifteen acres of land and built nearly thirty huts and tepees covered in cedar bark. They were well established on the land and planned to remain, summering farther north toward the Mackinac region and returning for the fall and winter to the Macatawa area.[1]

The Ottawas' natural rhythm was to spend part of the summer hunting, fishing, trapping, or visiting other villages. This was also necessary because throughout the 1830s and 1840s, settlers "destroyed the natural resources that the Ottawas of Southern Michigan relied upon." It is documented that often, "Americans declared that Ottawa homesteads had been abandoned and claimed the land for themselves."[2] The following spring the Native Americans sold their land to the settlers, exhumed their dead, and traveled north by canoe. They renamed the area Ana-mah-npo-nig, "the place where the Dutch live."[3]

> I would welcome immigrants and refugees with a pink and purple welcome sign.
> —Ruby, age 7

The eloquent Chief Simon Pokagon spoke six different languages and authored the book *Queen of the Woods*, thought of as a classic in Native American literature. In the words of Chief Pokagon, "The same forest that frowned upon you smiled upon us. The same forest that was ague and death to you was our bulwark and defense. The same forest you have cut down and destroyed, we loved, and our great fear was that the white man in his advance westward would mar or destroy it."[4] Native Americans were the original inhabitants of the land.

The words of Native Americans in response to the seizure of their lands are written in eloquent heartbreak. Chief Joseph of the Nez Percé tribe went to the Hayes Administration in Washington, DC, in 1879. There he said, "I have asked some of the Great White Chiefs where they get their authority to say to the Indian that he shall stay in one place, while he sees white men going where they please. They cannot tell me. I only ask of the Government to be treated as all other men are treated. If I cannot go to my own home, let me have a home in a country where my people will not die so fast."[5] This history speaks of how non–Native Americans were also immigrants. If you live in the United States, you may be able to trace your ancestry back to Ellis Island. More than twelve million immigrants entered through Ellis Island in the years between 1892 and 1954.[6] This life, this land, this freedom are all gifts.

Understanding the Issue

Precise definitions better explain the immigrant and refugee population. An *immigrant* is a person who moves to live permanently in a foreign country. A *refugee* is someone who has been forced to leave their country in order to escape war or religious, political, or ethnic persecution. A *migrant* is a worker who moves from place to place in order to work. An *internally displaced person* is a person who has been forced to move due to conflict but who has not crossed international borders.

We face a global refugee crisis. In 2015, more than a million refugees and migrants made perilous journeys into Europe.[7] According to "the United Nations Refugee Agency, UNHCR, 65.6 million people are currently living as refugees or as displaced persons inside their own countries."[8] An alarming number of displaced people are children, some traveling alone. According to Pew Research Center, in the United States there are an estimated one million undocumented immigrants.[9] Undocumented immigrants enter the United States to escape poverty and violence and to look for employment.

Global Concerns

The Transatlantic Council on Migration cites five main reasons why the public defaults to anxiety and fear about immigration: when (1) flow of immigrants outpaces preparation, (2) immigrants are viewed as competition for scarce resources and opportunities, (3) influx of different cultures threatens norms and values, (4) acts of terrorism and violence are attributed to a whole people group, and (5) trust is lost in government integration policies.[10]

The Israelites have a strong history of migration in the Bible. Jesus himself was a refugee as a young child. Major refugee populations today include

Palestinians, Afghans, Iraqis, Somalis, Congolese, Myanmarese, Colombians, Sudanese, and Syrians. An estimated 65.3 million refugees are displaced globally.[11] The Rohingya, a Muslim indigenous people group in Myanmar, have been subject to forced eviction recently. Over the past two years, one million refugees have escaped conflict by the Mediterranean Sea in overfilled boats, some nothing more than squishy inflatable rafts. More than seven thousand people have lost their lives in doing so; those who survive arrive in Europe struggling and at times unwelcome.

The Declaration of Human Rights, Article 14, Section 1 states: "Everyone has the right to seek and to enjoy in other countries asylum from persecution." Reading Scripture, we find God's word in Leviticus 19:33–34:

> "When a foreigner resides among you in your land, do not mistreat them. The foreigner residing among you must be treated as a native-born. Love them as yourself, for you were foreigners in Egypt. I am the LORD your God."

> I would ask, "Do you want to play with me?"
> —Carlito, age 8

We live during a time of refugee crisis. Refugees face deep trauma from war-torn lands. We saw the photographs of three-year-old Alan Kurdi lying dead on the shoreline of the Mediterranean Sea; the stunned little boy from Aleppo, covered in dust and blood, in the back of an ambulance; an Afghan baby in half-inflated water wings, cradled in the arms of his mother. We see the photographs of overloaded trucks, boats, and trains, and of people traveling many miles on foot. Refugee children find even greater challenges and are five times less likely to attend school.[12] Currently there are 2.6 million child refugees affected by the Syrian crisis alone.[13] Their little spirits find resilience in the strength of their families; their long-term fates are less certain.

Next-Door Concerns

The United States has documented a history of both welcoming immigrants and unwelcoming them. This history we need to acknowledge and teach. The Chinese Exclusion Act of 1882 suspended immigration for ten years from China after American citizens experienced declining wages. The law was later expanded to the Asiatic Barred Zone Act and overturned sixty-one years later in 1943. Japanese internment relocated 120,000 Japanese

Americans—including orphans of Japanese American descent and first-, second-, and third-generation Americans—into internment camps after the attack on Pearl Harbor. When the United States entered World War II, the agricultural community needed workers and instituted the Bracero Program. This program allowed legal temporary workers from Mexico to fill low-paying agricultural jobs. When wages stagnated in 1954, the Eisenhower administration instituted Operation Wetback, a mass deportation effort. By 1964, the Bracero Program had been completely terminated.

> I would welcome immigrants and refugees by saying, "Welcome to Spokane, I hope you like it here." I would try to be their friend.
> —Dannon, age 10

The goal of the Immigration and Nationality Act of 1952, "as described in the legislative language was to preserve the sociological and cultural balance of the United States."[14] The act continued selective and limited immigration. The quota system gave more visas to people of Northern and Western European descent. Although President Truman vetoed the law because he believed the quota should have been higher for Asian nations, Congress still passed it.

Today the United States uses a highly structured vetting process. Refugees pair with case managers, who collect identifying documents. They collect biological data like fingerprints and facial recognition and perform biometric security scans. Applicants are then interviewed, and documents reviewed again. Resettlement Support Centers receive the documents of strong candidates. Then US security agencies such as the FBI, CIA, Department of Health and Human Services, and the State Department screen candidates. Candidates then receive another interview and submit fingerprints. The fingerprints are then screened against the FBI, DHS, and Department of Defense databases. If these screenings are passed, refugees then undergo a medical exam. Applicants attend a cultural orientation class and are assessed for an appropriate resettlement area. At this time, refugees travel to the United States and have one year to apply for a green card. Throughout the process, cases continue to be checked against terrorist databases. Of the roughly 17.2 million refugees worldwide, only 1 percent are ever reestablished in another country.[15]

Crucial to understanding immigration is knowing the stories of those without legal documentation. Today 11 million undocumented immigrants are living in the United States.[16] They make up disproportionate amounts of the United States' low-skilled labor market: farm workers, construction workers, housekeepers, janitors, groundskeepers, and dishwashers. Today a group of people lives as a permanent underclass in our country. They pay taxes and contribute to Social Security benefits they will never receive themselves. They wake up each morning and provide the labor for the most underpaid, backbreaking, unnoticed jobs.

> Hi, I'm Kellan.
> We take care
> of this country.
> Maybe you could
> help us.
> —Kellan, age 7

They have undocumented status because acquiring permanent legal status in the United States is quite limited due to an outdated immigration system. Currently there is no way to correct an undocumented status even if you have been living in the United States for decades. There are three ways in which a person can enter the United States legally: through employment, family, or asylum. None of these ways guarantee immigrants a green card, and all have yearly caps.

Just over one million undocumented immigrant farm laborers in the United States do essential work for our agricultural system, filling jobs that citizens do not.[17] At least 50–70 percent of farm laborers in the country today are unauthorized.[18] If you were to read the job description for an agricultural worker, you would find the following: inspecting, planting, weeding and harvesting by hand, spraying fertilizer and pesticides. Workers often move from harvest to harvest. They work in all weather conditions—heat, rain, wind, and cold. There are between 1 and 2.5 million hired farmworkers in the United States.[19]

> I would invite
> them over
> for dinner.
> —Summer,
> age 10

This is the reality in which they live. Many immigrants are limited to the boundaries of the farm they work. Undocumented workers are at a high risk for exploitation. Employers could withhold wages or provide unfair working conditions without fear of retribution, because undocumented workers would be hesitant to seek help from law enforcement. They are at risk for hunger and face difficulties acquiring adequate shelter, health care, and education. It is estimated that 5.5 million children in the United States have at least one undocumented parent.[20] These families live with the constant fear of separation. Undocumented persons are only eligible for school and emergency room services, no other government benefits. Their story is a part of the history of the United States and the church.

Hope

My family attends a multilingual church; we sing in English and Spanish, sometimes Swahili or other languages. There I have learned it is a beautiful thing to know I'm not the center of the world. Suddenly, fear of what is not familiar does not seem so insurmountable. The world and its people grow softer and deeper. The multicultural church can be messy—the simplest things can be lost in translation—but there is power in being together and working to understand one another.

> Try some of their foods. Respect their beliefs, or (best of all) bring them some cookies.
> —Ellie, age 12

In his book *The Way of the Heart*, Henri Nouwen says, "To die to our neighbors means to stop judging them, to stop evaluating them, and thus to become free to be compassionate. Compassion can never coexist with judgment because judgment creates the distance, the distinction, which prevents us from really being with the other."[21]

When I was eight years old, the movie *An American Tail* came out. When a family of mice emigrates from Russia to the United States, their young son gets separated from them. In the quiet of the night, young Fievel sings a heartwarming song about the connection he feels to the family he misses. He knows that somewhere, wherever his family might be, there is someone saying a prayer for him. Our immigrant and refugee brothers and sisters need our prayers and our voices.

> I would give them some of my stuff, try to help them, and ask if they need anything.
> —Kabelo, age 14

> We could help immigrants and refugees by making sure they can participate in activities in the community.
> —Grace, age 10

The Christian Reformed Church Office of Social Justice teaches a class called Church Between Borders. That statement cannot be refuted; we are a church that resides between the borders of other countries. As God's church, we are called to show hospitality to the stranger. How will we respond? Matthew 25:35 says, "I was hungry and you gave me something to eat, I was thirsty and you gave me something to drink, I was a stranger and you invited me in."

INNOVATION TO EXPLORE

- *Using Advocacy*: Countless churches and individuals have adopted and helped refugee families settle into their new homes and communities.
- *Using Technology*: The organization Techfugees gathers people in the technology industry to collaborate and bring about response and solutions to the needs of refugees.
- *Using Education*: BorderLinks offers educational immersion trips to groups at the Arizona-Sonora region at the US-Mexico border near Chiapas, Mexico. Participants develop a deeper understanding of migration and life at the border through experiential learning and workshops (borderlinks.org).
- *Using Advocacy*: World Renew and the Office of Social Justice offer Blessing Not Burden events for people to share how immigrants have been a blessing to them, and to help people ask Congress to change the laws that prevent immigrants from getting legal status.
- *Using Community Development*: The Philadelphia Immigrant Innovation Hub works with entrepreneurs and small-business owners to provide tools, language classes, and free services to immigrants. Their work has renewed local neighborhoods and reenergized their economies.

Appreciate Partnership

The National Immigration Forum was established in 2013 to gather a network of advocates from faith communities, law enforcement, and business leadership. They seek to develop policy that grows the economy, is compassionate, and preserves security while respecting the law (immigrationforum .org).

TALK JUSTICE

Ages 3–6

What do you love about the city you live in?

_____

_____

Have you ever traveled away from your home? How did it feel?

_____

_____

What is your home like?

_____

_____

_____

If you had to leave your home with just one suitcase, what would you pack?

_____

_____

_____

How do you welcome guests to your home?

_____

_____

Ages 7–11

Families around the world live in constant fear of separation. Describe how you think that would feel.

_____

_____

_____

How can you welcome immigrants and refugees in your community?

_____

_____

How can you reach out to students in your school that are new immigrants and refugees?

_____

_____

What are some reasons you think people immigrate to other countries?

_____

_____

_____

Did anyone from your family immigrate to the United States? What is their story?

_____

_____

_____

Ages 12+

In what ways do immigrants and refugees contribute to communities?

_____

_____

_____

How can you honor cultures and traditions that are not your own?

_____

_____

_____

What would it feel like to be a refugee? If you had to leave your home immediately, what would you take with you?

_____

_____

If you were in danger in your home country, would you stay there even though it was dangerous, would you try to immigrate to another country, or would you escape as a refugee with the hope of returning someday?

_____

_____

_____

How do you feel we could make the process of immigration into the United States fair?

_____

_____

_____

STUDY GOD'S WORD

Deuteronomy 10:17–19

For the LORD your God is God of gods. . . . He defends the cause of the fatherless and the widow, and loves the foreigner residing among you, giving them food and clothing. And you are to love those who are foreigners, for you yourselves were foreigners in Egypt.

The Israelites were once strangers in Egypt; in this passage, God calls them to love the strangers living among them. As immigrants themselves, they should understand the difficulties faced by immigrants. Your personal experience may include immigration, but what if it does not? Hebrews 13:2 encourages all believers to show hospitality to strangers.

Kids know that the necessities for survival include food, water, shelter, and love. If you truly love someone, you want more for them than just the bare necessities. You want for them a life lived in hope, not fear. The stranger in our midst is close to the heart and thoughts of God, as seen in these verses and others throughout Scripture. Growing close to Jesus means learning to open our hearts to those whom he loves and what he calls us to do.

Extend Study of God's Word

Read Deuteronomy 10:17–19 aloud.

How could you follow the example of God in welcoming strangers?

_____

_____

_____

What does it mean to "love those who are foreigners"?

_____

_____

_____

Can you describe a time in your life when you felt like a stranger in a new place?

_____

_____

_____

Choose an organization that supports immigrants and refugees that your family or group can pray for:

_____

_____

_____

Choose a specific community of immigrants or refugees that your family or group can pray for:

_____

_____

_____

God, hold close those who have been displaced and need refuge. Thank you for remembering them with loving-kindness. Help us remember refugees fleeing conflict and persecution, and the immigrant seeking a better life. Give us eyes to see their contributions. Give us opportunities to love the stranger. Help us have courage to meet their needs when we can and give voice to the needs we cannot meet personally. Amen.

EXPLORE JUSTICE

Ages 3–6

Read: *Migrant* by Maxine Trottier

Anna's family migrates north in the summer and south in the winter. She wonders what it would be like to be rooted in one place year round.

Connection—This simple book with sweet illustrations helps the youngest children grasp the immigration journey.

Read: *A Gift from Papá Diego / Un Regalo de Papá Diego* by Benjamin Alire Sáenz

The beautifully illustrated English/Spanish bilingual story of Diego and his longing to see his Papá Diego, who lives across the border in Mexico.

Connection—Readers are introduced to the border between the United States and Mexico and how it separates many families.

Read: *We Came to America* by Faith Ringgold

We Came to America examines America's history of immigration and diversity and celebrates the unique gifts each person brings.

Connection—Readers learn that America was built on a history of immigration.

Read: *Lost and Found Cat: The True Story of Kunkush's Incredible Journey* by Doug Kuntz and Amy Shrodes

Based on the true story of an Iraqi refugee family who was traveling to Greece with their stowaway, beloved family cat Kunkush. When Kunkush's carrier breaks, he becomes separated from his family . . . then the worldwide community works to reunite them!

Connection—Children learn about the refugee journey through the highly relatable experience of a family pet.

Gather stones and try creating stone artwork to illustrate the story of Rama.

Read: *Stepping Stones: A Refugee Family's Journey* by Margriet Ruurs
A unique story in English and Arabic that features the stone artwork of Syrian artist Nizar Ali Badr. Rama and her family leave Syria and flee civil war for safety in Europe.

Connection—Readers experience the refugee journey through a unique art form.

Play: Packing a Bag
Gather supplies: a variety of suitcases and bags, clothing, bags of rice, food boxes, water bottles, bandages, stuffed animals, flashlights, blankets.
• Lay out all the supplies and allow kids time to pack the traveling bags.

Connection—Children think of the immigrant and refugee experience through the lens of packing belongings to travel to a new home. Ask what items they think might be important to pack for a long journey.

Ages 7–11
Read: *Good-Bye, 382 Shin Dang Dong* by Frances Park
In this beautiful picture book, Jangmi adjusts to leaving Korea for her new home in Massachusetts.

Connection—Children learn empathy for the immigrant experience and all that immigrants leave behind.

Read: *Harvesting Hope: The Story of Cesar Chavez* by Kathleen Krull
Weaving in the story of Cesar Chavez's life, *Harvesting Hope* focuses primarily on the 340-mile march he organized to protest the working conditions of migrant farmworkers in California. When Chavez spoke, a nation listened.

Connection—Readers learn about the story of Cesar Chavez, the difficulty of migratory farm labor, discrimination, and fair labor practices.

Read: *The Name Jar* by Yangsook Choi

Unhei, a recent immigrant from Korea, decides to choose a new name to fit in with her new classroom. Her classmates help by filling a glass jar with names for her to choose from. What name will she choose?

Connection—Children will understand the challenges of fitting into a new culture while retaining one's own culture. They also learn about the power of friendship in helping immigrants assimilate.

Read: *Inside Out and Back Again* by Thanhha Lai

Based on the author's childhood experiences as a refugee, *Inside Out and Back Again* relates Hà's immigration journey from Saigon to the United States in poetic verse.

Extend understanding by encouraging readers to write the next chapter of Hà's story.

Connection—Children are invited into the inner thoughts and feelings of a young girl leaving the only place she has known as home and settling in a new land.

Read: *Four Feet, Two Sandals* by Karen Lynn Williams and Khadra Mohammed

Lina and Feroza each find a single sandal in a refugee camp on the Afghanistan-Pakistan border. Their friendship grows when they decide to share the matching sandals as they experience life at the camp and wait for immigration to the United States.

Connection—Children learn what life is like in a refugee camp, as well as what it means to sacrifice for a friend.

Read: *Baseball Saved Us* by Ken Mochizuki

When a young boy and his family land in a Japanese American internment camp after the attack on Pearl Harbor, Shorty's dad decides baseball is the perfect distraction during their displacement. The entire community finds hope in the baseball games.

Connection—Readers learn about internment during World War II and the power of community.

Read: *The Red Pencil* by Andrea Davis Pinkney
When militia attack a peaceful Sudanese village, twelve-year-old Amira must escape to a refugee camp. Just as she is beginning to lose hope, a simple gift reminds her that the world is full of possibilities.

Connection—Readers experience a refugee journey and holding on to hope.

Read: *The Red Umbrella* by Christina Diaz Gonzalez
Fourteen-year-old Lucía Álvarez journeys from Cuba as part of an organized movement of fourteen thousand unaccompanied minors sent to America to escape Fidel Castro's revolution.

Connection—Readers learn what it means to have a dual identity and the great lengths people navigate to live in safety.

Read: *Pancho Rabbit and the Coyote: A Migrant's Tale* by Duncan Tonatiuh
Young Pancho goes on a journey to find Papá Rabbit, who went north to seek work.

Connection—Children gently enter into the hardships of families who cross from Mexico into the United States when undocumented to seek employment and a new life.

Observe: Study Art
Study the photograph *Migrant Mother* by Dorothea Lange.

Connection—Students study a photograph taken in 1932 of a destitute mother of seven, with three of her children. They are migrant pea pickers.

Create: Design a Postcard
Gather supplies: cardstock cut to postcard size (4" x 6"), decorating supplies (like crayons, colored pencils, or markers).

- Encourage students to design a postcard that welcomes refugees and immigrants to your city, school, church, or community.

Connection—Students think about how to welcome newcomers in their communities.

Create: Collage
Gather supplies: old magazines, decoupage, paintbrushes, poster board, scissors.

> **Try a collage for any of the *And Social Justice for All* topics.**

- Have each student cut out photographs, letters, and colors that represent the immigrant and refugee journey.
- Arrange the collage pieces on the poster board.
- When they feel they have their final work of art, decoupage it to the poster board using a paintbrush.
- When everyone is done with their poster, take turns sharing it with the group.

Connection—Students share their thoughts on immigration and refugees in the form of a collage. Encourage artists to share why they chose the images they did and what their collage means to them.

Ages 12+

Read: *Esperanza Rising* by Pam Muñoz Ryan
When tragedy strikes, Esperanza and her mother flee their family ranch in Mexico and seek work in California. Unprepared for the challenges and difficulties she now faces, Esperanza must find a way to rise above it all.

Connection—Readers learn about the immigration experience through Esperanza's family.

Read: *The Distance Between Us: Young Readers Edition* by Reyna Grande
An adaptation of her memoir, this story shares the experiences of young Reyna and her siblings crossing cultures and borders. The funny and heartbreaking account of an undocumented family.

Connection—Readers gain a deeper understanding of the challenges of assimilation.

Connect: Letters to Congresspeople
* Make a difference by sending thoughtful, respectful letters to Congress-people sharing your beliefs on laws affecting immigrants and refugees.
* Be brief. Use your own words even if using a form letter.
* Close the letter requesting action.
* Thank the Congressperson for his or her time.
* Find addresses by searching online, using search terms such as "write my US representatives and senators."

Connection—Join the political process by sharing your concerns and thoughts on relevant justice issues.

Discussion panels following documentary films are a powerful way to extend the conversation and build community connections.

Gather: Film Viewing and Panel Discussion
* Organize a screening of the documentary *Papers*. *Papers* tells the story of undocumented youth and their challenge of turning eighteen without legal status in the United States.
* Host a panel discussion following the movie. Select and invite knowledgeable panelists. Create an introduction for each panelist. Compile questions to ask the panelists and allow the audience space to ask questions.
* Find licensing information at grahamstreetproductions.com/papers-stories-of-undocumented-youth/.

Connection—Students witness the real stories of young people who do not have legal documentation.

CHALLENGE AND EXTEND AWARENESS AT HOME

* Read "30 Mealtime Facts About Immigrants and Refugees," found at lisavanengen.com.

- Practice "30 Days of Prayer for Immigrants and Refugees," found at lisavanengen.com.
- Play the online game *From Ellis Island to Orchard Street* at Tenement Museum (tenement.org).
- Visit and support your local farmers market.
- Follow the 40 Days of Scripture "I Was a Stranger" Challenge. Find a printable bookmark at evangelicalimmigrationtable.com.
- Download the app *My Life as a Refugee* and play the game together (mylifeasarefugee.org).
- On YouTube, watch the short documentary *Island of Hope—Island of Tears* from PublicResourceOrg.
- Take an interactive tour of Ellis Island from Scholastic (teacher .scholastic.com).
- Watch a short film or read a story about refugees from FilmAid (film aid.org).
- Watch an interactive time lapse of the loss of Native American land and the establishment of reservations, produced by Claudio Saunt, professor of history at the University of Georgia. Find the direct link for this map at lisavanengen.com.

The view from beneath the bridge is somewhat different:
reluctant refugees with an aching love of their forsaken
homeland, of a homeland that has forsaken them, refugees who
desire nothing more than to be home again.
—EDWIDGE DANTICANT, *THE BUTTERFLY WAY*

MAKING A DIFFERENCE

- Support Farmworker Justice (farmworkerjustice.org).
- Put together an infant care kit for refugees through the Mennonite Central Committee (mcc.org).

- Investigate how to help your own church or a local church prepare to help with refugee resettlement in your community.
- Bring the Church Between Borders simulation to your church. Learn more at justice.crcna.org/church-between-borders.
- Watch the eight-minute film *Making It in America* from the Global Oneness Project.
- Put together a CWS (Church World Service) blanket event for refugees at your church (cwsblankets.org).
- Watch short videos and read stories on Migrant Offshore Aid Station's blog (moas.eu).
- Donate a set of library books for a refugee camp through CARE (gifts .care.org).
- On YouTube, watch *Growth, Cities, and Immigration* from CrashCourse.
- Play the game *Against All Odds*, an interactive experience about what it is like to be a refugee (unhcr.org).

For direct links to any of these resources plus additional materials, go to lisavanengen.com and click the And Social Justice for All tab.

Local Ideas

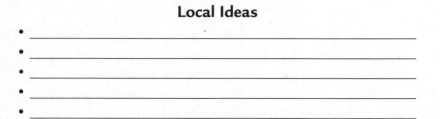

11

Peace: How We See Others

Returning hate for hate multiplies hate, adding deeper darkness
to a night already devoid of stars. Darkness cannot drive out
darkness; only light can do that. Hate cannot drive out hate;
only love can do that.

—MARTIN LUTHER KING JR., *STRENGTH TO LOVE*

Raise Awareness

February 12—International Day Against the Use of Child Soldiers
May (third Saturday)—Armed Forces Day
May (last Monday)—Memorial Day
September 21—International Peace Day
October—National Bullying Prevention Month
November—Military Family Appreciation Month
November (third Week)—International Restorative Justice Week
November 11—Veterans Day

At the close of a year, I enjoy looking at the best journalism photographs of the past twelve months. Leading into 2017, I was struck with the number of photos that captured violence. They were striking but also deeply despairing. Young people throwing bottle rockets, shelled-out buildings, burning barricades, riot police with shields, hands throwing rocks, empty bullet cartridges littering the ground, ammunition belts draped across a chest, mazes of barbed wire. Lives ended from explosives strapped to bodies, high-powered automatic weapons, and vehicles used as killing devices. Conflict has devastating effects on countries, lands, infrastructure, families, and children.

New York Times journalist Chris Hedges writes in his book *What Every Person Should Know About War*, "Of the past 3,400 years, humans have been entirely at peace for 268 of them, or just 8 percent of recorded history."[1] Conflict is interwoven with history and our human experience. Our only true peace is found in Christ. His Word calls for us to seek peace in relationship to others. Romans 12:18 states, "If it is possible, as far as it depends on you, live at peace with everyone." We can work to change how we see those we perceive as enemies and pursue peace as a result.

> I solve disagreements by asking their opinions.
> —Catherine, age 10

Understanding the Issue

Often, at the heart of conflict is inequality, such as food availability, the supply of fresh water, land and oil, resources (like diamonds), natural gas and minerals, and social tensions (including job loss). Conflict also emerges from religion, politics, governance, and territorial gain. Wars occur when groups desire to maintain cultural autonomy from another group. In all these factors, "wars in developing countries have heavy human, economic, and social costs and are a major cause of poverty and underdevelopment."[2]

> Rock, paper, scissors—shoot. That's a fun way to do it.
> —Micah, age 8

We can all attest that we live in a time of uncertainty. Nations face disagreement politically. Racial tension has been exposed. Terrorism occurs all too often. Anonymity and loss of face-to-face interaction with the rise of technology allow us to enter into conflict with ease. Conflict occurs not only in the settings of war but also on a microscale in homes, schools, workplaces, and places of worship.

Global Concerns

Thanks to world history classes, most students can identify critical points of conflict like the Crusades, the French Revolution, the World Wars, the Israeli-Palestinian conflict, the Cold War, the Gulf War, and Vietnam. Areas of global conflict continue to be fluid and continual over time. Presently, we might cite Syria, Yemen, Israel-Palestine, Afghanistan, and Myanmar as conflicted regions. Conflict in Syria alone has taken 500,000 lives and displaced 12 million citizens after six years of fighting.[3] We see conflict through a different lens than war alone with the rise of global terrorism. Terrorism threatens peace worldwide in unpredictable and unconventional ways.

> See whose idea is better and be OK with it.
> —Isaiah, age 9

In conflicts, we think of soldiers losing their lives, but we sometimes forget that civilians die too. "Between 1900 and 1990, 43 million soldiers died in wars. During the same period, 62 million civilians were killed."[4] Still others are uprooted from their homes and are displaced within their own country or become refugees. For those who survive in conflict areas, normal life can be greatly disrupted. Imagine losing basic infrastructure like electricity, water, and food sources. Often education is interrupted, and the ability to even move about freely is hindered. Civilians also experience the internal effects of trauma from what they experience and witness. The emotional scars can be debilitating without care and intervention.

> I would fix terrorism by telling people to be kind and not have hate for others.
> —Bess, age 14

Armed conflict in any form is horrifying, but imagine being a child soldier in the midst of the chaos of war. Anyone under the age of eighteen used for military purposes is categorized as a child soldier. The exact number of child soldiers globally is difficult to know for sure; in 2012, estimates were 300,000.[5] While some children are used as weapons of war, others are used as messengers, cooks, and spies, or for sexual violence. Those who find escape face a long road to recovery from trauma, abuse, and the memories of everything they have witnessed. The use of child soldiers in conflict has far-reaching effects on nations, families, and the children themselves.

Next-Door Concerns

Often unseen is the endless aftermath of warfare on soldiers and their families. In all of the United States' wars to date, we have lost 1.1 million people. The Department of Defense and the Department of Veterans Affairs record the most lives were lost in the Civil War, with the second largest number lost in World War II. War has lasting effects on all involved. Soldiers return with physical scars and injuries from war and also psychological trauma. They might face post-traumatic stress, depression, traumatic brain injury, and physical injuries. Although they have served our country, the quality of health care provided to them is often lacking. One-third of the homeless population is made up of armed forces veterans.[6] What these servicemen and women have experienced cannot be fully grasped and should not be minimized.

> **We need to come together and overlook our differences, which will make a difference in itself.**
> —Charlie, age 15

We owe great respect and honor to those who have defended us through our armed forces. Their sacrifice is not measurable, nor is that of their families. Warriors face long separations from their loved ones and the challenge of returning to civilian life after deployment. Military families relocate, on average, every two to three years. Solid community support and emotional care help families feel loved and cared for during difficult times. As we seek peace, it is important to remember those who are very much on the front lines of attaining resolution to conflict.

Hope

First Peter 3:11 says, "Seek peace and pursue it." While you may not be able to broker peace among nations, you can start right where you are. Very few people can influence whether one nation or another engages in war, but every person has the ability to influence relationships with the people they interact with every day. Many churches, schools, and organizations use the concept of restorative justice to pursue peace and mediate conflict.

> **Think. Take a breath.**
> —Jaeyiah, age 8

Zechariah 7:9 states, "This is what the LORD Almighty said: 'Administer true justice; show mercy and compassion to one another.'" Restorative justice uses responsibility, confession, repentance, forgiveness, amends, and reconciliation to lead to restoration. Restorative justice strives to meet the needs of both victim and offender as well as others affected. For instance, instead of suspension, school leaders might use parentally approved mental health screenings, individual counseling, and group counseling. Those who commit an offense use collaborative problem solving to understand their actions and repair harm to those involved. The Oakland Unified School district uses restorative justice by engaging classrooms in community-building circles to voice concerns. Data shows these efforts have reduced suspensions and increased student attendance.[7]

> **We should have branches of politicians in every country's government that strengthen alliances with other countries and make new alliances with other countries.**
> **—Eli, age 10**

The US Institute of Peace holds a teacher's program that provides curriculum and educates teachers. Teachers train on the topics of mediation, negotiation, and dialogue. Even introducing vocabulary like *collaboration* makes a difference in students' ability to interact with one another. Many schools have shifted focus to increase the teachings of social-emotional learning, a process to deepen self-awareness, self-management, relationship skills, social awareness, and responsible decision-making. If children learn these skills when they are young, they will carry them into adulthood and their interactions with others.

These practices also lend to competence in engaging in civil discourse. Productive discussions focused on respect toward one another allow peace to emerge from conflict situations. We can teach our children that we will have differing opinions from others, but that should not hinder our ability

> **If I have a disagreement, I solve it by looking for clues.**
> **—Elijah, age 12**

to listen respectfully. When we listen, we allow the walls we build between one another to crumble. Being heard is a gift of compassion we can give and receive. Building trust and relationships allows us to have conversations that lead to a place of peaceful understanding. Our views may not ever align, but that should never give us an excuse to turn our face from those we disagree with.

We understand the fragility of peace. We live with ongoing tension internally, interpersonally, and globally. Attaining peace has never been simple, but we must seek and pursue it. In John 14:27 Jesus left his disciples with these words: "Peace I leave with you; my peace I give you. I do not give to you as the world gives. Do not let your hearts be troubled and do not be afraid." Jesus left us with the gift of peace to reside in our hearts. The absence of peace produces trouble and fear. We long to give that gift of peace to others just as Jesus gave it to us.

INNOVATION TO EXPLORE

- *Using Communication Leadership*: Seeds of Peace equips new generations of leaders in areas of war and conflict to promote peace. Leaders start with personal transformation and grow into facilitating societal change.
- *Building Community*: The Japanese-based nongovernment organization Peace Boat embarks on peace voyages. Docking at ports around the world, they offer forums, workshops, seminars, and cultural events based on building a peaceful culture.
- *Using Policy*: The work of Association for a More Just Society in Honduras supports projects that advocate for peace and justice at a grassroots level. Their work has reduced homicide levels by 75 percent in one of the most violent communities of Honduras.[8]
- *Using Communication*: The National Institute for Civil Discourse seeks to revive civility and champions respect by creating community solutions to strengthen democracy.
- *Using Technology*: The International Crisis Group tracks conflict worldwide. Interact with their Crisis Watch map at crisisgroup.org/crisis watch to pray for the people affected by conflict.

Appreciate History

The Peace Trail on the National Mall in Washington, DC, promotes a self-guided walking tour of thirteen key sites, accompanied by stories that demonstrate America's enduring commitment to peace.

TALK JUSTICE

Ages 3–6

What makes you feel safe and peaceful? A hug from Mom or Dad? A grand-parent? A special stuffed animal? A warm blanket? A prayer to Jesus?

_____

_____

How can you share your feelings with family and friends?

_____

_____

Why should you share toys with friends?

_____

_____

What is hard about sharing?

_____

_____

What helps when you disagree with someone?

_____

_____

_____

Ages 7–11

Why do you feel people have conflict?

_____

_____

_____

In what situations do you experience the most conflict?

_____

_____

_____

What do you think are good listening skills?

_____

_____

Do you think bullying breaks down peace?

_____

_____

How do you show good teamwork when working in a group or playing a team sport?

_____

_____

Ages 12+

If there was a war in your country, how would your life change?

_____

_____

How can you work collaboratively with others? What about people you disagree with?

_____

_____

What do you think it means to restore a relationship?

_____

_____

_____

What have wars accomplished? What have they destroyed?

_____

_____

What actions could you take to promote peaceful interactions among peers?

_____

_____

STUDY GOD'S WORD

Luke 6:27–28, 31, 35–36

To you who are listening I say: Love your enemies, do good to those who hate you, bless those who curse you, pray for those who mistreat you. . . . Do to others as you would have them do to you. . . . Love your enemies, do good to them, and lend to them without expecting to get anything back. . . . Be merciful, just as your Father is merciful.

The opposites of peace are hatred, fighting, war, discord. What we intuitively feel toward our enemies Jesus asks us to profoundly turn on its head. He asks us to love when we want to hate; choose kindness instead of fighting; be peacemakers instead of revenge seekers; find common ground where there is discord. He asked us to love in a way that broadens our capacity to forgive.

But forgiveness doesn't start with us. It starts with Christ. Ephesians 4:32 says, "Be kind and compassionate to one another, forgiving each other, just as in Christ God forgave you." It's the forgiveness of Christ in our lives that enables us to forgive others, and forgiveness is a key to peace.

We attain peace through the work of Christ in our lives. Luke 6:36 says, "Be merciful, just as your Father is merciful." Jesus is our example and our anchor in allowing peace to rule our hearts.

Extend Study of God's Word

Draw a picture that represents Luke 6:27–36. Share and explain your thinking with others.

Whom could you treat with more kindness and compassion?

_____

_____

Whom could you forgive?

_____

_____

_____

If you imagine God's mercy, what might you change in your life?

_____

_____

Choose an organization that works for peace or restorative justice your family or group can pray for:

_____

_____

Choose a specific community or place in need of peace or restorative justice your family or group can pray for:

_____

_____

> *God, help us love our enemies, be merciful, and forgive.*
> *Help us remember those entangled in conflict. Thank you for those*
> *in the military and their families, who face long separations in order*
> *to protect us. Our hearts are especially broken for children used as*
> *soldiers in wars and conflicts. Please watch over them and*
> *help them find freedom. Help us pursue peace and seek justice*
> *that is restorative. Amen.*

EXPLORE JUSTICE

Ages 3–6
Read: *Can You Say Peace?* by Karen Katz
The word *peace* is shared in twenty-two different languages with colorful drawings featuring children from around the world.

Connection—Children learn about kids from around the world and are encouraged to embrace peace.

Read: *The Peace Tree from Hiroshima: The Little Bonsai with a Big Story* by Sandra Moore

Based on a true story, *The Peace Tree from Hiroshima* tells the story of a more than three-hundred-year-old bonsai tree that was given by a family in Japan as a gift to the United States. The little tree was a token of peace and friendship between the two countries that were enemies during World War II.

> *Connection—Readers consider friendship, forgiveness, and peace in spite of war.*

Read: *Peace Is an Offering* by Annette LeBox
In poetic verse and gentle illustrations, this book shares how a community of neighbors finds peace in ordinary things.

> *Connection—Children learn to find peace in their environment and among one another.*

Play: Telephone
Gather children in a circle. Pick one student to think of a short phrase or sentence. They whisper the message to the student next to them, who passes it to the next student, and so on until the message circles back to the original student. When the message has traveled all the way around the circle, compare the original statement and what the message turned out to be.

> *Connection—Talk to students about listening skills. Ask them what made hearing the message easier or harder. Try the game multiple times to see if they can improve.*

Play: Pass the Parcel
Gather supplies: small box, olive branch, wrapping paper, tape.
- Ahead of time, place the olive branch inside the box, then wrap the box in enough layers of paper to allow each child to unwrap at least one layer.
- Have the participants sit in a circle.
- Tell the children that the box contains a symbol of peace. Pass the wrapped box around the circle.
- Allow each child to guess what might be in the box and unwrap one

layer. Affirm each child by saying, "Good guess," as the box continues on to the next child in the circle.

- When they reach the olive branch, explain its significance. Read about the time after the flood when Noah sent out a dove that returned with an olive branch, indicating that life had been restored to the land (Gen. 8).

Connection—Children learn about a biblical symbol of peace.

Play: Seek and Find

Gather supplies: art supplies to make many different peace signs (suggestions include construction paper, felt, foam board, or wood cutouts).

- Before the event, create many different colorful and easy-to-find peace signs.
- Hide the peace symbols all around the area where you will play seek and find. Keep count so you'll know when all have been found.
- When children arrive, show them an example of what you've hidden and give them time to search for the signs.
- Come back together when all the symbols have been found.

Connection—Ask the kids what each peace symbol means. Challenge them to share what they think being peaceful means.

Create: Calming Bottle

Gather supplies: bottle for each child (smartwater and VOSS brands found at most grocery stores work well, but any sturdy, see-through water bottle would do the job), water, 6-oz. bottle of glitter glue per child, 10-g. jar of fine glitter per child, hot glue gun, hot glue sticks, clear glue (optional).

- Fill the bottle three-fourths full of hot water.
- Add in the entire bottle of glitter glue and the jar of glitter. (If you want the glitter to settle, slowly add half a bottle of clear glue to the mixture.)
- Hot-glue the top to the bottle so it is secure.
- Encourage kids to use the calming bottle as a tool to self-regulate. Self-regulate by taking the calming bottle to a quiet space to watch the glitter settle on the bottom of the bottle. Flip the bottle and watch the glitter fall again.

Connection—Kids create a tool to help them feel peaceful in times of stress or sadness.

Ages 7–11

Read: *The Butter Battle Book* by Dr. Seuss
The Yooks and Zooks like buttered bread, but bad feelings erupt when the groups discover that they like to eat it differently.

Connection—With whimsical characters and a gentle story line, children are introduced to the concept of respecting others' differences.

Read: *Brothers in Hope: The Story of the Lost Boys of Sudan* by Mary Williams
Garang, only eight years old, must leave his home in Sudan. He joins other boys fleeing violence as they walk to Ethiopia and on to Kenya. During the hard journey, they must support and encourage one another in the hope of finding a safe home.

Connection—Children are exposed to the difficulties of war while focusing on resilience and the power of hope when we care for each other. Children make the connection that war often leads to people taking on refugee status.

Read: *Hiawatha and the Peacemaker* by Robbie Robertson
Based on Native American oral tradition, this story tells how Hiawatha translated the Peacemaker's message of unity to five warring Iroquois tribes. His work united the tribes and also inspired those who wrote the US Constitution.

Connection—Readers learn more about the concept of peaceful interaction and a historical figure who fought for peace.

Create: Poppy
Gather supplies: poppy template (found at lisavanengen.com), scissors, red tissue paper, pencils, glue, small paper plates.
  • Give each child a pencil and a small paper plate with a quarter-size circle of glue on it.

• Instruct children to cut small squares of red tissue paper, wrap one square at a time around the eraser of a pencil and dip the paper into the glue. Use the pencil to press each square onto the poppy, covering it with red squares. When finished you will have a fully covered poppy of red tissue paper squares.

Connection—Students create something that symbolizes the sacrifice of veterans. Read the poem "In Flanders Fields," written by Canadian doctor John McCrae during World War I in memory of a friend killed during battle.

Create: Writing
Gather supplies: paper, pens and pencils.
• Prompt: A peacemaker is . . .

Connection—Writers are encouraged to think about what peace means to them personally and how to be a peacemaker to others.

Gather: Veteran's Home Visit
Gather a group and visit a local veteran's home. Call ahead to arrange the visit and see if you can bring anything along to do together, like games or snacks. Take time to visit with the veterans and ask them to share their stories.

Connection—Students experience intergenerational stories and have an opportunity to personally encourage veterans.

Ages 12+

Read: *The Breadwinner* by Deborah Ellis
Parvana and her family live under Taliban rule in Afghanistan. When her father is imprisoned, eleven-year-old Parvana must pretend to be a boy in order to work and help her family survive.

Continuing the story: *Parvana's Journey, Mud City, and My Name Is Parvana.*

Connection—Students learn about the conditions of war-torn areas, gender roles, and the cost of survival.

Read: *Where the Streets Had a Name* by Randa Abdel-Fattah
Thirteen-year-old Hayaat and her family present one side of the Israeli-Palestinian conflict, told from the perspective of Palestinian refugees.

Connection—Readers receive a personal look at an age-old conflict between two nations.

Read: *A Long Way Gone: Memoirs of a Boy Soldier* by Ishmael Beah
The heart-wrenching true story of a former child soldier in Sierra Leone, his escape, and his struggle for redemption.

Connection—Students read a firsthand account of a child soldier and his journey to healing.

Read: *Child Soldier: When Boys and Girls Are Used in War* by Michel Chikwanine and Jessica Dee Humphreys
When Michel was five years old, he was abducted into a rebel militia group in the Congo. This is his true story of being forced to become a child soldier, eventually escaping the militia, and ultimately being reunited with his family.

Connection—Readers learn about child soldiers through graphic novel form.

Create: Writing
Gather supplies: paper, pens and pencils.
- Prompt: I encourage global peace by . . .

Connection—Writers think about tools they might use to encourage global peace.

Try blackout poetry with any justice issue. Share your work with others.

Create: Blackout Poetry
Gather supplies: printed newspapers and magazines, black markers.
- Provide each child a printed page and a black marker.

- Instruct children to use the marker to black out words, leaving only words to form a poem about conflict and peace.

Connection—Poets use the creative form of blackout poetry to share their thoughts about global peace.

Play: Dodgeball Game
Gather supplies: playground balls.
- Gather two or more groups from different schools or church youth groups. Break the groups into teams, but mix the students up. Make sure there is an equal number of students from each group on the teams.
- Play a dodgeball game or even a tournament, depending on how many teams you have.

Connection—Students learn to work together in a group with people they don't know well. Talk about the experience afterward. What made teams work well together? What did not? How did it feel to be teammates with someone you did not know?

Study: Nobel Peace Prize Winners
Choose a Nobel Peace Prize winner (an individual or organization) to learn more about at nobelprize.org. Study what they contributed to make the world a more peaceful place.

Connection—Students learn about people and organizations that have led movements of peace globally throughout history.

CHALLENGE AND EXTEND AWARENESS AT HOME

- Read "30 Mealtime Conversations About Peace," found at lisavan engen.com.
- Practice "30 Days of Prayer for Peace," found at lisavanengen.com.
- Consider using restorative justice in your school or church. Edutopia has an extensive list of resources (edutopia.org).

- Read through the Glossary of Nonviolence from The King Center (thekingcenter.org).
- Read 2 Thessalonians 3:16 together. Why do you think Paul gave this as his final greetings to the Thessalonians? What can these words mean for your family?
- The Carter Center offers printable pdf teacher resources for social studies focusing on critical thinking and resolving global conflict (cartercenter.org).
- Choose a specific need for a military family through Operation Homefront (operationhomefront.org).
- Celebrate Peace Day on September 21 with Peace One Day. Listen to their curated playlist together. Learn more at peaceoneday.org.
- Make a pinwheel for peace to display in your yard. A template can be found at pinwheelsforpeace.com.
- Create a paper crane and take part in the Peace Crane Project exchange at peacecraneproject.org.

"Though the mountains be shaken and the hills be removed, yet my unfailing love for you will not be shaken nor my covenant of peace be removed," says the LORD, who has compassion on you.
—ISAIAH 54:10

MAKING A DIFFERENCE

- Donate hotel reward points for families of wounded soldiers with Hotels for Heroes (fisherhouse.org).
- Make cards for A Million Thanks (amillionthanks.org).
- Support ShelterBox, which provides lifesaving aid to those affected by conflict (shelterboxusa.org).
- Buy a light and give a light through LuminAID (luminaid.com).

- Get involved with a peace project through the work of World Renew (worldrenew.net).
- Organize a One Day One Dance flash mob to celebrate Peace Day (September 21) at peaceoneday.org/campaigns/one-day-one-dance.
- Write a lobbying letter to encourage action for a landmine-free world through the International Campaign to Ban Landmines.
- Install a Peace Pole through the World Peace Prayer Society in your community. The pole is a symbol of unity and displays the words "May peace prevail on earth" (worldpeace.org).
- Organize an old cell phone drive to benefit Cell Phones for Soldiers (cellphonesforsoldiers.com).
- On February 12, bring Red Hand Day (also called International Day Against the Use of Child Soldiers) to your school (redhandday.org).

For direct links to any of these resources plus additional materials, go to lisavanengen.com and click the And Social Justice for All tab.

Local Ideas

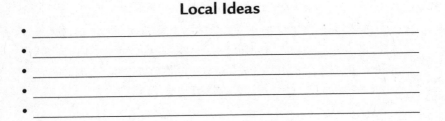

12

Poverty: Having Been Entrusted Much

*I wonder how many people I've looked at all my life
and never seen.*

—JOHN STEINBECK, AMERICAN AUTHOR

Raise Awareness

April—National Fair Housing Month

May 1—International Workers' Day

October (first Monday)—World Habitat Day

October 15—International Day of Rural Women

November 25—International Day for the Elimination of Violence Against
Women

The book *My Name Is Asher Lev* by Chaim Potok follows a young Hasidic Jew and artist, who comes of age while struggling with injustices in the world. One passage from this novel always pierces my heart.

Asher says, "It's not a pretty world, Papa."

"I've noticed," his father said softly.[1]

Have you noticed? The challenges of poverty are interwoven into all the

237

other justice subjects in this book. Poverty brings heartbreak and sorrow. The challenge of living in poverty deepens when onlookers assume the worst of those already dealing with trying circumstances. This response is not a pretty part of the world.

Have you played the game Jenga with your family? A stack of wooden blocks climbs up from the surface of a table. The goal is to remove a block and lay it on the top of the tower without the tower toppling down. The rising tower becomes more and more precarious until it completely topples, leaving rubble. Living in poverty is like balancing a tower of Jenga blocks all the time. All it takes is one little wobble, and the whole structure crumbles.

Understanding the Issue

Poverty largely comes in three forms: generational, situational, and absolute. These forms of poverty can occur in rural and urban settings. When two or more generations of a family have lived in poverty, it is called generational poverty. These families do not have the job training, life skills, or capital needed to move out of poverty. They have limited support networks and often unstable family structures.

A crisis or loss forces a family into situational poverty. This type of poverty is often temporary. Examples of situations that cause poverty for a period of time are disasters like a hurricane, divorce, death, or health problems such as cancer or a heart attack.

In developing countries, families experience absolute poverty. All energy is invested in the day-to-day survival of acquiring clean water, food, and shelter. According to the World Bank, in 2013 absolute poverty included 767 million people in the world who live on less than $1.90 a day.[2]

Urban poverty occurs in areas with fifty thousand residents or more. In these spaces, people have limited access to jobs, housing, education, and resources. Poverty in rural areas includes subsistence farmers and migrant workers. Families in rural areas have less access to social services, infrastructure, and jobs.

Families that live in poverty often lack one or more types of capital. Economic capital encompasses money like a savings account, a down payment, or credit for a loan. Poor families have no economic capital to utilize or fall back on.

The people you know in your life, from relatives to friends, are social capital. Your social capital would be those you turn to in a crisis. Families in poverty often do not have social capital with resources to offer loans or assistance.

Poverty also means low human capital. People in poverty might not have skills or education to make their employment options vast, limiting them to low-paying job choices. Though they work, they do not make a living wage.

> **Everyone needs someone who cares about them.**
> **—Cheyenne, age 11**

Institutional capital reaches to institutions such as the government and church to help provide for needs. Although institutional capital does bridge gaps, it does not meet the needs of those in poverty in their entirety.

Hope shrinks when survival becomes an all-consuming effort—imagine a puddle languishing in the sun over the course of many days, shrinking to nothing. Hardship piles up like snowbanks on the edges of vast parking lots. Long-term goals wear thin when it seems impossible to even dream; the wanting, the deprivation, the unrealized hope lead to a fragile cynicism.

In the iconic film *A Christmas Story*, young Ralphie hears once again a warning that the very thing he wants most is too dangerous: the Red Ryder Range Model 1938 200-shot air rifle. At his limit of disappointment, he finds himself in an alley once again being bullied by Scut Farkus and Grover Dill. He utterly loses his mind, beating Scut with his hands covered in mittens, breaking his eyeglasses, crying in rage. His mother comes to stop him and bring him home. She helps him wash his face, lie down, and assures him he can wear his old glasses until the new ones are fixed. He lies in bed silently crying. And in that moment we know we have all been in that very space at times—utterly exposed and scared, brokenhearted. People who experience poverty feel this acutely and daily. They have little control, fight exhaustion, feel vulnerable, and their hearts hurt.

When my son was young, he would line up his toy cars over and over again. This ordering of playthings is a common toddler phase of development. Children learn about order and sorting by engaging their toys in this way.

People in poverty do an enormous amount of lining up too. They order and sort the resources they have again and again: substandard housing, a food budget that won't stretch through the month, limited health care, inconsistent childcare, and unreliable transportation. No matter how many times they rearrange what they have, they can't get the right formation that allows them to break out of the cycle of poverty.

> **People need a house, heat, food, and water to survive.**
> **—Paisley, age 8**

All forms of poverty put children and families at risk for acute and chronic stressors. Those in poverty may have limited access to the basic necessities of life such as shelter, health care, food, and clean water. Others in poverty may have these resources, but not enough or the quality needed to thrive. People in poverty adapt by using survival strategies like delaying payments or forgoing dental or medical care. They might stretch a diaper change, mix water with milk, or go without a meal so their children can eat. One family may pool resources with another family, doubling up in an apartment or sharing a car or a bus pass; another family might pawn jewelry or anything of worth they can find. Families purchase clothing at thrift shops, stand in food bank lines, and use internet at the local library. Their housing might lack a functional kitchen, so they cook with a hot plate. People bike through all the seasons of the year—even winter. They might toil at any income-generating method they can find, like collecting cans and scrap metal or donating plasma. They might utilize payday loan shops, getting stuck in a cycle of high-interest borrowing.

When people are poor and struggling to survive, the line between illegal and legal blurs. Wires are connected to a neighbor's power supply for electricity. Vehicles are driven with expired registrations; otherwise, jobs will be lost. Children might be left in a car during a job interview or sleep in a car during a parent's night shift. A family might squat in an empty home for a safe place to sleep. An outdoor hose connected to the neighbor's house might provide an indoor water supply. Homeless loiterers receive fines. "The experience of surviving a spell of extreme destitution often leaves deep physical and emotional wounds—wounds that further serve to separate, not incorporate."[3] Poverty complicates lives.

Global Concerns

Paging through a photography book, I stop to look at the picture of a little boy who is warming his hands over a portable stove. His extended family, consisting of four adults with ten children, live in a bus and trailer in Spain. They will be evicted later that morning.[4] Further in the book, additional photographs document other scenes of human desperation, such as eight children on the Gulf Coast crowded into a mobile home; the eldest, perhaps eight years old, pours Coke into cups and plops cottage cheese onto his siblings' plates. A young couple lives under a bridge overpass. Two babies sleep in strollers outside a burned-out trailer. Homeless individuals live out of storage units, under a plastic tarp, in underground heating and sewer spaces, and at train stations. Young people sniff glue to suppress their appetites.

Photographer Johnny Miller captures disparity in his work *Unequal Scenes*. Gated communities stand alongside concrete low-income homes in Mexico City. The Kibera slum in Nairobi, Kenya, borders the Royal Nairobi Golf Club. Low-income neighborhoods around the world buffer high-rise skyscrapers and affluent streets. In the book *Beyond the Beautiful Forevers*, Katherine Boo focuses on the Indian settlement of Annawadi in proximity to luxury hotels near the Mumbai airport. In slum areas around the world, you find spaces densely populated, streams of floating garbage, and substandard housing. In Lagos, Nigeria, resides the historic water community of Makoko, a slum area built on stilts. Alongside skyscrapers in the South American metropolises of Santa Marta and Rio de Janeiro stand slums called *favelas*, with tightly packed homes painted in stunning colors. Would you see poverty differently if it lived next door?

> Make more jobs for everyone to make more money. Then you can give away more money to those who need it.
> —Calvin, age 10

The poorest countries in the world are in Africa; however, because of population, three-fourths of the world's poor live in India.[5] Worldwide, women disproportionately experience extreme poverty. Microfinance and training for entrepreneurship open the door for women to earn their own income. Giving girls access to education and women access to vocational training alleviates poverty in families. When organizations invest in crops like maize, cassava, and millet, women are able to feed their families and sell the extra for income. Not only are women supporting their families and communities, they are also more likely to build cooperatives with one another. The fight to end child marriage offers girls the chance to attain education.

Next-Door Concerns

In the United States, poverty contributes to family breakdown and homelessness. In homes at the poverty line, it is not uncommon for adults to have multiple jobs and still struggle to earn a living wage. "About one in four jobs pays too little to lift a family of four out of poverty."[6]

> I care a lot about homeless people. I think about them a lot in the winter when it's cold and they have nowhere to go.
> —Auburn, age 13

Intense poverty leads to chaotic and unstable households. The stress of poverty lends itself to chemical dependence, depression, violence, and trauma. The consequences of these behaviors can lead to the intervention of child protective services. Pediatricians have found that childhood trauma can change the actual chemistry of a child's brain.[7] Children learn to function in a state of constant fight or flight. The landscape of their future stands altered.

According to the National Alliance to End Homelessness, 564,708 people experienced homelessness in 2015. They were either living in a shelter, on the streets, or, in some cases, in cars, tents, or abandoned buildings. One of the biggest contributors to homelessness is the lack of affordable housing in so many areas. "Housing costs now absorb a staggeringly high percentage of any low-income household's earnings."[8] If a family is paying more than 30 percent of their salary to housing, they will struggle to buy other necessities. A full-time worker at minimum wage will struggle to rent a two-bedroom apartment. Section 8 housing vouchers provide subsidized housing through the US Department of Housing and Urban Development to low-income families, but the waiting lists for such subsidies are typically long because demand exceeds resources.

Hope

When looking at models of organizations fighting poverty, community-based ideas stand out. The organization Libraries Without Borders provides access to information, education, and culture. They bring their Idea Box, a mobile pop-up with a multimedia center, to areas of poverty.

The Bible shares three examples of giving those in poverty an opportunity for new life. In Deuteronomy 15, debts are canceled every seven years. In Leviticus 25, whatever the land yields during the Sabbath year is food for you, your male and female servants, and the hired worker and temporary resident who lives among you. Finally, also in Leviticus 25, the Year of Jubilee is counted off from seven sabbatical years, roughly every fifty years. During that year, slaves are freed and land returned to original owners. In all three examples, the people were called to not be hard-hearted or tightfisted. They were asked to be openhanded and to freely lend.

Thomas Merton, a Catholic writer and Trappist monk, wrote, "Our job is to love others without stopping to inquire whether or not they are worthy. That is not our business and, in fact, it is nobody's business. What we are asked to do is to love, and this love itself will render both ourselves and our neighbors worthy."[9] We know what to do, and judgment and poverty don't belong together. Proverbs 22:2 states, "Rich and poor have this in common: The LORD is the Maker of them all." Unlike math, there are no greater-than or less-than signs for people. Can you sit with someone for more than a minute and hear the slightest edge of his or her story and not feel that way? We all carry layers. Some are just stacked more precariously than others.

> **What advice would you give to grown-ups about making the world a better place? Nothing, because they already know what to do.**
> **—Ian, age 7**

How we perceive poverty changes when we think about the individual lives affected. Growing up in close proximity to poverty changed my life. Being surrounded by families that struggled changed something inside of me. All I had—a loving family, food, and shelter—became more deeply appreciated. My heart grew softer and more empathetic. Maybe most transforming of all was understanding that most people who live in poverty work hard, care deeply about their families, and want a better life.

Journalist Sasha Abramsky wrote *The American Way of Poverty: How the Other Half Still Lives*. His well-researched work largely tells the stories of those in poverty from all around the United States. He closes the book with the following: "And now, knowing the challenges, and hearing the demands of conscience, our task is to act."[10]

INNOVATION TO EXPLORE

- *Using Community Development*: City planners have sought to alleviate poverty by placing anchor institutions in low-income areas in cities such as Cleveland, El Paso, and Memphis. Institutions including hospitals, universities, museums, sports facilities, and corporations all provide job opportunities (livingcities.org).
- *Using Design and Engineering*: In San Francisco, developers have envisioned a 160-square-foot MicroPAD to combat homelessness.[11] PAD stands for a "prefabricated affordable dwelling" that offers a living space, kitchen area, and bathroom.
- *Using Construction and Volunteerism*: Retired "habitat gypsies" travel in RVs around the United States, working to build homes for Habitat for Humanity.
- *Using Social Enterprise*: World Bicycle Relief provides bicycles in rural areas, creating access to education, health care, and farming delivery. Their model, the Buffalo Bicycle, is simple to maintain.
- *Using Community Development*: Christian Community Development Association, pioneered by John Perkins, is a network of Christians seeking spiritual, emotional, physical, economic, and social restoration in broken communities.

Appreciate Global Cooperation

The Sustainable Development Goals of the United Nations provide a guide for all nations to fight poverty globally. Many different countries, organizations, and communities have been working in cooperation with one another to end global poverty through the guidance of these seventeen goals. Visit sustainabledevelopment.un.org/sdgs with your family and talk about the goals. Which goals resonate most strongly with your family?

Why do think it might be a good idea for nations to work toward the same goals together?

TALK JUSTICE

Ages 3–6

What does your family have that you could share with others?

_____

_____

What things do you think a person needs in order to survive?

_____

_____

What do you use money for?

_____

_____

_____

Would it be hard to only eat one meal a day and have no snacks?

_____

_____

_____

Does everyone in the world have a car? What are other ways people get from place to place?

_____

_____

_____

Ages 7–11

If you wanted to play soccer or checkers but didn't have the money to buy a ball or board game, what are innovative ways you could still play?

_____

_____

Would you enjoy washing your laundry by hand in a river? How much time would that take each week?

_____

_____

How would you feel about using an outhouse to go to the bathroom in all weather conditions?

_____

_____

If your school did not have heat during the winter, what all would be hard to do with your coat and mittens on?

_____

_____

What might be the pros and cons of not having many material things?

_____

_____

Ages 12+

If you had no money to pay your heating bill in the winter, how would you stay warm?

_____

_____

_____

What does home mean to you?

_____

_____

_____

Can you imagine sharing your home with two other families? How about shrinking your house in half and sharing it with two other families?

_____

_____

What would it be like to spend a night outside without shelter? What about sleeping in a car?

_____

_____

What are your family's most valued possessions?

_____

_____

_____

STUDY GOD'S WORD

Luke 12:48
From the one who has been entrusted with much, much more will be asked.

Have you been entrusted with much? Think of all the things that are a part of your life: family, friends, food, pets, shelter, education, community, and health care. Write a list of everything that has been entrusted to you. If you have a warm home, enough food, clean water, a chance to visit the doctor's office, a school to attend, and religious freedom, you have been entrusted with much. Beyond necessities, you could list extra things you have been given, like toys, bicycles, or an opportunity for a vacation.

Most of us have been entrusted with more than enough to survive. The Bible says that when we have been given much, God will ask much more of us. Do you think something he might ask of us would be to have thankful hearts and giving spirits? We can think about what we have been given beyond material possessions too. What about the special gifts God gave you? Think of the things you are very good at or all the things you know. How can we be faithful stewards of our gifts and knowledge? God entrusted us with these gifts and calls us to use them to give back to his people—not only material things but our spiritual gifts too.

Extend Study of God's Word
Make a list of all the gifts God has given your family. Write a prayer thanking God for these gifts.

How can you show thankfulness for the things that have been entrusted to you?

_____

_____

_____

What could you give to others in response to the gifts that God has given to you?

_____

_____

_____

What is one thing God has helped you be very good at doing? How could you use this gift to help others?

_____

_____

_____

Choose an organization that fights poverty that your family or group can pray for:

_____

_____

_____

Choose a specific community or place that experiences poverty that your family or group can pray for:

_____

_____

_____

Thank you for all you have entrusted us with, God. We pray for those who do not have basic necessities or a high quality of life. Teach us to look at systems that contribute to poverty. Help us know how to be sensitive to the pain of poverty. Open our hearts to others before we judge them. Teach us to listen. Amen.

EXPLORE JUSTICE

Ages 3–6
Read: *A Chair for My Mother* by Vera B. Williams
When their home is destroyed by fire, Rosa, her grandma, and mother save their coins in a jar so they can buy a new chair.

Connection—A warm and loving family finds joy in simple things like a chair.

Create: Collaborative Mural
Gather supplies: brightly colored construction paper, scissors, glue, a large poster board.
- Encourage each artist to create their own home out of construction paper, including a roof, door, and windows. (The finished mural will look even more colorful if artists use different colors of construction paper for different parts of the home.)
- Each child then glues their completed home to the poster board, creating a community of homes.

Connection—Children think about the concept of community through creative design.

Create: Fort Building
Gather supplies: anything for building a blanket fort—blankets, sheets, pillows, clothespins, rope, flashlights.
- Work together as a family to build a fort.
- When you are finished, read a story together inside the fort using a flashlight.

Connection—Talk about the importance of having a safe place to live and call home.

Create: Loose Parts Building
Gather supplies: twigs, rocks, grass, flowers, and so on.

- Use the loose parts to build a community with homes, land features, and community buildings such as a hospital, school, post office, and stores.

Connection—Kids use play and creativity to design what they think is important in a community.

Ages 7–11

Read: *Sélavi: That Is Life—A Haitian Story of Hope* by Youme Landowne
Sélavi, a young homeless boy, finds family in a group of homeless children in Port-au-Prince, Haiti.

Connection—In the most difficult circumstances, people can join together to make a difference.

Read: *If the World Were a Village: A Book About the World's People* by David J. Smith
By imagining that the world is a village of one hundred people, children discover that people in other nations often live very differently than the reader does.

Connection—The world is shrunk to a smaller scale to make statistics easier to grasp while learning about our global neighbors.

Read: *If America Were a Village: A Book About the People of the United States* by David J. Smith
Imagine the United States as a village of one hundred people. Cheerful acrylic illustrations accompany easy-to-comprehend statistics.

Connection—The United States is shrunk to a smaller scale to make statistics easier to grasp while learning about the people of America.

Read: *Joelito's Big Decision: La Gran Decisión de Joelito* by Ann Berlak
Two fourth-grade friends face the issues of economic justice and workers' rights. A bilingual story told from the perspective of the worker, the child, and the immigrant.

Connection—Students learn about the relationship between consumption and the rights of those who make and serve products.

Read: *The Hundred Dresses* by Eleanor Estes
Wanda says she has one hundred dresses at home, but she wears the same faded blue dress to school every day. Her classmates tease her mercilessly until she simply doesn't return to school. A story of learning to do the right thing, even when it's hard.

Connection—Readers learn the impact of bullying due to one's economic situation.

Read: *Crenshaw* by Katherine Applegate
Jackson and his family face eviction and may have to live in their van again. His imaginary friend, Crenshaw the cat, might be just who he needs to navigate the challenges of his life.

Connection—Readers build empathy for children who experience homelessness and poverty.

Create: Pass the Story
Direct participants to form a circle to play Pass the Story. Choose one student to start the story. Use a prompt such as, "Once upon a time, a brother and sister had nowhere to call home." Set a timer, and allow each participant fifteen seconds to add to the story. Work your way around the circle until each participant has had two or three turns.

Connection—Students collaborate with one another to create a story about homelessness.

Observe: Study Art
Picasso's Blue Period, marked by monochromatic blues and blue-greens, reflected a time of sadness and instability in his life. Observe paintings from this period such as *The Tragedy, Blind Man's Meal, The Old Guitarist,* and *The Soup.*

Connection—What do the Blue Period paintings teach you about poverty? Why do you think Picasso used the colors and style he did during this period?

Ages 12+

Read: *Material World: A Global Family Portrait* by Peter Menzel
Photographs of "statistically average" families from thirty countries. A great visual of the inequities in our world.

Connection—Visual images show the disparity between what global families own. What did you learn from these photographs? What does this book tell us about global poverty?

Read: *Lyddie* by Katherine Patterson
The story of Lyddie, who, during the Industrial Revolution, is hired out as a servant at age ten and determines to create a better life by working in a textile mill.

Connection—Readers are exposed to poverty, factory working conditions, women's rights, and education.

Read: *Paper Things* by Jennifer Richard Jacobson
When siblings Ari and Gage leave their guardian's home for a life of their own, they step into the world of homelessness. Ari promised her dying mother that she would attend the middle school for gifted students, but will all their moving around ruin her chances?

Connection—Readers get an insider's view of homelessness and the strength of family.

Read: *Trash* by Andy Mulligan
Three "dumpsite boys" uncover a mystery and find themselves on a twisting and turning quest to right a terrible wrong.

Connection—Through the eyes of three boys living in extreme poverty, readers uncover corruption, the abuse of the poor, and the disparity of wealth.

Gather: Photo Scavenger Hunt
Provide students with a list of local nonprofits. Their goal is to take a group selfie in front of each organization's sign. After the scavenger hunt, encourage the kids to use their group pictures to promote and share the work of the nonprofits on social media.

Connection—Students raise awareness of local nonprofits.

Study: History
President Franklin D. Roosevelt created a number of federal programs called the New Deal to help those affected by the Great Depression. Research and study some of those programs, such as the Agricultural Adjustment Administration, Works Progress Administration, Social Security Act, National Youth Administration, Civilian Conservation Corps, Federal Housing Administration, and the Public Works Administration.

Connection—What programs worked well during the Great Depression? What programs are still in existence today? What could you learn from these ideas? What type of New Deal program would you create today to meet a need?

Observe: Personal Budget Simulation
Gather supplies: Monthly Budget Worksheet (see below), pencils, calculators.
- Divide students into three groups.
- Give each group a Monthly Budget Worksheet, which includes basic necessities, a pencil, and a calculator.
- Each group will pretend to be a single parent with two children. See below for group assignments.

Monthly Budget Worksheet

Housing (choose one)
❑ Two-bedroom apartment: $890
❑ Rental home: $950
❑ Mortgage: $1,061

Transportation (choose one)
❏ Car: $482
❏ Public transportation: $85
❏ Bicycle: $29

Food/household supplies
$700

Health insurance
$300

Telephone
$73

Utilities
$60

Group 1: Works two part-time minimum wage jobs at a fast-food restaurant ($8.50 an hour at 30 hours) and security ($11.07 an hour at 10 hours), making $1,462 a month.

Group 2: Works one full-time minimum wage job as a certified nursing assistant in a nursing home ($11.68 an hour at 40 hours), making $1,868 a month.

Group 3: Works three part-time jobs in hotel housekeeping ($10.00 an hour at 15 hours), as a waitress ($5.00 an hour plus tips at 15 hours), and at a hairdresser ($10.00 an hour at 5 hours), making $1,100 a month.

Ask
- Were you able to pay for all your basic necessities?
- Was any money left over? How much?
- What categories did the budget leave out that would contribute to quality of life?
- How would it feel to work so many hours yet struggle to meet basic needs?
- If you wanted to find a job that paid more money, what challenges might you face?

Connection—Students think about how much basic necessities actually cost and how difficult it can be to cover all the needed categories while living in poverty.

CHALLENGE AND EXTEND AWARENESS AT HOME

- Read "30 Mealtime Facts About Poverty," found at lisavanengen.com.
- Practice "30 Days of Prayer for Poverty," found at lisavanengen.com.
- Take a free leadership course through +Acumen, which works to create a world beyond poverty (plusacumen.org).
- Make a card through Habitat for Humanity for donors, volunteers, and homeowners (habitat.org).
- Look at the UNICEF photo essays of their global work (unicef.org).
- Invite friends for a Souper Bowl event and raise money for your local food pantry (souperbowl.org).
- Use AmazonSmile, which donates 0.5 percent of the price of your eligible Amazon purchase toward the charitable organization of your choice.
- Populate your home with living gift catalogs from any of the following nonprofits to spark conversations and set giving goals: American Red Cross, CARE, Feeding America, Heifer International, International Justice Mission, Kiva, Mercy Corps, Oxfam, UNICEF, World Help, World Relief, World Renew, World Vision.
- Look through the photographs of *Unequal Scenes* by Johnny Miller (unequalscenes.com).
- Watch the short film *Journey to Freedom* from the National Underground Railroad Freedom Center (freedomcenter.org).

The test of our progress is not whether we add more to the abundance of those who have much; it is whether we provide enough for those who have too little.

—FRANKLIN D. ROOSEVELT, 32ND PRESIDENT OF THE UNITED STATES

MAKING A DIFFERENCE

- Choose a microfinance loan to support from kiva.org.
- Help your group participate in a housing simulation through Habitat for Humanity (habitat.org).
- Find an organization that supports fair housing in your community and see how your group can get involved through justshelter.org.
- Donate to One Day's Wages with your wages for a day of work (one dayswages.org).
- Consider participating in Trick-or-Treat for UNICEF.
- Contribute to Foster Care to Success, a college fund for foster youth (fc2success.org).
- Bring the Two Dollar Challenge to your campus or community, to promote "a more mindful movement to end global poverty" (twodollar challenge.org).
- Shop the Habitat for Humanity gift catalog (secure.habitat.org).
- Watch the Change Series from Living on One Dollar (livingonone .org).
- Stage a Sweatshop Relay to support Labour Behind the Label (labour behindthelabel.org).

For direct links to any of these resources plus additional materials, go to lisavanengen.com and click the And Social Justice for All tab.

Local Ideas

- _____
- _____
- _____
- _____
- _____

Race: Mend Our Fractures

It means a great deal to those who are oppressed to know that they are not alone. Never let anyone tell you that what you are doing is insignificant.

—DESMOND TUTU, BISHOP AND ANTI-APARTHEID ACTIVIST

Raise Awareness

January 27—International Holocaust Remembrance Day

February—Black History Month

February 19—Day of Remembrance (Japanese Americans)

March 21—International Day for the Elimination of Racial Discrimination

March 25—International Day of Remembrance for the Victims of Slavery and the Transatlantic Slave Trade

May—Asian Pacific American Heritage Month

May—Jewish American Heritage Month

May 5—Cinco de Mayo

May 21—World Day for Cultural Diversity for Dialogue and Development

June 19—Juneteenth

August 9—International Day of the World's Indigenous Peoples

September 15–October 15—National Hispanic-Latino Heritage Month

November—National American Indian Heritage Month

n 2014, Lupita Nyong'o stood on the Oscar stage to accept the award for Best Performance by an Actress in a Supporting Role for the film *12 Years a Slave*. She ended her acceptance speech with these words: "No matter where you're from, your dreams are valid."[1] Those nine words took my breath away that evening, and they still do today. There may be no other societal issue more delicate today than race. Psalm 60:2 says, "You have shaken the land and torn it open; mend its fractures, for it is quaking." We are a nation and world that desperately need to mend our fractures. We are a nation and a world that are hurting.

While I worked on the rewrites of this book in the summer of 2017, a white nationalist rally in Charlottesville, North Carolina, led to protests and violence. As a part of Be the Bridge, an organization that seeks to inspire and equip the church to engage in the work of reconciliation, I listened to the response of people of color. What I heard the most was how much silence hurts. If you are able to turn off racial injustice, gloss over it, pretend it doesn't have anything to do with you, you reveal a societal advantage. What our brothers and sisters in Christ need is for us to stand beside them and proclaim that hate is not what Jesus died on the cross for.

Understanding the Issue

According to the *Merriam-Webster Collegiate Dictionary*, prejudice is "an adverse opinion or leaning formed without just grounds or before sufficient knowledge."[2] Prejudice, if we are honest, is something every person confronts. Bias might emerge in our subconscious and be terribly subtle, but it still resides. The subterranean occurs underground; sometimes our feelings happen in that space. There is a danger in saying we are not prejudiced or racist without ever challenging structures like education, housing, employment, and health care that can keep racism in place.

> What scares me about the world is people hurting other people because of their skin color or religion.
> —Savannah, age 14

Engaging in building bridges between races and standing against racism is difficult work. If you are willing to learn and engage in these conversations, they may be uncomfortable and painful, but they are so worth your effort. Acknowledging discomfort—sometimes presenting as anger, defensiveness, or silence—but still being willing to engage in that tension-filled space opens the door for working through reconciliation.

Microaggressions happen all the time in communities, but many people are unaware that hidden bias occurs. These take place in the context of environment, verbally and nonverbally. An example of an environmental microaggression might be the flying of a Confederate flag. Someone unconsciously locking his or her car door when a person of color walks by would be a nonverbal example. A verbal microaggression might be asking a person of color where they were born, assuming it was not the United States. Even if they seem harmless, microaggressions point out differences, "often causing anxiety and crises of belonging on the part of minorities."[3] In the big picture, words and actions can be symptomatic of discriminatory systems in a society.

Demographics are ever changing. There are 7.3 billion people living on the planet. There are 10,000 different ethnic groups and 7,100 documented languages.[4] The countries of Africa are the most diverse. Chad, in north-central Africa, is home to one hundred different ethnic groups.[5] Analyzing census data, Pew Research Center estimates, "By 2055, the U.S. will not have a single racial or ethnic majority."[6] God created a uniquely diverse planet of human beings who reflect his image. We take to heart Genesis 1:27: "God created mankind in his own image, in the image of God he created them; male and female he created them."

> God made it that way that we have different skin colors. I feel normal.
> —Vismai, age 14

Global Concerns

Discrimination because of one's race happens all over the world. When one people group believes they are greater or better than another, a hierarchy occurs. Consider India's caste system, one of the world's oldest stratification systems, which divides Hindus into four different castes. Outside the caste system are the Dalits, or untouchables. An ancient Japanese stratification system counts Burakumin the lowest of a four-tier system. The North Korean system of Songbun assigns social classification upon birth.

Ethnic cleansing is an attempt to get rid of an unwanted people group through mass killing or displacement. The German Nazi Holocaust killed six million Jews during a brief four-year period. The Khmer Rouge's reign led to the death of between 1.5 and 2 million Cambodians. Their bodies were buried in mass graves called killing fields. In 1994, in three short months, up to a million Tutsi minorities were killed at the hands of the Hutu majority in Rwanda. Today an ongoing crisis of genocide continues as the government of Sudan kills Darfuri men, women, and children. In Syria, a civil war has all but destroyed the city of Aleppo and caused an enormous humanitarian crisis of internally displaced peoples and refugees. These are horrible parts of world history, but if we don't teach young people that they happened and continue to, we are destined to keep repeating profoundly heartbreaking loss and unfathomable atrocity.

> I feel shy at first, but when I get to know them I feel like a friend.
> —Anna, age 10

Elie Wiesel, Holocaust survivor and Nobel Peace Prize–winning author, said of his work, "My goal is always the same: to invoke the past as a shield for the future."[7] Knowing about atrocities of the past can inform our present, leading to a better future. History can be a powerful tool to fight racism. Know history. Learn from the past. Be honest about the ugly chapters. Humbly listen to how history affects the lives of people of color today. In that knowledge, seek to build a future free from discrimination, hate, displacement, and killing due to ethnicity and race.

Next-Door Concerns

The founding of the United States and the expansion of the West happened when settlers invaded and conquered the Native Americans who resided on the land. President Andrew Jackson's Indian Removal Act, signed in 1830 and forcibly enacted in 1838, asked the Cherokee Nation to give up its land and migrate to Oklahoma. The journey became known as the Trail of Tears as thousands died over the 1,200 miles traveled. Every year classrooms re-enact this walk across the freshly fallen snow of playgrounds, and every few seconds they leave a classmate behind.

Though you and I did not physically remove Native Americans from their land or personally own slaves, being a part of community, being brothers and sisters in Christ, means acknowledging that these real events in history shaped our country. They had and continue to have a lasting impact. An organization called Facing History and Ourselves encourages students to wrestle with complex parts of history. The organization teaches young people to become an ally to people of all races through civics, community building, and the study of history and human behavior.

The economic foundation of our country was built on the four million slaves who were freed only after the Civil War. These freed slaves faced an uphill battle to equality, one that continues today in educational opportunities, housing options, health care, and income gap, as well as other ways. The Fifteenth Amendment, passed in 1870, gave voting rights to all men despite race, color, or previous servitude. A march from Selma to Montgomery, Alabama, set the stage for the passing of the Voting Rights Act in August 1965. The act banned literacy tests and federal oversight, and it challenged poll tax. Nearly a century after the Fifteenth Amendment was passed, the barriers that still hindered voting rights were removed. Change has occurred slowly.

> People have different amounts of pigment and are born from different parts of the world, but when it comes down to it, it's not what is on the outside, it's what's on the inside that counts.
> —Navaeh, age 15

We need to acknowledge this happened in the not-so-distant past. People living today have witnessed segregation firsthand. Beginning in the 1890s, Jim Crow laws outlined "separate but equal" treatment. "Whites only" and "Colored" signs drew lines in public spaces. There were separate bathrooms, water fountains, waiting rooms, laundries, theaters, and railroad cars. Not until May 17, 1954, did the Supreme Court pass *Brown v. Board of Education of Topeka*, which stated segregated schools are inherently unequal. Author Ta-Nehisi Coates writes in *Between the World and Me*, "Never forget that we were enslaved in this country longer than we have been free. Never forget that for 250 years black people were born into chains—whole generations followed by more generations who knew nothing but chains."[8]

> I would risk my life to help slaves. My skin is brown, it could be me.
> —Adalyn, age 9

Martin Luther King Jr. gave a speech entitled "The Other America" on March 14, 1968, at Grosse Point High School. He said, "It [America] has failed to hear that the promises of freedom and justice have not been met."[9] Two phrases he used to describe this failure of realizing not everyone has attained equality are "appalling silence" and "indifference of the good people." He also invoked Jesus's last words on the cross from Luke 23:34: "Father, forgive them, for they don't know what they are doing."

In August 2005, Hurricane Katrina hit the Gulf Coast as a Category 3 hurricane. The hurricane brought catastrophic destruction when levees of the low-lying land were breached and massive flooding occurred. Before the hurricane hit, around ten thousand citizens took shelter in the Superdome. Those who sheltered there were families with the least amount of resources to evacuate. Once the storm took hold, nearly fifteen thousand more citizens flooded the evacuation center before its doors were locked. It was overcrowded and without adequate supplies, and when the flooding began, generators shut down, leaving the Superdome without air-conditioning, lighting, and sanitation. Resources dwindled. In the days after, evacuation from the Superdome was slow at best. When evacuation buses finally arrived, it took two days to bring everyone to safety. An estimated 986 people were killed during the storm and more than a million displaced.[10] It should be astounding that these human tragedies occur in the United States, yet they continue to happen in impoverished areas that are disproportionately populated by minority people groups.

> MLK was black and he changed the world. He's my hero.
> —Joshua, age 11

Activist movements seek to build connections, spark dialogue, and facilitate social action and engagement. When we, as Christians, react with defensiveness instead of empathy, we lose a chance to talk about justice and build bridges. Defensiveness thrives on a scarcity model. Scarcity thinks that if *your* life matters, *mine* does not. Our human nature positions us to create our own narrative about how others' should feel. We oversimplify and generalize. When we don't listen, it's easy to decide what other people should feel, let go of, or overcome. When it comes to the fractures we need to mend, it is imperative that we listen.

Hope

When we forget our commonalities, we miss out on amazing things like intricate henna designs from India, beignet from New Orleans, elephant polo in India, prayer flags that line the mountains of Nepal, paper-cut designs of Polish folk art, the beat of a djembe drum of West Africa, and mackerel sushi in a bento box from Japan. We discover new cultures when we try different foods, watch international sports, or play global games. Reading books from other cultures, admiring art from around the world, and listening to global music also expand our borders.

> **If I feel someone is different from me, I feel it's a friend.**
> **—Jayden, age 8**

Henri Nouwen said in *Bread for the Journey: A Daybook of Wisdom and Faith*, "We become neighbors when we are willing to cross the road for one another. There is so much separation and segregation: . . . There is a lot of road crossing to do. We are all very busy in our own circles. We have our own people to go to and our own affairs to take care of. But if we could cross the road once in a while and pay attention to what is happening on the other side, we might indeed become neighbors."[11]

> **There is no nobody, everyone is someone, and everyone plays a part in this world.**
> **—Miguel, age 12**

The children at the school where I work are so used to being together, despite the many races and ethnicities represented within our walls, they do not think much of differences. One day I walked into a classroom, and loaded on two chairs sat about half a dozen students chatting, all from different ethnicities. Being a neighbor becomes effortless; their commonalities far outweigh their differences.

I attended a panel on race as I wrote this book. One panelist's statement stayed with me. The young woman said that with race, the place she feels most alone is at church. At a lecture at Western Michigan University, Martin Luther King Jr. stated, "The church is still the most segregated major institution

> **I bet if everyone was blind or couldn't tell what they looked like, they wouldn't think twice about discrimination.**
> **—Amelia, age 14**

in America. At 11:00 on Sunday morning when we stand and sing and Christ has no east or west, we stand at the most segregated hour in this nation. This is tragic."[12] We need to pray for God to mend our racial fractures. The next generation desperately needs to hear us tell them how important all God's people are to him. We need to stand beside one another.

INNOVATION TO EXPLORE

- *Building Community*: Be the Bridge, founded by LaTasha Morrison, seeks to unite through racial reconciliation. Small groups form around conversations and building bridges between races.
- *Using Community Development*: Communities around the nation intentionally work toward open discussion between law enforcement and stakeholders to build trust and shared partnership in safe communities.
- *Using Science, Research, and Geography*: Since 2005, the National Geographic Genographic Project has used DNA analysis to map personal genetic stories. They have studied more than 800,000 participants in 140 countries. The project reveals how closely we are all genetically linked.
- *Using Community Development*: The organization Partners for a Racism-Free Community offers an Intercultural Development Inventory to increase intercultural competence.
- *Using Film*: World Trust offers five films that talk about race using the voices of real people (world-trust.org/films/).

Appreciate a Voice of Racial Equality

Read the transcript of the last speech given by Martin Luther King Jr. the evening before his assassination. The speech is entitled "I've Been to the Mountaintop," given April 3, 1968, in Memphis, Tennessee.

TALK JUSTICE

Ages 3–6
What color is your skin?

Do you know anyone with skin a different color than yours?

_____

_____

What makes people different from one another? What makes us the same?

_____

_____

What is something that is special about you?

_____

_____

What is something special about someone you know who doesn't look the same as you?

_____

_____

Ages 7–11

What do you know about history and the way people were treated because of the color of their skin?

_____

_____

Are people still treated differently because of the color of their skin?

_____

_____

How does it feel when you are judged by your appearance?

_____

_____

How often do you see people with different skin colors in television, movies, and books?

_____

_____

How can we listen well to other people's stories?

_____

_____

Ages 12+

Why do you think race can be such an uncomfortable topic of conversation?

_____

_____

How can you respect people even when they don't do things the same way you do?

_____

_____

What is a stereotype? How can you move a relationship beyond stereotypes?

_____

_____

How often do you describe someone by what race or culture they belong to?

_____

_____

_____

How honest are we about history? Are we honest about how history affects the present?

_____

_____

_____

STUDY GOD'S WORD

Acts 17:26

From one man he made all the nations, that they should inhabit the whole earth; and he marked out their appointed times in history and the boundaries of their lands.

We are people of routine and pattern. We sleep in the same spot in our beds, choose the same church pew, take the same route to school, or sit in the same spot on the couch. Have you ever tried sitting somewhere different or traveling a new route? Most likely you will notice something you had not previously. It might even be something you pass every day but never noticed before.

God designed the nations that inhabit the earth. He chose our time to live and the lines and boundaries that make up our countries. The people in our path are not there by chance. Be mindful of the people around you and in your life. God placed us in this very time and place for a reason. How do you feel about the fact that God designed the time and location in history he wanted you to live your life?

Have you ever thought about the fact that from one ancestor, Adam in the garden of Eden, God made all the nations that inhabit the whole earth? We are joined together and linked by a common beginning despite our cultural, ethnic, and racial differences. God chose to begin his creation this way. Perhaps he longs for us to remember where we came from and that the spaces between us are not insurmountable. We are God's people, every one of us.

Extend Study of God's Word

Take time to look at a globe. Read Acts 17:26 again.

Who has God put in your path who is from a different place?

_____

_____

_____

_____

What do you think about God designing the time and place where each person lives?

_____

_____

_____

_____

When you consider the fact that we are all God's people, who in your life could you see differently?

_____

_____

_____

Choose an organization that supports racial reconciliation that your family or group can pray for:

_____

_____

_____

Choose a specific place or community in need of racial reconciliation that your family or group can pray for:

_____

_____

> *God, thank you for making so many unique people in our world.*
> *Help our hearts be sensitive to people of all colors, ethnicities, cultures,*
> *and backgrounds. Teach us to widen our circles and boundaries.*
> *Teach us to support and create systems that are fair and just for*
> *everyone. Mend our fractures. Amen.*

EXPLORE JUSTICE

Ages 3–6

Read: *Mama Panya's Pancakes: A Village Tale from Kenya* by Mary and Rich Chamberlin

Adika invites friends and neighbors to come for a pancake dinner at his house. Will Mama Panya be able to stretch their food far enough to feed everyone?

Who could you share pancakes with?

Connection—This sweet tale teaches children about community, sharing, and the culture of Kenya.

Read: *The Colors of Us* by Karen Katz
Seven-year-old Lena learns that skin color comes in many different shades.

Connection—Students explore the many different colors of humans and how to celebrate those differences.

Read: *The Skin You Live In* by Michael Tyler
Beautiful illustrations and poetic verses explore skin color in children.

Connection—Students learn to appreciate the beauty of diversity.

Read: *My Granny Went to Market: A Round-the-World Counting Rhyme* by Stella Blackstone
This international counting rhyme sends Granny on an adventure to many different countries.

Connection—Young children experience new places and cultures in a fun counting format.

Consider having boxes of multicultural crayons, colored pencils, and markers in your home, classroom, or group. Crayola sells boxes with eight different skin tones.

Read: *This Is the Rope: A Story from the Great Migration* by Jacqueline Woodson
Follow an African American family's journey north during the early twentieth century, looking for better opportunities.

Connection—Readers understand the journey of a black family adapting to change and seeking freedom and opportunity.

Play: Volleyball
Gather supplies: inflatable world globe beach balls (available at Oriental Trading Company).
- Play a game of your choice using the globe balls. You could pass the beach balls back and forth in pairs, across a net for a "volleyball" game, or grab a parachute and add the balls.

- While playing, talk about all of the different countries and continents where people of the world live.

Connection—Kids play with a tangible representation of a globe while learning some world geography.

Multicultural colored play dough can be purchased at many retailers, such as Discount School Supply.

Create: Play Dough

Gather supplies: multicultural colored play dough.
- Provide the kids with multicultural colored play dough.
- Encourage the kids to model children from all around the world.

Connection—Children use their creativity to think about different skin tones.

Try a creative message for any justice topic using sidewalk chalk.

Create: Sidewalk Art

Gather supplies: sidewalk chalk, outdoor space.
- Encourage children to draw pictures of kids from all around the world.

Connection—Children decorate community spaces with representations of kids from all around the world.

Ages 7–11

Read: *Same, Same but Different* by Jenny Sue Kostecki-Shaw
Pen pals from America and India exchange letters and discover that in many ways their lives are the same . . . but different.

Connection—Readers witness a friendship built between kids from different parts of the world.

Read: *Separate Is Never Equal* by Duncan Tonatiuh
The story of Sylvia Mendez and her family's legal fight for school desegregation in 1940s California.

Connection—Children learn that schools were segregated and how families went to great lengths to secure a right to equal educational opportunities.

Read: *28 Days: Moments in Black History That Changed the World* by Charles R. Smith Jr.
Twenty-eight daily readings, each featuring different influential black Americans and crucial events that changed the history of the United States.

Connection—Readers learn about influential figures in black history and their contributions to the world.

Read: *Freedom over Me: Eleven Slaves, Their Lives and Dreams* by Ashley Bryan
The story of eleven slaves and their lives and dreams contrasted with their monetary value from estate and slave auction documents.

Connection—Students learn how our lives are not something to be bought or sold. Students also learn about the history of slavery.

Read: *Gordon Parks: How the Photographer Captured Black and White America* by Carol Boston Weatherford
Gordon Parks, a self-taught photographer, captured images of segregation in the United States. He took a stand against racism and got America to notice.

Connection—Children learn about the tenacity and courage it takes to document inequalities.

Read: *Lillian's Right to Vote: A Celebration of the Voting Rights Act of 1965* by Jonah Winters
One-hundred-year-old Lillian travels to vote with her family and remembers her history, voting rights history, and the civil rights movement.

Connection—Readers appreciate the long fight citizens endured to attain an equal right to vote in the United States.

Read: *Journey to Jo'Burg: A South African Story* by Beverly Naidoo
When their baby sister becomes deathly ill, siblings Naledi and Tiro travel
to Johannesburg where their mother works. On their journey, they become
aware of the suffering of people in apartheid South Africa.

*Connection—Readers are introduced to the history of apartheid in South
Africa and draw parallels to other times in history when people of color faced
segregation.*

Observe: Study Art
Study the oil-on-canvas painting *The Problem We All Live With* by Norman
Rockwell.

*Connection—Students study the painting of Ruby Bridges being escorted by
federal marshals to an all-white school in New Orleans following the 1954*
Brown v. Board of Education of Topeka *ruling.*

Write a personal diary entry for other historical justice figures you discover. Putting yourself in someone else's shoes builds empathy.

Create: Diary Entry
Gather supplies: *I Am Rosa Parks* by Brad Meltzer or
Who Was Rosa Parks? by Yona Zeldis McDonough,
paper, pens and pencils.
• Read the book *Who Was Rosa Parks?* by Yona
  Zeldis McDonough or *I Am Rosa Parks* by Brad
  Meltzer.
• Write a diary entry from the perspective of Rosa
  Parks. Include what she might have been experi-
  encing and feeling.

*Connection—Writers think about race from the per-
spective of someone who lived through the civil rights
movement.*

Ages 12+

Read: *Nelson Mandela* by Kadir Nelson
With glorious illustrations and free verse, Kadir Nelson tells the story of

Nelson Mandela, who sought equality for all people in his country of South Africa.

   Connection—Readers learn about apartheid and Mandela's lifelong quest for equality and just practices.

Read: *Brown Girl Dreaming* by Jacqueline Woodson
Jacqueline Woodson tells her story, in vivid poetry, of growing up during Jim Crow and the civil rights movement.

   Connection—Young people are connected to US history through the eyes of Jacqueline Woodson, who graciously invites readers into her world.

Read: *Turning 15 on the Road to Freedom: My Story of the 1965 Selma Voting Rights March* by Lynda Blackmon Lowery with Elspeth Leacock and Susan Buckley
Lynda Blackmon Lowery was the youngest marcher in the 1965 voting rights march during the civil rights movement.

   Connection—Readers are inspired to make a difference despite their age.

Read: *The Absolutely True Diary of a Part-Time Indian* by Sherman Alexie
Junior grows up on the Spokane Indian Reservation. This is his story of trying to escape the life he was destined to live. Based on Sherman Alexie's personal experience.

   Connection—Students get a glimpse into Native American life and living on a reservation.

Read: *The Latte Rebellion* by Sarah Jamila Stevenson
Asha and Carey led a student group that raises awareness of mixed-race students. Their cause goes viral, and Asha is faced with a difficult decision between her dreams and her beliefs.

   Connection—Students consider ethnic identity and standing up for a cause.

Read: *The Watsons Go to Birmingham—1963* by Christopher Paul Curtis
The Watson family of Flint, Michigan, travels to visit Grandma in Birmingham, Alabama. Both comical and serious in turn, the Watsons arrive in Birmingham in time to witness a very dark day in American history.

Connection—Readers experience a pivotal moment in history and learn about the effects that racism has on families and communities.

Read: *Maniac Magee* by Jerry Spinelli
Maniac Magee, an orphaned boy, runs away to find a home and confront racism in the divided town of Two Mills, Pennsylvania. But he doesn't just run away, he runs . . . and that is where the legend begins.

Connection—Readers gain a deeper understanding of racial tension and the ability each of us has to become a bridge builder in our communities.

Read: *Maus: A Survivor's Tale* by Art Spiegelman
The Pulitzer Prize–winning graphic novel tells the survival story of a Holocaust survivor.

Connection—Readers face the haunting history of the Holocaust and are challenged to learn from the past.

Read: *The Hate U Give* by Angie Thomas
Starr Carter moves between the poor neighborhood she lives in and the suburban private school she attends. Her divided life comes to a head when she is the sole witness to the shooting of her unarmed childhood friend at the hands of a police officer.

Connection—Students read an important, honest work about racial tension through the empathetic voice of Starr and her family, friends, and community.

Read: *All American Boys* by Jason Reynolds and Brendan Kiely
Alternating narrators Quinn and Rashad are classmates who become entan-

gled in an act of police violence that results in racial tension in their community and nation.

Connection—Readers experience racial tension through the voices of two narrators, one white and one black. The story will raise questions and allow readers to process current racial tension.

Gather: Mix It Up at Lunch Day

To encourage students to meet new classmates, host a Mix It Up at Lunch Day at school lunch. Mix It Up at Lunch Day is a national campaign from Teaching Tolerance, a project of the Southern Poverty Law Center. Schools are asked to participate the last Tuesday of October.

> **Read 1 Peter 4:10: "Each of you should use whatever gift you have received to serve others, as faithful stewards of God's grace in its various forms."**

Connection—Consider debriefing during homeroom to help students share the new things they learned about their classmates.

Gather: Blind Date with a Book

Gather supplies: various books with diverse characters and places in the world, brown wrapping paper, scissors, tape.

- Wrap each book in brown paper packaging.
- Gather a group of students to meet and have them each pick a wrapped book.
- Unwrap the books at your gathering and have students express their initial thoughts on the book they selected.
- Set a date to come together again and discuss the books they read.

Connection—Students experience people and places they might not have otherwise. Talk about what they learned. What surprised them? Would they read a similar story again?

Connect: Coffee Date

Invite someone of a different race to have a coffee date with you. Talk about your families, traditions, and cultures. Listen and ask thoughtful questions about challenges they face.

Read Proverbs 27:17: "As iron sharpens iron, so one person sharpens another."

Connection—Build a relationship with someone from a different race.

Connect: Ancestry
Spend time with someone from your family (e.g., a parent, grandparent, or great grandparent). Talk to them about your ancestry and where your family originated.

Connection—Were you surprised by where your ancestors were from? The journeys they made? The things they experienced?

Gather: Mash-Up Talent Show
Organize a talent show with a twist. For students to participate they need to combine their act with another act. Encourage them to think about unique mash-ups that bring together different talents. (Mash-up act examples: rap and ballet, poetry and karate, magic and hip-hop, improvisation and strings, beat boxing and acrobatics.)

Connection—Students learn to work in community, value differences, and witness the fusion of various cultures.

CHALLENGE AND EXTEND AWARENESS AT HOME

- Read "30 Mealtime Facts About Race," found at lisavanengen.com.
- Practice "30 Days of Prayer for Race," found at lisavanengen.com.
- Look at a United States map that shows population and race. What does your city look like?
- Try some interactive table discussion guides through Repair the World's Turn the Tables program (werepair.org).
- Pick a book to read from Lee and Low Books, the largest multicultural children's book publisher in the United States (leeandlow.com).
- Visit kidworldcitizen.org for a variety of fun resources.

- Read articles in *Faces—The Magazine of People, Places, and Cultures*.
- Watch the TED Talk "The Danger of a Single Story" by Chimamanda Ngozi Adichie.
- Read stories from the project Humans of New York (humansof newyork.com).
- Look at the anatomy of a slave ship from *Roots* and the History Channel (history.com).

Without our faith, without the spirit and spiritual bearings and underpinning, we would not have been so successful. Without prayer, without faith in the Almighty, the civil rights movement would have been like a bird without wings.

—JOHN LEWIS, CIVIL RIGHTS ACTIVIST AND US SENATOR

MAKING A DIFFERENCE

- Explore diversity resources from the website Teacher Vision (teacher vision.com).
- Join or invest in a Be the Bridge group in your community (beabridge builder.com).
- Support UNCF, the United Negro College Fund (uncf.org).
- Watch the episode "Mainstream, USA" by America by the Numbers, about one of the most diverse square miles in the country (pbs.org).
- Read and hear stories from men and women born into slavery through the "WPA Slave Narrative Project" sponsored by a Federal Writers' Project. Go to lisavanengen.com for a direct link.
- Watch the YouTube video "Civil Rights and the 1950s: Crash Course US History #39," narrated by John Green.
- Watch the YouTube video "The Atlantic Slave Trade: Crash Course World History #24," narrated by John Green.
- Look up UnidosUS and learn more about issues facing Latinos.

- Explore five lesson plans on hate crimes from the Anti-Defamation League (adl.org).
- Look at the photographic work of the Gordon Parks Foundation (gordonparksfoundation.org).

For direct links to any of these resources plus additional materials, go to lisavanengen.com and click the And Social Justice for All tab.

Local Ideas

- _____
- _____
- _____
- _____
- _____

14

Changemakers: Fierce Light

Although the world is full of suffering,
it is also full of the overcoming of it.

—HELEN KELLER, AUTHOR, ACTIVIST, AND LECTURER

Raise Awareness

January (third Monday)—Martin Luther King Jr. Day (National Day of Service)

February 20—World Day of Social Justice

July 30—International Day of Friendship

August 12—International Youth Day

August 17—National Nonprofit Day

August 19—World Humanitarian Day

November 13—World Kindness Day

November (Tuesday after Thanksgiving)—Giving Tuesday

December 5—International Volunteer Day

American painter Thomas Kinkade was known as the "painter of light" because his work features strong contrasts between light and dark. Many people will say that when they pass a Kinkade painting, the first thing they see is the light. And like a painting in its earliest stages, children have all the potential in the world to exude brilliant warmth and a fierce light. They possess potential to be changemakers wherever they are. Proverbs 22:6 states, "Start children off on the way they should go, and even when they are old they will not turn from it." We as parents and educators have an opportunity to paint light into the lives of young people. They are uniquely designed by God to make a difference. What qualities can children grow in order to be brilliant warmth and fierce light for justice in the world? What defines changemakers who lead with audacious courage and compassionate mercy?

It's a challenge to make a difference, but it's worth it.
—Leah, age 10

Fresh out of college and newly married, Kris and I led a middle school mission trip to Chicago. Our group led a vacation Bible school in the mornings and explored the city in the afternoons. The book of Nehemiah was the topic of our devotions. One evening I sat on the top of the steps of a church sanctuary sharing evening prayers with a small group. One family had brought along their twin daughters, just going into sixth grade. They were young but wise beyond their years. At the time I was still searching for my first post-college job. I remember one of the girls, Ellen, praying for me that evening, "Dear God, if Nehemiah could rebuild the wall in fifty-two days, then Lisa can find a job too. Amen." Those sweet words of faith have remained with me all these years.

God, grant us childlike faith that trusts in your promises.

When Ellen prayed for my life, she modeled caring for an individual story. When we focus on individuals and not just huge numbers, everything changes. In the three years since I began Talk Justice Playgroups, each gathering has surprised me. There were events when the turnout wasn't stunning, and I felt inadequate. My mind would spiral downward. Maybe I had advertised poorly or my activities were not exciting enough. Perhaps I had chosen the wrong cause. The evening we partnered with a local library and high school to make cards for servicemen and women, it rained buckets and the group was tiny. As we cleaned up, we found that the students had made the most stunning cards. I was honored to send the breathtaking artwork on to A Million Thanks for distribution.

Another week at a local park, close to the July Fourth holiday, the group that gathered was small. That evening a number of children from the playground gravitated to us to participate, including a sibling group without parents accompanying them. A little boy from this group stayed close to the sidewalk chalk during playtime. Afterward, while we cleaned up, he approached my friend Jen quietly. He asked if he could take a piece of sidewalk chalk because he didn't have any of his own at home. She packed up a plastic grocery bag full for him. I remember watching him walk back down the grassy incline to the playground with the bag dangling off his wrist.

Life is a gift. So don't take it for granted—make the world a better place.
—Bryanna, age 11

Lord Jesus, teach us to look at each individual life and not just impressive numbers.

When we think about each individual life, we must consider each individual story too. My husband once ran into a man he had previously met in a church parking lot through Feeding America, a nationwide food distribution organization. The man had a story to share with him. He told how he stopped by Panera Bread for a small cup of coffee one morning before work. There a lady from the church that hosted Feeding America recognized him. She greeted him and pulled him aside. She shared with him that if she saw him buying coffee in a place like Panera again, she hoped to never see him in line for food because surely he could afford it. He went on to tell my husband how ashamed that had made him feel. He apologized for not being at church again; he could not bear to go after the exchange. What she might not have known was that the help from Feeding America might have allowed him to get a cup of coffee before work for the very first time, empowering and helping him feel like a part of the community.

You are old enough—go do something.
—Gessel, age 13

Lord Jesus, help us to think about each person as your creation, to be greatly loved even when no one else is looking.

Empathy understands backstory and history. Possessing empathy means kneeling with someone, not towering above them and looking down.

Empathy acknowledges that in a different time and place, our own circumstances could be precarious. Before empathy speaks, it listens. In the classic writing book *The Elements of Style*, authors William Strunk and E. B. White encourage writers to place themselves in the background. Empathy means stepping outside of ourselves to see a larger picture. When we frame our hearts around empathy, we learn the art of restraint.

Restraint challenges big and small people alike. A child tries to be happy for the friend who snatches the last piece of candy or an adult attempts to stop typing harsh words behind a computer screen. If we truly contemplate our thoughts throughout the day, we bend toward judgment. Restraint means recognizing our thoughts of what others *should* feel, overcome, or let go of, acknowledging the potential unfairness of those thoughts, and not voicing them. We do not need to say everything. We can offer only what is life giving and affirming to those in our wider circles.

> **It's not always easy for kids to make a difference, so grown-ups need to help us.**
> **—Evan, age 13**

Lord Jesus, move our hearts to see with empathy and act with restraint when we bend toward judgment.

The acts of empathy and restraint take a great deal of courage. A fifth-grade student from India reminded me of this. The class was exploring historical figures for a wax museum project. This student discussed Nelson Mandela with his partner, and in the conversation mentioned that Mandela spent time in jail. Some students were surprised and dismayed at this realization, assuming someone who had been to jail was a bad person. His perspective was that many people who fought for justice ended up in jail. He was right, and we know many died for the cause of justice too.

> **To make a difference means to change something major or minor.**
> **—Aiden, age 12**

Defending justice takes courage. Students often learn about two types of bystanders when discussing bullying. One type might bring you back to high school. During fights, these bystanders stand in a crowd and yell, "Fight, fight, fight." This bystander perpetuates injustice. The other bystander risks himself or herself to stand alongside those facing injustice. This bystander moves to the role of an ally.

With fortitude, such a person conveys that unkindness and injustice are not acceptable.

Lord Jesus, teach us to have the courage to be an ally to those facing injustice.

Courage is strengthened by the concept of community. One spring a gaga ball pit was installed on our school playground. Standing outside of the octagonal space looking in, I wondered how long it would take for the grass to wear thin. The gaga pit became wildly popular, and two days later the ground was reduced to dirt. One student could not have done that, but with a group, it was no problem. Keep standing up. Keep marching on. Together.

I like to say, if we want to make a difference, it doesn't have to be your own way. —Nayeli, age 8

Together we can offer space to create. When you give children a palette of paints, something interesting occurs. I've witnessed the hardest, most resistant kids melt into the methodic movements of a paintbrush, carefully selecting colors and watching the paints bleed into one another. I always tell them how amazing it is that no two pictures turn out exactly alike. Often we hear the phrase "thinking outside the box," but for many kids, the box does not even exist. Their creativity and imaginations are a magnificent gift. If we allow them space, they will change the world.

Lord Jesus, thank you for the power of creative collaboration and for allowing us to be stronger together.

In the year 2000, the Grand Valley State University Campus Ministry took many fifteen-passenger vans to Shelby Farms, Tennessee, to attend a large worship gathering. Thousands of students arrived to camp—and to not shower for days. One night the rain was unyielding, and in the very early morning hours, I woke to my feet in a puddle of rain that had seeped into the tent. I tried to curl away from the dripping canvas sides. I was uncomfortable, but I still would have chosen to be in that very place. My natural tendency, and maybe yours, is not to wade into uncomfortable spaces. Staying complacent is not an option when seeking justice. Our lives should reflect that we are willing to be uncomfortable if it means loving others. The children in our lives will notice.

Loving others means really seeing them. I was born in the late seventies, and my parents were huge fans of Christian singer Keith Green. His prophetic lyrics filled the background of my growing-up years. The lyrics of his song "Asleep in the Light" have always remained with me and remind me of Ephesians 5:14: "Wake up, sleeper, rise from the dead, and Christ will shine on you." Are we asleep or do we see? Are we looking away or placing ourselves in proximity to people who are struggling? Renee C. Byer, a documentary photographer, wrote about her experience taking the photographs for the book *Living On a Dollar a Day*: "If we cannot connect, cannot imagine, cannot see, we can never hope to change."[1]

> We live in our own little bubbles and don't notice what's happening around us. To fix it we could help people be more informed.
> —Aliyah, age 16

We pray for God to help us see the needs of people around us and then respond by giving of ourselves. First Peter 4:10 says, "God has given each of you a gift from his great variety of spiritual gifts. Use them well to serve one another" (NLT). Our call is to use our gifts well. I often pause and ask myself, Am I giving my very best in gifts, time, and resources? Does it cost me anything, or do I just skim off the top? When pondering these questions, I remember the story of the widow's offering. Jesus searched the crowd as the people gave their offerings, most throwing in large amounts of money haphazardly. Eventually the widow entered with her two copper coins, all that she had. Jesus declared that she had "put in more than all the others" (Luke 21:3). We are to give sacrificially to others and use our gifts well.

Lord Jesus, teach us to see others, love well, and use our gifts well.

The last two chapters of *Living On a Dollar a Day* are entitled "And Yet the Children Play" and "Hope." Photographs of children with practically no material possessions are shown playing peek-a-boo with a recycling net, sparring with found sticks, jumping rope with a vine, playing soccer with a homemade ball, wrestling, and swimming together. Children are innovative. They offer us hope. All these qualities of faith—caring for individual lives, showing empathy, practicing restraint, acting with courage, being an ally, collaborating creatively, truly seeing someone, loving well, and using gifts well—can be developed in children and young people. I see the thoughtful lives and the work previous youth group and camp ministry students went on to accomplish. They inspired me then, and they continue to now. I am convinced we have great hope, because kids are brilliant warmth and fierce light. That will change everything for them and for us.

Lord Jesus, thank you for the gift of allowing us to be changemakers and to live a life worthy of the calling you have given us.

TALK JUSTICE

Ages 3–6

What things are you really good at?

_____

_____

Who is great at taking care of you?

_____

_____

Who are you great at taking care of?

_____

_____

What is your favorite way to help others?

_____

_____

How do you hope to help other people when you get bigger?

_____

_____

Ages 7–11

How can one person bring about change? How can a community bring about change? How can a family bring about change?

_____

_____

_____

Who is a person in your community who makes a difference for social justice?

_____

_____

In what way would you like to make a difference?

_____

_____

What are challenges that come with trying new things?

_____

_____

What do you want to remember about making a difference?

_____

_____

Ages 12+

What does it mean to you to make a difference?

_____

_____

What are qualities of people who make a difference in your community?

_____

_____

How do we make a difference by just listening to others' stories?

_____

_____

How are our actions as powerful as words?

_____

_____

What changemaker (past or present) would you like to invite to dinner? Why?

_____

_____

STUDY GOD'S WORD

1 Samuel 3:10

The LORD *came and stood there, calling as at other times, "Samuel! Samuel!" Then Samuel said, "Speak, for your servant is listening."*

In 1 Samuel 3, we read the story of Samuel. Before Samuel was born, he was dedicated to the Lord. He ministered in the temple under Eli, the high priest of Israel. As a young boy, he lay in the dark night hearing the voice of God calling to him. Jewish historians estimate that Samuel's age at the time was around twelve years old. A message from God in those days was a rare occurrence. The people of Israel had hard hearts, and there was corruption in the priesthood, even in Eli's own family.

Samuel answered God's call with three simple words: "Here I am." After returning to Eli three times, Eli instructed Samuel to lie down. If God was speaking to Samuel, Eli instructed him to say, "Speak, for your servant is listening." The prophecy God gave Samuel was not good news for Eli. Samuel told Eli God's message in its entirety, even though it was a hard one to share. Verse 19 says, "The LORD was with Samuel as he grew up, and he let none of Samuel's words fall to the ground."

Though Samuel was young, he set an example for believers in responding to God's call. Samuel listened. Samuel was responsive. Samuel was faithful. "Here I am." Think about those three words and let them soak into your heart. What could they mean for you in your relationship with God? What would it mean for you to sincerely pray "Here I am" to God?

Extend Study of God's Word

Read 1 Samuel 3:4–10, 19, but substitute your name for Samuel's in the passage. What new insight did you gain?

_____

_____

_____

_____

_____

_____

_____

How can you make space in your life to listen to God?

_____

_____

_____

To answer, "Here I am," what would you need to change in your life?

_____

_____

What gifts can you offer to others?

_____

_____

Choose an organization that makes a difference that your family or group can pray for:

_____

_____

Choose a specific place or community that is in need that your family or group can pray for:

_____

_____

God, we are listening. We want to tell you we are here.
Help us not to fear. Teach us to be brave. Shape our hearts to listen
and feel genuine empathy. Don't let us stand by when others face
injustice, but help us stand with them. Help us use all the gifts you
have given us to make a difference. Amen.

EXPLORE JUSTICE

Ages 3–6
Read: *The Giving Tree* by Shel Silverstein
A little boy forms a friendship with an apple tree that is willing to sacrificially

give of itself to the boy, who turns into a young man, who eventually turns into an old man.

Connection—Readers consider selflessness and selfishness, caring and giving.

Read: *To Be an Artist* by Maya Ajmera
Children from around the world share how they express themselves through the arts.

Connection—Children see examples of how other children make a difference with their art and are encouraged to use their own gifts.

Read: *Be My Neighbor* by Maya Ajmera
Be My Neighbor is a book about community and being a neighbor. Beautiful photographs show neighborhoods all around the world.

Connection—Children are challenged to think about how they can be a neighbor to others.

Read: *One* by Kathryn Otoshi
Colors and numbers stand together against a bully and learn to accept one another's differences.

Connection—A sweet way to connect children with the ideas that everyone counts and it only takes one person to make a difference.

Read: *Same Kind of Different as Me for Kids* by Ron Hall and Denver Moore
Whether big or small, we can all make a difference when we choose to help others. A true story accompanied by colorful illustrations.

Connection—Students are encouraged that we all can make a difference, even by just being a friend to someone.

Gather: Treasure Hunt
Gather supplies: 5–10 squares of cardboard paper, 5–10 resealable baggies,

treasure for each participant (party bags filled with supplies: see ideas below).

- Plan a series of 5–10 clues that each lead to another (clue one takes you to clue two, clue two takes you to clue three, and so on).
- A variety of puzzles can be used to solve each clue. Ideas: an anagram, a word scramble, picture matching, directions to follow a certain pathway, a clue hidden in certain boundaries, a picture of the spot where the clue is hiding.
- After you write out the clues, place them in resealable baggies and then hide them in the predetermined spaces.
- The last clue should lead the students to the treasure.
- Provide each student with a small party bag filled with supplies for making a difference. Ideas: blank encouragement notes, travel-size toiletries, protein bars, small coffee or grocery gift card, food pantry staple, or new socks.

Connection—Students receive the gift of supplies they can use to make a difference and talk justice. Encourage each recipient to talk with their family about how they want to use the supplies.

Play: Bike Obstacle Course

Gather supplies: items for obstacle course can include cones for bikes to weave through, sidewalk chalk for paths to follow, obstacles to navigate around, a water element to go through on hot summer days, a bridge or rumble strip to ride over, or streamers (hung from overhead) to ride underneath.

- Find a large play space that would accommodate riding bicycles.
- Before the event, create an obstacle course for the bicycles to travel through.
- Invite neighborhood kids to come ride their bikes through an obstacle course. Remind them to wear their helmets.
- Have fun and work together to conquer the course!

Connection—Making a difference can be challenging. There will be obstacles to overcome. When we work together and don't give up, we can complete our mission, just like this bicycle obstacle course.

Ages 7–11

Read: *Of Thee I Sing: A Letter to My Daughters* by Barack Obama
Encourage children to be good and kind through stories honoring thirteen great American men and women.

Connection—Students learn about thirteen people who made a difference.

Read: *Red Bicycle: The Extraordinary Story of One Ordinary Bicycle* by Jude Isabella
When a boy in North America outgrows his bike, he donates it to an organization that ships it to Africa. In West Africa, Alisetta uses the bike to take sorghum to the market, and Haridata uses it as a type of ambulance.

Connection—The book shows how one gift can make a difference and demonstrates the importance of bicycles all around the world.

Read: *Who Says Women Can't Be Doctors? The Story of Elizabeth Blackwell* by Tanya Lee Stone
The inspiring story of the first female doctor.

Connection—Readers learn that just because something hasn't been done before doesn't mean it can't or shouldn't be done.

Read: *Brave Girl: Clara and the Shirtwaist Makers' Strike of 1909* by Michelle Markel
Clara Lemlich, a Ukrainian immigrant, led the largest strike of women workers from the garment industry in US history.

Connection—Readers learn that everyone should have a fair chance, and when we stand together, change can come.

Read: *Brick by Brick* by Charles R. Smith Jr.
When the first White House was built, there were no machines to complete the project. Many slaves did the hard work of laying the bricks. The contribution of those slaves is shared in poetic verse.

Connection—Readers get a deeper look at how an iconic symbol of freedom was built and the strength of the slaves who contributed to its construction.

Read: *The Lions of Little Rock* by Kristin Levine
Middle schoolers Marlee and Liz take on segregation and face the dangers their friendship could trigger in 1958 Little Rock, Arkansas.

Connection—The power of friendship makes a difference in fighting injustice.

Read: *Sit-In: How Four Friends Stood Up by Sitting Down* by Andrea Davis Pinkney
This picture book depicts four young friends who peacefully protested segregation during the historic Woolworth's lunch counter sit-in of 1960.

Connection—Readers learn civil rights history and the power of peaceful protest.

Read Jeremiah 29:12: "Then you will call on me and come and pray to me, and I will listen to you."

Create: Dream Catcher
Gather supplies: wooden hoop, string, feathers, beads.
• To make a dream catcher, use the string to weave a net through the middle of the hoop.
• Attach feathers and beads to pieces of string to hang down from the sides of the hoop.

Connection—As students make a dream catcher, encourage them to think about their dreams of being a changemaker. Encourage them to say a prayer for God to be a part of their dreams. The dream catcher reminds us that God hears our hopes and dreams through prayer.

Create: Write a Fairy Tale
Encourage students to write a fairy tale around the theme of making a difference. Key elements to include in a fairy tale: "Once upon a time," a distant land, imaginary characters, good overcomes evil, a magical component, and a "happily ever after."

Connection—Writers explore making a difference through creative writing.

Ages 12+

Read: *Taking Flight: From War Orphan to Star Ballerina* by Michaela DePrince
Born in war-torn Sierra Leone, fighting a medical condition, and orphaned, Michaela DePrince defied odds and went on to become a principal ballerina in a major company.

Connection—Despite difficult circumstances, we can make a difference and inspire others.

Read: *Hoot* by Carl Hiaasen
Unlikely friendships result in a hilarious adventure to save endangered miniature owls.

Connection—Readers are challenged to think about working together to make a difference.

Read: *Take Your Best Shot: Do Something Bigger Than Yourself* by Austin Gutwein
Teenager Austin Gutwein founded Hoops of Hope, the world's largest free-throw marathon, supporting AIDS orphans. *Take Your Best Shot* is Austin's story of response to God that resulted in the building of a medical clinic and school.

Connection—Readers learn about a teenager who responded to God's call in his life, and they are encouraged to do the same.

Read: *Rise: Get Up and Live God's Great Story* by Trip Lee
Hip-hop artist and church planter in Atlanta Trip Lee encourages young people to wake up, rise up, and live life for Christ.

Connection—Readers are inspired to live their life for Christ and make a difference.

Create: Writing
Gather supplies: paper, pens and pencils.
 • Prompt: In order to be a changemaker today, I can . . .

Connection—Challenge writers to think about what practical things they could do in their everyday lives to be changemakers.

Create: Changemakers Playlist
Compile an inspiring playlist using Spotify or YouTube for others who hope to make a difference in the world. Add a mission statement to the description box. Encourage other changemakers by sharing your playlist.

Connection—Students curate songs and lyrics that convey the message of making a difference.

Connect: Rock the Vote
Rock the Vote is a nonprofit organization that uses pop culture and technology to mobilize young voters. Bring the Rock the Vote Democracy Class to your high school.

Connection—Students are educated and empowered to be a part of the voting process.

Gather: Face Painting
Gather supplies: water-based face paint, sponges, brushes, cotton swabs, bowl of water, towels, baby wipes, handheld mirrors.
 • Before the event, research how to face-paint superhero masks or paint superhero symbols on top of hands. Print off ideas for children to choose from.
 • Enlist teens and young adults to offer face- and hand-painting to small children.

Connection—Young people encourage small children through the art of face painting. When children leave, remind them that when they make a difference, they are like powerful superheroes.

CHALLENGE AND EXTEND AWARENESS AT HOME

- Read "30 Mealtime Facts for Changemakers," found at lisavanengen.com.
- Practice "30 Days of Prayer for Changemakers" found at lisavanengen .com.
- Does your family travel? Check out Pack for a Purpose for information on supplies needed for community-based projects both at home and abroad (packforapurpose.org).
- Make a pillowcase dress together through Little Dresses for Africa (little dressesforafrica.org).
- Make blankets together through the Snuggles Project, Project Linus, or Project Night Night.
- Check out the work of UNICEF Kid Power, pairing active lives with saving lives (unicefkidpower.org).
- Read excerpts from Humans of New York to remember there is more to the story of a life (humansofnewyork.com).
- Take the "Changemaker Personality Quiz" from The Story of Stuff (story ofstuff.org).
- Read about the work of Theirworld, which helps make a brighter future for every child (theirworld.org).
- Go to parenttoolkit.com and work through the social and emotional development toolkit.

We shall awaken from our dullness and rise victoriously toward justice.

—HILDEGARD VON BINGEN, GERMAN BENEDICTINE ABBESS

MAKING A DIFFERENCE

- Learn about bottle-brick schools through Hug It Forward (hugitfor ward.org).

- Connect with the organization More Love Letters and write letters to people who need encouragement (moreloveletters.com).
- On YouTube, watch "Women's Suffrage: Crash Course US History #31."
- Watch the video "The Power of Advocacy" at plan-international.org.
- Use discussion playlists with a variety of topics from Bystander Revolution. Have a discussion about bullying by using the discussion materials found at bystanderrevolution.org.
- Work with a global network of young people making real change through Map Your World. Find a direct link at lisavanengen.com.
- Join a global game of Mystery Skype with your classroom (education .microsoft.com).
- Connect with Global Oneness Project and choose a lesson plan to work through (globalonenessproject.org).
- Learn about the difference communities are making for people with disabilities through a Makeathon with the organization Tom Global (tomglobal.org).
- Check out the innovative Toy Like Me collective (toylikeme.org). What would you invent?

For direct links to any of these resources plus additional materials, go to lisavanengen.com and click the And Social Justice for All tab.

Local Ideas

- _____
- _____
- _____
- _____
- _____

Epilogue: Let This Be Written

You may choose to look the other way, but you can never say
again that you did not know.

—WILLIAM WILBERFORCE, ENGLISH ABOLITIONIST

Poised along the coast of the Great Lakes stand 388 lighthouses. Lighthouses mark dangerous or hard-to-navigate spaces of coastline. Lamps and lenses at the top of the structures help guide maritime navigators away from the rocky shoreline, through darkness and gathering fog, and reference their navigational point. Not all lighthouses are still functional or updated with technological advances such as GPS, but they still remain a symbol of strength and light. The winter can be brutal on the coastline of the Great Lakes. The lakes often freeze over, creating beautiful icebergs. In certain conditions of wind and ice, lighthouses can become completely frozen over. Encased in ice, they must await a warming to be freed.

There are lives all over the world waiting to be freed from the icy grip of injustice. We are called to be that strength and light to others, and in turn we free others to be strength and light.

> What do I want to share about making a difference? Truthness.
> —Liam, age 6

The road from Jerusalem to Jericho stretched eighteen miles along a rocky path. Travelers faced not only difficult terrain but wild animals and bandits. The evening before his assassination, Martin Luther King Jr. delivered a speech entitled "I've Been to the Mountaintop," in which he spoke of the Bible story of the Good Samaritan, a man who traveled that route from Jerusalem to Jericho. King shared his perspective of why the Levite and priest did not stop to help the man beaten and left for dead by robbers. "It's possible that those men were afraid. You

> **Making a difference means standing out, like the one leper out of ten who came back to thank Jesus after he'd been healed, but the other nine didn't.**
> —Eli, age 10

see, the Jericho road is a dangerous road." King goes on to ask that we reverse the question from "If I stop to help this man, what will happen to me?" to "If I do not stop to help this man, what will happen to him?"[1] Fighting injustice can be dangerous. Navigating the complicated waters will never be simple or easy. Even though we are afraid, let us ask for the courage to flip the question and think about our neighbors before ourselves.

For others to be freed from injustice, a warming needs to take place in our own lives. Often, for us to notice our frozen tendencies, we need to create marginal space in our lives to intentionally draw near to God. We stand up to injustice from this space. We slow down and intentionally make social justice a priority of our Christian life. As we slow down, we find ways to place our families, groups, classrooms, and communities in proximity to injustice.

This is my prayer for you:

Do not be afraid; do not be discouraged.
—Deuteronomy 31:8

We must not look away.
Draw up in proximity.
Be a fierce light.
A sanctuary.
Do not let injustice stand.

Not knowing when the dawn will come I open every door.
—Emily Dickinson, American poet

Let this be written:
We listened.
We were people who cared
Deeply, openly, and expansively
For all of God's people.

Acknowledgments

Ellie and Josiah, you are my fierce lights. You have been so good to me through this process. You are wise beyond your years, forgiving, loving, creative, and just plain fun.

Kris, you have taught me so much about justice, unconditional love, and never giving up. You believe in me, and it makes all the difference.

Dad and Mom, from your work the deepest reflections of my heart emerged when I was so little. Thank you for making proximity one thing that was certain in our home. I know Jesus because of your hearts for those in need. To my brother, Jeff, thank you for always pushing me to be stronger.

Thank you, Amy Sullivan, for always believing in my writing, helping this idea expand, challenging me, and making me better than I am. Your friendship means so much to me. You are a champion of the struggling, a bridge builder, an idea machine, and full of a compassionate Jesus.

To Kregel Publications, thank you for your patience, guidance, and excitement for this project. Thank you to Dawn Anderson for your initial shaping and development of the manuscript. Sarah De Mey, you have patience, warmth, and an incredible eye for detail that strengthened these words beyond what I thought possible.

I owe a great thanks to the Breathe Christian Writers Conference for all the encouragement and connections you facilitate for writers in our community. Thank you, Chad Allen—your class and resources make so many writers better, including me.

To Janyre Tromp, thank you for taking a chance on me and offering me friendship. You see the beautiful in the ugly, and it's a wonderful gift.

Thank you, Lori and Amy, for retreating and brainstorming at the exact time I needed it. I'm so thankful for your contributions to this book.

Thank you to my strong and supportive brothers- and sisters-in-law. My in-laws, Allen and Judy. So many family and friends have encouraged and inspired me. I want to especially thank my girls Becky, Lisa, and Julie. Also Kim, Jen, Jenn, and Jennifer. Diane, Wendi P., Mickie, Allison, Shannon. My EC para team.

Thank you to all the powerful voices that contributed to the Kids Talk Justice surveys: the Bing, Woolsey, Meyers, Putzke, Petersen, Devries, Egedus, Sullivan, Motaung, Taneti, Manlapig, Hubbard, Fomunung, Van Kampen, Lappenga, Howard, Sorenson, Takenaka, Pitcher, Zandstra, and Elenbaas families. Thank you to Eaglecrest's Calling All Colors, New Community Reformed Youth Group, Boys and Girls Club of Holland, and Goldsboro Presbyterian Youth in North Carolina.

Thanks to so many who have shaped my life and my story through Grand Valley State University's Campus Ministry, GVSU School of Social Work, Camp Geneva, the youth of First Reformed Church and Harlem Reformed Church, the students, staff, and families of Eaglecrest, my Be the Bridge small group, and New Community Fourth Reformed Church.

To my Lord and Savior Jesus Christ, thank you for saving my life. I only hope to do you justice in loving others.

Appendix A

How to Plan a Community Gathering

Step 1
- Choose a justice theme.
- Pick a justice project or organization to partner with.
- Identify a location, date, and time. (We often choose early evening so parents who work can attend with their children.)

Step 2
- Plan the event.
- Choose a book to share about the justice issue.
- Create play stations that educate around the issue.
- Pick a justice project or partnership to complete together.

Step 3
- Advertise and share the event with the community.
- Gather supplies.

Step 4
- Hold the event.

Step 5
- Follow up with participants about the results of the justice project or partnership via email, blog post, or social media account.

Example

Project: Support a local rescue mission organization.

Book: *If the World Were a Village* by David J. Smith.

Activities: Make birthday kits for the rescue mission, walk through local organizations' mobile art gallery (based on *If the World Were a Village*), sidewalk chalk, bubbles, inflatable world volleyball, collaborative village art project.

Project: Donate birthday kits for families at the rescue mission.

Follow Up: Deliver birthday kits to the rescue mission, update social media with the number of kits donated and a thank-you for participation, ask for feedback from attending families.

Appendix B

Book Resources for Adults to Deepen Understanding of Global Issues

Changemakers

A Path Appears: Transforming Lives, Creating Opportunity by Nicholas D. Kristof and Sheryl WuDunn

Bowling Alone: The Collapse and Revival of American Community by Robert D. Putnam

Tattoos on the Heart: The Power of Boundless Compassion by Gregory Boyle

To Repair the World: Paul Farmer Speaks to the Next Generation by Paul Farmer

When More Is Not Enough: How to Stop Giving Your Kids What They Want and Give Them What They Need by Amy L. Sullivan

World Peace and Other 4th-Grade Achievements by John Hunter

Clean Water

Drinking Water: A History by James Salzman

One Thousand Wells: How an Audacious Goal Taught Me to Love the World Instead of Save It by Jena Lee Nardella

The Ripple Effect: The Fate of Fresh Water in the Twenty-First Century by Alex Prud'homme

Conflict

Burning Down the House: The End of Juvenile Prison by Nell Bernstein

Creation Care

Food, Inc: How Industrial Food Is Making Us Sicker, Fatter, and Poorer—and What You Can Do About It edited by Karl Weber

The Story of Stuff: How Our Obsession with Stuff Is Trashing the Planet, Our Communities, and Our Health—and a Vision for Change by Annie Leonard

Disabilities

A Good and Perfect Gift: Faith, Expectations, and a Little Girl Named Penny by Amy Julia Becker

Different: The Story of an Outside-the-Box Kid and the Mom Who Loved Him by Sally and Nathan Clarkson

Real Family, Real Needs by Joni and Friends

Refresh: Spiritual Nourishment for Parents of Children with Special Needs by Kimberly M. Drew and Jocelyn Green

Education

A Mind Shaped by Poverty: Ten Things Education Should Know by Regenia Rawlinson

Creating Room to Read: A Story of Hope in the Battle for Global Literacy by John Wood

I Am Malala: The Girl Who Stood Up for Education and Was Shot by the Taliban by Malala Yousafzai

I Wish My Teacher Knew: How One Question Can Change Everything for Our Kids by Kyle Schwartz

The Promise of a Pencil: How an Ordinary Person Can Create Extraordinary Change by Adam Braun

Fair Trade

Fair Trade: A Human Journey by Éric St-Pierre

Javatrekker: Dispatches from the World of Fair Trade Coffee by Dean Cycon

50 Reasons to Buy Fair Trade by Miles Litvinoff and John Madeley

Health Care

Keeping Hope Alive: One Woman—90,000 Lives Changed by Dr. Hawa Abdi

Preemptive Love: Pursuing Peace One Heart at a Time by Jeremy Courtney

Human Trafficking

A Long Way Gone: Memoirs of a Boy Soldier by Ishmael Beah

Five Thousand Years of Slavery by Marjorie Gann and Janet Willen

Girls Like Us: Fighting for a World Where Girls Are Not for Sale by Rachel Lloyd

Not for Sale: The Return of the Global Slave Trade—and How We Can Fight It by David Batstone

Refuse to Do Nothing: Finding Your Power to Abolish Modern-Day Slavery by Shayne Moore and Kimberly McOwen Yim

Sold by Patricia McCormick

The Locust Effect: Why the End of Poverty Requires the End of Violence by Gary A. Haugen and Victor Boutros

The White Umbrella: Walking with Survivors of Sex Trafficking by Mary Frances Bowley

Hunger

A Place at the Table: The Crisis of 49 Million Hungry Americans and How It Can Be Solved edited by Peter Pringle

Exodus from Hunger: We Are Called to Change the Politics of Hunger by David Beckmann

The Color of Food: Stories of Race, Resilience and Farming by Natasha Bowens

The Last Hunger Season: A Year in an African Farm Community on the Brink of Change by Roger Thurow

We the Eaters: If We Change Dinner, We Can Change the World by Ellen Gustafson

Immigrants and Refugees

Enrique's Journey: The Story of a Boy's Dangerous Odyssey to Reunite with His Mother by Sonia Nazario

Love Undocumented: Risking Trust in a Fearful World by Sarah Quezada.

Seeking Justice: On the Shores of the Global Refugee Crisis by Stephan Bauman, Matthew Soerens, and Dr. Issam Smeir

The Distance Between Us: A Memoir by Reyna Grande

The Invisible Girls: A Memoir by Sarah Thebarge

The Middle of Everywhere: Helping Refugees Enter the American Community by Mary Pipher

Welcoming the Stranger: Justice, Compassion, and Truth in the Immigration Debate by Matthew Soerens and Jenny Hwang Yang

Microfinance

Banker to the Poor: Mirco-Lending and the Battle Against World Poverty by Muhammad Yunus

Clay, Water, Brick: Finding Inspiration from Entrepreneurs Who Do the Most with the Least by Jessica Jackley

Teach a Woman to Fish: Overcoming Poverty Around the Globe by Ritu Sharma

The Blue Sweater: Bridging the Gap Between Rich and Poor in an Interconnected World by Jacqueline Novogratz

Poverty

$2.00 a Day: Living on Almost Nothing in America by Kathryn J. Edin and H. Luke Shaefer

Behind the Beautiful Forevers: Life, Death, and Hope in a Mumbai Undercity by Katherine Boo

Criminal of Poverty: Growing Up Homeless in America by Tiny aka Lisa Gray-Garcia

Evicted: Poverty and Profit in the American City by Matthew Desmond

Hillbilly Elegy: A Memoir of a Family and Culture in Crisis by J. D. Vance

Living On a Dollar a Day: The Lives and Faces of the World's Poor by Thomas A. Nazario

Nickel and Dimed: On (Not) Getting By in America by Barbara Ehrenreich

Same Kind of Different as Me: A Modern-Day Slave, an International Art Dealer, and the Unlikely Woman Who Bound Them Together by Ron Hall and Denver Moore

The Hole in Our Gospel: What Does God Expect of Us? by Richard Stearns

The Working Poor: Invisible in America by David K. Shipler

Race

All the Colors We Will See: Reflections on Barriers, Brokenness, and Finding Our Way by Patrice Gopo

A Sojourner's Truth: Choosing Freedom and Courage in a Divided World by Natasha Sistrunk Robinson

Beasts of No Nation: A Novel by Uzodinma Iweala

Birmingham Revolution: Martin Luther King Jr.'s Epic Challenge to the Church by Edward Gilbreath

I'm Still Here: Black Dignity in a World Made for Whiteness by Austin Channing Brown

Let Justice Roll Down by John M. Perkins

One: Unity in a Divided World by Deidra Riggs

Prophetic Lament: A Call for Justice in Troubled Times by Soong-Chan Rah

Raise Your Voice: Why We Stay Silent and How to Speak Up by Kathy Khang

Shalom Sistas: Living Wholeheartedly in a Broken World by Osheta Moore

The Warmth of Other Suns: The Epic Story of America's Great Migration by Isabel Wilkerson

Twelve Years a Slave by Solomon Northup

Women and Girls

Half the Sky: Turning Oppression into Opportunity for Women Worldwide by Nicholas D. Kristof and Sheryl WuDunn

However Long the Night: Molly Melching's Journey to Help Millions of African Women and Girls Triumph by Aimee Molloy

Women in the Material World by Faith D'Aluisio and Peter Menzel

Appendix C

Film Guide for Adults to Deepen Understanding of Global Issues

Changemakers
A Path Appears, directed by Maro Chermayeff

Conflict
Hotel Rwanda, directed by Terry George
Pray the Devil Back to Hell, directed by Gini Reticker

Creation Care
Before the Flood, directed by Fisher Stevens
Planet Earth, BBC One, produced by Alastair Fothergill
Rancher, Farmer, Fisherman, directed by Susan Froemke and John Hoffman
The True Cost, directed by Andrew Morgan

Education
Girl Rising, produced by Priyanka Chopra and Freida Pinto
Half the Sky, directed by Maro Chermayeff

Fair Trade
A Thousand Fibers, produced by Partners for Just Trade
Black Gold, directed by Marc Francis and Nick Francis

The Dark Side of Chocolate, directed by U. Roberto Romano and Miki
   Mistrati
The Price of Sugar, directed by Bill Haney

Families

ReMoved, directed by Nathanael Matanick
The Drop Box, directed by Brian Ivie

Human Trafficking

Born into Brothels: Calcutta's Red Light Kids, a documentary
Not Today, directed by Jon Van Dyke
The Long Night, directed by Tim Matsui

Hunger

A Place at the Table, directed by Kristi Jacobson and Lori Silverbush
Food, Inc., directed by Robert Kenner

Immigrants and Refugees

Documented: A Film by an Undocumented American, by Jose Antonio Vargas
The Stranger, produced by Linda Midgett

Poverty

Landfill Harmonic, directed by Brad Allgood, Graham Townsley, and Juli-
   ana Penaranda-Loftus
Living On One Dollar a Day, directed by Chris Temple, Zach Ingrasci, and
   Sean Leonard

Race

Crash, directed by Paul Haggis
Eyes on the Prize: America's Civil Rights Era 1954–1965, created by Henry
   Hampton
Freedom Riders, directed by Stanley Nelson
The Color Purple, directed by Steven Spielberg

Appendix D

Raise Awareness by Month

January

National Braille Literacy Month

National Mentoring Month

National Slavery and Human Trafficking Prevention Month

January (third Monday)—Martin Luther King Jr. Day (National Day of Service)

January 1—Global Family Day

January 27—International Holocaust Remembrance Day

February

Black History Month

National Children's Dental Health Month

February (last day)—Rare Disease Day

February 1—National Freedom Day

February 4—World Cancer Day

February 12—International Day Against the Use of Child Soldiers

February 14—National Donor Day

February 19—Day of Remembrance (Japanese Americans)

February 20—World Day of Social Justice

March

National Cerebral Palsy Awareness Month

National Developmental Disability Awareness Month

March (last week)—National Farmworker Awareness Week

March 1—International Wheelchair Day

March 2—Read Across America

March 14—International Day of Action for Rivers

March 21—National Single Parent Day

March 21—World Down Syndrome Day

March 21—International Day for the Elimination of Racial Discrimination

March 22—World Water Day

March 24—World Tuberculosis Day

March 25—International Day of Remembrance for the Victims of Slavery and the Transatlantic Slave Trade

March 31—Cesar Chavez Day

April

National Child Abuse Prevention Month

National Fair Housing Month

April (first week)—World Health Workers Week

April (week surrounding Earth Day)—Faith Climate Action Week

April (last Friday)—Arbor Day

April 2—World Autism Awareness Day

April 10—National Siblings Day

April 22—Earth Day

May

Asian Pacific American Heritage Month

Better Hearing and Speech Month

Jewish American Heritage Month

Lyme Disease Awareness Month

National Foster Care Month

National Mental Health Month

May (first week)—National Children's Mental Health Awareness Week

May (first full week)—Teacher Appreciation Week

May (second Saturday)—World Fair Trade Day

May (third Friday)—National Bike to Work Day

May (third Saturday)—Armed Forces Day

May (last Monday)—Memorial Day

May 1—International Workers' Day

May 1—World Day for Cultural Diversity
May 5—Cinco de Mayo
May 21—World Day for Cultural Diversity for Dialogue and Development

June

Great Outdoors Month
National Fresh Fruit and Vegetable Month
National Wildlife Federation's Great American Campout
June 1—Global Day of Parents
June 6—National Higher Education Day
June 12—World Day Against Child Labor
June 14—World Blood Donor Day
June 16—Disability Awareness Day
June 16—International Domestic Workers' Day
June 19—Juneteenth
June 20—World Refugee Day

July

July 30—International Day of Friendship
July 30—World Day Against Trafficking in Persons

August

National Breastfeeding Month
National Immunization Awareness Month
August (first full week)—National Farmers Market Week
August (begins the first Sunday)—International Assistance Dog Week
August 9—International Day of the World's Indigenous Peoples
August 9—National Book Lovers Day
August 12—International Youth Day
August 17—National Nonprofit Day
August 19—World Humanitarian Day

September

Childhood Cancer Awareness Month
Hunger Awareness Month

National Hispanic-Latino Heritage Month (September 15–October 15)
September (first Sunday)—National Grandparents Day
September (second Friday)—Stand Up to Cancer Day
September 8—International Literacy Day
September 10—World Suicide Prevention Day
September 21—International Peace Day

October

National Bullying Prevention Month
National Disability Employment Awareness Month
National Farm to School Month
Pregnancy and Infant Loss Awareness Month
October (first Monday)—World Habitat Day
October (first Wednesday)—National Walk to School Day
October (second Sunday)—Disability Awareness Sunday
October (second Thursday)—World Sight Day
October 5—World Teachers' Day
October 10—World Mental Health Day
October 11—International Day of the Girl
October 15—Global Handwashing Day
October 15—International Day of Rural Women
October 16—World Food Day

November

Military Family Appreciation Month
National Adoption Awareness Month
National American Indian Heritage Month
November (third week)—International Restorative Justice Week
November (third Thursday)—National Parental Involvement Day
November (third Thursday)—Children's Grief Awareness Day
November (Saturday before Thanksgiving)—National Adoption Day
November (Tuesday after Thanksgiving)—Giving Tuesday
November 11—Veterans Day
November 13—World Kindness Day
November 19—World Toilet Day

November 25—International Day for the Elimination of Violence Against Women

December

December 1—World AIDS Day

December 2—International Day for the Abolition of Slavery

December 3—International Day of Persons with Disabilities

December 5—International Volunteer Day

December 10—Human Rights Day

Notes

Introduction

1. Henri Nouwen, *Making All Things New: An Invitation to the Spiritual Life* (New York: HarperOne, 1981), 55.

Chapter 1: Clean Water and Sanitation

1. Anne Marie Helmenstine, "How Much of Your Body Is Water?," ThoughtCo, March 15, 2018, https://www.thoughtco.com/how-much-of-your-body-is-water-609406.
2. Dina Spector, "Here's How Many Days a Person Can Survive Without Water," *Business Insider*, March 8, 2018, http://www.businessinsider.com/how-many-days-can-you-survive-without-water-2014-5.
3. "The World's Water," USGS, December 2, 2016, https://water.usgs.gov/edu/earthwherewater.html.
4. Marq De Villiers, *Water: The Fate of Our Most Precious Resource* (New York: Houghton Mifflin, 2000), 25.
5. "Transboundary Waters: Sharing Benefits, Sharing Responsibilities," UN-Water, May 6, 2008, http://www.unwater.org/publications/transboundary.
6. *Progress on Drinking Water, Sanitation and Hygiene: 2017 Update and SDG Baselines* (Geneva: World Health Organization and UNICEF, 2017), 24, https://www.unicef.org/publications/files/Progress_on_Drinking_Water_Sanitation_and_Hygiene_2017.pdf.
7. Tessa Wardlaw et al., *Committing to Child Survival: A Promise Renewed* (New York: UNICEF, 2014), 24, https://www.unicef.org/philippines/APR2014_Sep2014.pdf.
8. Kevin Watkins et al., *Human Development Report 2006: Beyond Scarcity: Power, Poverty and the Global Water Crisis* (New York: United Nations Development Programme, 2006), 5, http://hdr.undp.org/sites/default/files/reports/267/hdr06-complete.pdf.
9. "What We Do: Water, Sanitation and Hygiene Overview," Bill and

Melinda Gates Foundation, accessed September 17, 2018, http://www
.gatesfoundation.org/What-We-Do/Global-Growth-and-Opportu
nity/Water-Sanitation-and-Hygiene.

10. Kristin Myers, "Women, Water, and the Cycle of Poverty," Concern
Worldwide US, August 10, 2017, https://www.concernusa.org/story
/women-water-the-cycle-of-poverty/.

11. *UNHCR Somalia: Drought Displacements in Period 1 Nov 2016 to 30
June 2017*, UN Refugee Agency, accessed September 17, 2018, http://
reliefweb.int/sites/reliefweb.int/files/resources/58534.pdf.

12. Grace Hood and Lauren Sommer, "High Demand, Low Supply:
Colorado River Crisis Hits Across the West," National Public Radio,
December 30, 2016, transcript and audio, 5:05, https://www.npr.org
/2016/12/30/507569514/high-demand-low-supply-colorado-river
-water-crisis-hits-across-the-west.

13. Henry Cisneros, "A National Water Crisis: Fixing the Water Infrastructure Is One of the Greatest Challenges of Our Time," *U.S. News
and World Report*, June 29, 2016, https://www.usnews.com/opinion
/articles/2016-06-29/the-united-states-faces-a-national-water-crisis.

14. Jacey Fortin, "American's Tap Water: Too Much Contamination, Not
Enough Reporting, Study Finds," *New York Times*, May 14, 2017,
https://www.nytimes.com/2017/05/04/us/tapwater-drinking-water
-study.html.

15. Tim Friend, "Water in America: Is It Safe to Drink?," *National Geographic*, February 17, 2014, http://news.nationalgeographic.com/news
/2014/02/140217-drinking-water-safety-west-virginia-chemical-spill
-science.

Chapter 2: Creation Care

1. Aaron Bernstein and Eric Chivian, *Sustaining Life: How Human
Health Depends On Biodiversity* (New York: Oxford University Press,
2008), 3.

2. Alister Doyle, "Oceans Yield 1,500 New Creatures, Many Others
Lurk Unknown," March 11, 2015, Reuters, https://www.reuters.com
/article/us-environment-seas/oceans-yield-1500-new-creatures-many
-others-lurk-unknown-idUSKBN0M800720150312.

3. "Sea Level Rise," *National Geographic*, January 13, 2017, https://www
.nationalgeographic.com/environment/global-warming/sea-level-rise.

4. Ron Kwok and D. Andrew Rothrock, "Decline in Arctic Thickness
from Submarine and ICESAT Records: 1958–2008," *Geophysical
Research Letters* 36, no. L15501 (2009): 1–5.

5. "WHO Releases Country Estimates on Air Pollution Exposure and
Health Impact," World Health Organization, September 27, 2016,
http://www.who.int/en/news-room/detail/27-09-2016-who-releases
-country-estimates-on-air-pollution-exposure-and-health-impact.

6. Brady Dennis and Chris Mooney, "WHO: Global Air Pollution Is
Worsening, and Poor Countries Are Being Hit the Hardest," *Washington Post*, May 12, 2016, https://www.washingtonpost.com/new
/energy-environment/wp/2016/05/12/who-global-air-pollution-is
-worsening-and-poor-countries-are-being-hit-the-hardest.

7. Elizabeth Grossman, *High Tech Trash: Digital Devices, Hidden Toxins,
and Human Health* (Washington, DC: Island Press, 2007), 5.

8. Carolyn VanHouten, "First Official Climate Change Refugees in the
U.S. Race Against Time," *National Geographic*, May 25, 2016, https://
news.nationalgeographic.com/2016/05/160525-isle-de-jean-charles
-louisiana-sinking-climate-change-refugees/.

9. Robinson Meyer, "The Standing Rock Sioux Claim 'Victory and Vin-
dication' in Court," *Atlantic*, June 14, 2017, http://www.theatlantic
.com/science/archive/2017/06/dakota-access-standing-rock-sioux
-victory-court/530427.

10. "The State of Consumption Today," Worldwatch Institute, accessed
October 10, 2018, http://www.worldwatch.org/node/810.

11. Derrick Jensen and Aric MacBay, *What We Leave Behind* (New York:
Seven Stories, 2009), 25.

12. Annie Leonard, *The Story of Stuff: The Impact of Overconsumption on
the Planet, Our Communities, and Our Health—and How We Can
Make It Better* (New York: Free Press, 2010), 251.

13. Joshua Glenn and Elizabeth Foy Larsen, *Unbored: The Essential Field
Guide to Serious Fun* (New York: Bloomsbury, 2012), 226.

14. "Svalbard Global Seed Vault," CropTrust, accessed September 17, 2018,
https://www.croptrust.org/our-work/svalbard-global-seed-vault/.

Chapter 3: Disabilities

1. "Nearly 1 in 5 People Have a Disability in the US, Census Bureau Reports," United States Census Bureau, July 25, 2012, http://www .census.gov/newsroom/releases/archives/miscellaneous/cb12-134 .html.

2. *All Children in School by 2015: Global Initiative on Out-of-School Children, South Asia Regional Study* (Kathmandu: UNICEF Regional Office for South Asia, 2014), vi, http://unesdoc.unesco.org/images /0022/002262/226221e.pdf.

3. Brian Delozier, *Dot Nation*, ArtPrize, accessed September 17, 2018, https://www.artprize.org/62794.

4. *WHO Global Disability Action Plan 2014–2021: Better Health for All People with Disabilities* (Geneva: World Health Organization, 2015), 1, http://www.who.int/disabilities/actionplan/en.

5. "Greece: Refugees with Disabilities Overlooked, Underserved," Human Rights Watch, January 18, 2017, https://www.hrw.org/news/2017 /01/18/greece-refugees-disabilities-overlooked-underserved.

6. Katherine Reynolds Lewis, "Why Schools Over-Discipline Children with Disabilities," *Atlantic*, July 24, 2015, https://www.the atlantic.com/education/archive/2015/07/school-discipline-children -disabilities/399563.

7. "Mayor Thomas M. Menino Park," Landscape Structures, accessed September 17, 2018, https://www.playlsi.com/en/playground-design-ideas /featured-playgrounds/thomas-m.-menino-park-detail-page.

8. "Disability Concerns," Christian Reformed Church, accessed September 17, 2018, https://www.crcna.org/disability.

9. Larry Greenemeier, "5 Mobile Technologies Help Level the Playing Field for People with Disabilities," *Scientific American*, August 5, 2015, https://www.scientificamerican.com/article/5-mobile-technologies -help-level-the-playing-field-for-people-with-disabilities-video.

10. Colin Lecher, "Dean Kamen's DARPA-Funded Prosthetic Arm Gets FDA Approval," *Popular Science*, May 12, 2014, http://www.popsci .com/article/technology/dean-kamens-darpa-funded-prosthetic-arm -gets-fda-approval.

Chapter 4: Education

1. Cynthia E. Lamy, "How Preschool Fights Poverty," *Educational Leadership* 70, no. 8 (May 2013): 32.

2. "Literacy," UNESCO, accessed September 17, 2018, https://en.unesco.org/themes/literacy.

3. Réka Vágvölgyi et al., "A Review About Functional Illiteracy: Definition, Cognitive, Linguistic, and Numerical Aspects," *Frontiers in Psychology* 7 (November 2016): 4.

4. Michael Sainato, "US Prison System Plagued by High Illiteracy Rates," *Observer*, July 18, 2017, https://observer.com/2017/07/prison-illiteracy-criminal-justice-reform.

5. Phineas Rueckert, "10 Barriers to Education Around the World," Global Citizen, January 24, 2018, https://www.globalcitizen.org/en/content/10-barriers-to-education-around-the-world-2/.

6. Jonathon Kozol, *The Shame of the Nation: The Restoration of Apartheid Schooling in America* (New York: Broadway Books, 2006), 316.

7. Ken Robinson, *Creative Schools: The Grassroots Revolution That's Transforming Education* (New York: Penguin, 2016), xv.

8. "Education and the Developing World," Center for Global Development, June 12, 2006, https://www.cgdev.org/publication/education-and-developing-world.

9. "The Positive Effects of Teacher Home Visits," Project Appleseed, accessed September 17, 2018, http://www.projectappleseed.org/teacher-home-visits.

Chapter 5: Fair Trade

1. Branislav Pekic, "Serbia Becomes the World's Largest Exporter of Raspberries," *European Supermarket Magazine*, May 24, 2016, http://www.esmmagazine.com/serbia-becomes-worlds-top-raspberry-producer/27910.

2. "Malaysia Cocoa Industry Report 2017—Research and Markets," Business Wire, May 3, 2017, http://www.businesswire.com/news/home/20170503005811/en/Malaysia-Cocoa-Industry-Report-2017---Research.

3. "Made in China?," *Economist*, March 12, 2015, http://www.economist

.com/news/leaders/21646204-asias-dominance-manufacturing-will
-endure-will-make-development-harder-others-made.

4. Colleen Haight, "The Problem with Fair Trade Coffee," *Stanford Social Innovation Review* 9, no. 3 (Summer 2011): 76, https://ssir.org/pdf/2011SU_CaseStudy_Haight.pdf.

5. Emily Jane Fox, "Shoppers Face Tough Choices over Bangladesh," CNNMoney, May 1, 2013, https://money.cnn.com/2013/05/01/news/companies/bangladesh-garment-factory/index.html.

6. "Buyer's Guide," Student Action with Farmworkers, accessed October 11, 2018, https://saf-unite.org/content/buyers-guide.

7. Mary Bauer and Mónica Ramírez, *Injustices on Our Plates: Immigrant Women in the U.S. Food Industry* (Montegomery, AL: Southern Poverty Law Center, 2010), 4, https://www.splcenter.org/sites/default/files/d6_legacy_files/downloads/publication/Injustice_on_Our_Plates.pdf.

8. Rachel Dixon, "Teach Us How to Fish—Do Not Just Give Us the Fish," *Guardian*, March 12, 2008, https://www.theguardian.com/environment/2008/mar/12/ethicalliving.lifeandhealth.

9. "Sukambizi Association Trust, Malawi," Fairtrade Foundation, accessed September 14, 2018, https://www.fairtrade.org.uk/en/farmers-and-workers/tea/sukambizi-association-trust.

10. "The Impact of Fair Trade Certification," Fair Trade USA, accessed September 14, 2018, http://www.fairtradecertified.org/why-fair-trade/our-impact.

11. "Nearly 385 Million Children Living in Extreme Poverty, Says Joint World Bank Group-UNICEF Study," World Bank, October 3, 2016, http://www.worldbank.org/en/news/press-release/2016/10/03/nearly-385-million-children-living-extreme-poverty-joint-world-bank-group-unicef-study.

12. Brad Kent, ed., *George Bernard Shaw in Context* (New York: Cambridge University Press, 2018), xxv.

13. "Kroger Expands Fair Trade Certified Offerings," PR Newswire Association, January 8, 2018, https://www.prnewswire.com/news-releases/kroger-expands-fair-trade-certified-offerings-300579075.html.

14. "The Power of Fair Trade Coffee in La Revancha, Nicaragua," Fair

Trade USA, November 5, 2015, https://www.fairtradecertified.org
/news/power-of-fair-trade-coffee-la-revancha-nicaragua.

Chapter 6: Families

1. Philip Bashe, *Caring for Your Teenager: The Complete and Authoritative Guide* (New York: Bantam, 2013), 108.
2. *Introduction to Family Strengthening: Policy Brief No. 1*, Family Strengthening Policy Center (Washington, DC: National Human Services Assembly, 2004), http://www.aecf.org/m/resourcedoc/fspc -IntroductiontoFamilyStrengthening-2004.pdf.
3. Vanessa Sacks, David Murphy, and Kristin Moore, *Adverse Childhood Experiences: National and State Level Prevalence* (Bethesda, MD: Child Trends, 2014), 10, https://www.childtrends.org/wp-content /uploads/2014/07/Brief-adverse-childhood-experiences_FINAL.pdf.
4. Children's Bureau, *The AFCARS Report* (Washington, DC: US Department of Health and Human Services, 2016), https://www.acf.hhs.gov /sites/default/files/cb/afcarsreport24.pdf.
5. Jo Jones and Paul Placek, "Adoption by the Numbers," National Council for Adoption, February 15, 2017, http://www.adoptioncouncil.org /publications/2017/02/adoption-by-the-numbers.
6. Ola Barnett and Cindy Miller-Perrin, *Family Violence Across the Lifespan*, 3rd ed. (Thousand Oaks, CA: Sage, 2011), 2.
7. Alessondra Villegas, "The Influence of Technology on Family Dynamics," *Proceedings of the New York State Communication Association* 2012 (2013): 12, https://docs.rwu.edu/nyscaproceedings/vol2012/iss1/10.
8. Catherine E. Snow and Diane E. Beals, "Mealtime Talk That Supports Literacy Development," *New Directions for Child and Adolescent Development* 111 (March 2006): 51–66.
9. Jerica M. Berge, "The Protective Role of Family Meals for Youth Obesity: 10 Year Longitudinal Associations," *Journal of Pediatrics* 166, no. 2 (February 2015): 296–301.
10. Jayne A. Fulkerson, "Family Dinner Meal Frequency and Adolescent Behavior: Relationships with Developmental Assets and High-Risk Behaviors," *Journal of Adolescent Health* 39, no. 3 (September 2006): 337–45.

11. Lisa Hoeve, "When We're Done," *Community in Action* (blog), Hope Pkgs, December 23, 2016, http://www.hopepkgs.org/community-in -action/when-were-done.

12. Margaret Wise Brown, *The Runaway Bunny* (New York: Harper-Collins, 2017), 1.

Chapter 7: Health Care

1. Gabriela Flores et al., *Tracking Universal Health Coverage: 2017 Global Monitoring Report* (Geneva: World Health Organization and International Bank for Reconstruction and Development, 2017), http:// documents.worldbank.org/curated/en/640121513095868125/pdf /122029-WP-REVISED-PUBLIC.pdf.

2. "Access to Medicines," Médecins Sans Frontières, accessed October 11, 2018, https://www.doctorswithoutborders.org/what-we-do/medical -issues/access-to-medicines.

3. *Children's Grief Awareness Day: 10th Anniversary*, Children's Grief Awareness Day, accessed September 14, 2018, https://www.childrens griefawarenessday.org/cgad2/pdf/factsheet.pdf.

4. "About Child Trauma," National Child Traumatic Stress Network, accessed September 14, 2018, http://www.nctsn.org/what-is-child -trauma/about-child-trauma.

5. James B. Kirby and Toshiko Kaneda, "Neighborhood Socioeconomic Disadvantage and Access to Healthcare," *Journal of Health and Social Behavior* 46, no. 1 (March 2005): 15–31.

6. Tiffany Dovydaitis, "Human Trafficking: The Role of the Health Care Provider," *Journal of Midwifery and Women's Health* 55, no. 5 (June 2011): 462–67.

7. "Antibiotic Resistance," World Health Organization, February 5, 2018, http://www.who.int/news-room/fact-sheets/detail/antibiotic-resistance.

8. "Global Health Workforce Shortage to Reach 12.9 Million in Coming Decades," World Health Organization, November 11, 2013, http:// www.who.int/mediacentre/news/releases/2013/health-workforce -shortage/en.

9. *How AIDS Changed Everything: 15 Years, 15 Lessons of Hope from the*

AIDS Response (Geneva: UNAIDS, 2015), http://www.unaids.org
/sites/default/files/media_asset/MDG6Report_en.pdf.

10. *Towards an AIDS-Free Generation: Children and AIDS: Sixth Stock-
taking Report, 2013* (New York: UNICEF, 2013), 3, http://www.unaids
.org/sites/default/files/media_asset/20131129_stocktaking_report
_children_aids_en_0.pdf.

11. *Immunization: Keeping Children Alive and Healthy* (New York:
UNICEF, 2014), https://www.unicef.org/immunization/files/Immuni
zation_brochure.pdf.

12. "Maternal, Newborn, and Child Health: Strategy Overview," Bill and
Melinda Gates Foundation, accessed September 14, 2018, http://www
.gatesfoundation.org/What-We-Do/Global-Development/Maternal
-Newborn-and-Child-Health.

13. Betsy Teutsch, *100 Under $100: One Hundred Tools for Empowering
Global Women* (Berkeley, CA: She Writes Press, 2015), 5.

14. "Obesity Information," American Heart Association, accessed Sep-
tember 14, 2018, http://www.heart.org/HEARTORG/HealthyLiving
/WeightManagement/Obesity/Obesity-Information_UCM_307908
_Article.jsp#.W3iwA-hKhPY.

15. Colleen Kane, "Why Americans Just Won't Take Time Off,"
Fortune, May 1, 2015, http://fortune.com/2015/05/01/paid-time-off
-vacation/.

16. James R. Knickman and Emily K. Snell, "The 2030 Problem: Caring
for Aging Baby Boomers," *Health Services Research* 37, no. 4 (August
2002): 849–84.

17. Kate Kelland, "Study Shows Health Improving Globally, but Progress
Is Patchy," Reuters, October 6, 2016, http://www.reuters.com/article
/us-health-disease-global-idUSKCN1260KX.

Chapter 8: Human Trafficking

1. Thomas A. Nazario, *Living On a Dollar a Day* (New York: Quantuck
Lane, 2014), 179.

2. Ayperi Karabuda Ecer, *Reuters: Our World Now*, vol. 5 (London:
Thames and Hudson, 2012), 270.

3. Claudio Montesano Casillas, "Beyond the Label #7," 2016, http://www
.claudiomontesanocasillas.com/photogallery/beyond-the-label/#7.

4. Vlad Solkin, "Restaveks: Haitian Slave Children," End Slavery Now,
January 1, 2015, http://www.endslaverynow.org/blog/articles/restaveks
-haitian-slave-children.

5. "Universal Declaration of Human Rights," United Nations, accessed
September 14, 2018, http://www.un.org/en/universal-declaration
-human-rights/index.html.

6. *New ILO Global Estimate of Forced Labour: Results and Methodology*
(Geneva: International Labor Organization, 2012), 13, https://www
.ilo.org/wcmsp5/groups/public/---ed_norm/---declaration/documents
/publication/wcms_182004.pdf.

7. *Accelerating Action Against Child Labour* (Geneva: International Labour
Organization, 2010), ix, http://www.ilo.org/wcmsp5/groups/public
/@dgreports/@dcomm/documents/publication/wcms_126752.pdf.

8. *Global Estimates of Child Labour: Results and Trends, 2012–2016*
(Geneva: International Labour Organization, 2017), 5, http://www
.ilo.org/wcmsp5/groups/public/---dgreports/---dcomm/documents
/publication/wcms_575499.pdf.

9. Flannery O'Connor, *The Habit of Being: Letters of Flannery O'Connor*,
ed. Sally Fitzgerald (New York: Farrar, Straus and Giroux, 1988), 100.

10. Ronald D. Lankford, ed., *Slavery Today* (San Diego: Greenhaven,
2010), 69.

11. "Human Trafficking by the Numbers," Human Rights First, January
7, 2017, https://www.humanrightsfirst.org/resource/human-trafficking
-numbers.

12. Ken Bales, *Disposable People: New Slavery in the Global Economy*
(Berkeley: University of California Press, 2004).

13. Gary Haugen and Victor Boutros, *The Locust Effect* (New York: Oxford
University Press, 2014), 98.

14. Omar Martinez and Guadalupe Kelle, "Sex Trafficking of LGBT Individuals: A Call for Service Provision, Research, and Action," *International Law News* 42, no. 4 (Fall 2013), https://www.ncbi.nlm.nih.gov
/pmc/articles/PMC4204396.

15. Guillermo Contreras and Emilie Eaton, "San Antonio Death Toll in

'Horrific' Human Trafficking Reaches 10," July 24, 2017, *San Antonio Express-News*, https://www.mysanantonio.com/news/local/article/San -Antonio-death-toll-in-horrific-human-11308288.php.

16. Upton Sinclair, *The Jungle* (Chicago: Doubleday, Page and Company, 1906), 121.

17. "Unpacking the Rapid Response Backpack," *146* (blog), Love146, May 20, 2018, https://love146.org/unpacking-the-rapid-response-backpack.

Chapter 9: Hunger

1. "Hunger in the United States," Feeding America, accessed September 14, 2018, https://www.feedingamerica.org/hunger-in-america/the -united-states.

2. "The Year in Review 2016," World Food Programme, accessed September 14, 2018, https://publications.wfp.org/en/annual-report/2016 /section_1.html.

3. *Hunger in Our Schools* (Washington, DC: No Kid Hungry, 2015), 4, https://nkh-development-s3-bucket.s3.amazonaws.com/sites/default /files/pdfs/HIOS_2017.pdf.

4. Eric Holt-Giménez et al., "We Already Grow Enough Food for 10 Billion People . . . and Still Can't End Hunger," *Journal of Sustainable Agriculture* 36, no. 6 (July 2012): 595.

5. "Save Food: Global Initiative on Food Loss and Waste Reduction," Food and Agriculture Organization of the United Nations, accessed September 14, 2018, http://www.fao.org/save-food/resources/keyfind ings/en.

6. Dana Gunders, *Wasted: How America Is Losing Up to 40 percent of Its Food from Farm to Fork to Landfill* (New York: Natural Resources Defense Council, 2012), https://www.nrdc.org/sites/default/files/wasted-food-IP .pdf.

7. *The State of Food Security and Nutrition in the World 2017: Building Resilience for Peace and Food Security* (Rome: FAO, IFAD, UNICEF, WFP, and WHO, 2017), http://www.fao.org/3/a-I7695e.pdf.

8. Katarina Wahlberg, "Food Aid for the Hungry?," Global Policy Forum, January 2008, https://www.globalpolicy.org/component/con tent/article/217-hunger/46251-food-aid-for-the-hungry.html.

328   Notes

9. Steven Were Omamo, Ugo Gentilini, and Susanna Sandstrom, *Revolution: From Food Aid to Food Assistance—Innovations in Overcoming Hunger* (Rome: World Food Programme, 2010), 65–74.

10. Max Kutner, "The Number of People on Food Stamps is Falling. Here's Why," *Newsweek*, July 22, 2017, http://www.newsweek.com /people-food-stamps-snap-decline-participation-640500.

11. Mary Babic et al., *From Paycheck to Pantry: Hunger in Working America* (Chicago: Feeding America; Boston: Oxfam, 2014), 8, https:// www.oxfamamerica.org/static/media/files/From-Paycheck-to-Pantry -Oxfam-FeedingAmerica.pdf.

12. Theresa DelVecchio Dys et al., *Baby Boomers and Beyond: Facing Hunger After Fifty* (Chicago: Feeding America, 2015), http://www .feedingamerica.org/research/senior-hunger-research/baby-boomers -executive-summary.pdf.

13. Dys et al., *Baby Boomers and Beyond*, 6.

14. J. P. Faber, *The New Pioneers* (Dallas: BenBella, 2017).

15. Elaine Waxman, Susan J. Popkin, and Martha Galvaz, *Bringing Teens to the Table: A Focus on Food Insecurity in America* (Chicago: Feeding America, 2015), http://www.feedingamerica.org/research/teen-hunger -research/bringing-teens-to-the-table.pdf.

16. Eliza Barclay, "Rooftop Farming Is Getting Off the Ground," National Public Radio, September 25, 2013, http://www.npr.org/sections/thesalt /2013/09/24/225745012/why-aren-t-there-more-rooftop-farms.

Chapter 10: Immigrants and Refugees

1. James M. McClurken, *Our People, Our Journey: The Little River Band of Ottawa Indians* (Lansing: Michigan State University Press, 2009), 19–20.

2. W. Vernon Kinietz, *The Indians of the Western Great Lakes, 1615–1760* (Ann Arbor: University of Michigan Regional, 1965), 38, 88.

3. Cornelia Van Voorst, "Holland's Early Colonists Befriended by Indians but Indians Left Area Around 1948," *Holland Sentinel*, May 17, 1972.

4. Randy VandeWater, "Pokagon One of Most Famous Native Americans in West Michigan," *Holland Sentinel*, February 21, 2010.

5. "Chief Joseph Speaks: Selected Statements and Speeches by the Nez Percé Chief," New Perspectives on the West, PBS, accessed September 14, 2018, https://www.pbs.org/weta/thewest/resources/archives/six/jospeak.htm.

6. "Ellis Island," History.com, October 27, 2009, http://www.history.com/topics/ellis-island.

7. "Migrant Crisis: Migration to Europe Explained in Seven Charts," BBC, March 4, 2016, http://www.bbc.com/news/world-europe-34131911.

8. Jason Beaubien, "5 Surprising Facts About the Refugee Crisis," National Public Radio, June 20, 2017, http://www.npr.org/sections/goatsandsoda/2017/06/20/533634405/five-surprising-facts-about-the-refugee-crisis.

9. Jens Manuel Krogstad, Jeffrey S. Passel, and D'Vera Cohn, "5 Facts About Illegal Immigration in the U.S.," Pew Research Center, April 27, 2017, https://www.pewresearch.org/fact-tank/2017/04/27/5-facts-about-illegal-immigration-in-the-u-s/.

10. Demetrios G. Papademetriou and Natalia Banulescu-Bogdan, *Understanding and Addressing Public Anxiety About Immigration* (Washington, DC: Migration Policy Institute, 2016).

11. *Global Trends: Forced Displacement in 2015* (Geneva: UNHCR, 2015), http://www.unhcr.org/576408cd7.pdf.

12. *No More Excuses: Provide Education to All Forcibly Displaced Peoples* (Paris: UNESCO, 2016), http://unesdoc.unesco.org/images/0024/002448/244847E.pdf.

13. "Child Refugee and Migrant Crisis: Syrian Crisis," UNICEF USA, April 16, 2018, https://www.unicefusa.org/mission/emergencies/child-refugees/syria-crisis.

14. Tom Gjelten, *A Nation of Nations: A Great American Immigration Story* (New York: Simon and Schuster, 2015), 93.

15. Johan Bävman, "Resettlement," UNHCR, accessed September 14, 2018, http://www.unhcr.org/en-us/resettlement.html.

16. Krogstad, Passel, and Cohn, "5 Facts About Illegal Immigration."

17. Andrew Wainer, *Farm Workers and Immigration Policy* (Washington, DC: Bread for the World Institute, December 2011), 5, http://www.bread.org/sites/default/files/downloads/briefing-paper-12.pdf.

18. "Economic Impact of Immigration," American Farm Bureau Federation, 2018, http://www.fb.org/issues/immigration-reform/agriculture-labor-reform/economic-impact-of-immigration.

19. William Kanel, "Profile of Hired Farmworkers: A 2008 Update," USDA, July 2008, https://www.ers.usda.gov/publications/pub-details/?pubid=46041.

20. "Undocumented Americans," American Psychological Association, accessed October 15, 2018, http://www.apa.org/topics/immigration/undocumented-video.aspx.

21. Henri Nouwen, *The Way of the Heart: Desert Spirituality and Contemporary Ministry* (New York: HarperCollins, 1991), 35.

Chapter 11: Peace

1. Chris Hedges, *What Every Person Should Know About War* (New York: Free Press, 2003), 1.

2. Frances Steward, "Root Causes of Violent Conflict in Developed Countries," *BMJ* 324, no. 7333 (February 9, 2002), https://www.ncbi.nlm.nih.gov/pmc/articles/PMC1122271.

3. Jean-Marie Guehenno, "10 Conflicts to Watch in 2017," *Foreign Policy*, January 5, 2017, https://foreignpolicy.com/2017/01/05/10-conflicts-to-watch-in-2017.

4. Hedges, *War*, 7.

5. Siddharth Chatterjee, "For Child Soldiers, Every Day Is a Living Nightmare," *Forbes*, December 9, 2012, http://www.forbes.com/sites/realspin/2012/12/09/for-child-soldiers-every-day-is-a-living-nightmare/#2ab15fe2603e.

6. Philip Brookman and Jane Slate Siena, *The Way Home: Ending Homelessness in America* (New York: Harry N. Abrams, 1999), 143.

7. Matt Davis, "Restorative Justice: Resources for School," Edutopia, October 29, 2015, https://www.edutopia.org/blog/restorative-justice-resources-matt-davis.

8. Devin Thorpe, "Christian Organization Works to Restore Peace in Violent Honduras," *Forbes*, October 7, 2015, https://www.forbes.com/sites/devinthorpe/2015/10/07/christian-organization-works-to-restore-peace-in-violent-honduras/#191013a16deb.

Chapter 12: Poverty

1. Chaim Potok, *My Name Is Asher Lev* (New York: Anchor, 1972), 33.
2. José Cuesta et al., *Poverty and Shared Prosperity 2016: Taking on Inequality* (Washington, DC: World Bank Group, 2016), 3, https://openknowledge.worldbank.org/bitstream/handle/10986/25078/9781464809583.pdf.
3. Kathryn J. Edin and H. Luke Shaefer, *$2.00 a Day: Living On Almost Nothing in America* (New York: Houghton Mifflin Harcourt, 2015), 173.
4. Susana Vera, *Reuters: Our World Now*, vol. 5 (London: Thames and Hudson, 2012), 42.
5. "Poverty and Equity Data Portal," World Bank, 2012, http://povertydata.worldbank.org/poverty/home.
6. Edin and Shaefer, *$2.00 a Day*, 43.
7. J. D. Vance, *Hillbilly Elegy: A Memoir of Family and Culture in Crisis* (New York: HarperCollins, 2016), 227.
8. Philip Brookman and Jane Slate Siena, *The Way Home: Ending Homelessness in America* (New York: Harry N. Abrams, 1999), 142.
9. Thomas Merton, *Disputed Questions* (New York: Harcourt Brace, 1985), 125.
10. Sasha Abramsky, *The American Way of Poverty: How the Other Half Still Lives* (New York: Nation Books, 2013), 327.
11. "Cityspaces MicroPAD," Panoramic Interests, accessed October 15, 2018, https://www.panoramic.com/cityspaces-location/cityspaces-micropad.

Chapter 13: Race

1. Academy of Motion Picture Arts and Sciences, "Lupita Nyong'o Winning Best Supporting Actress," YouTube video, 3:33, March 11, 2014, https://www.youtube.com/watch?v=73fz_uK-vhs.
2. *Merriam-Webster's Collegiate Dictionary*, 11th ed. (2003), s.v. "prejudice."
3. Simba Runyowa, "Microaggressions Matter," *Atlantic*, September 18, 2015, http://www.theatlantic.com/politics/archive/2015/09/microaggressions-matter/406090.
4. Catherine Herbert Howell, K. David Harrison, and Spencer Wells,

People of the World: Cultures and Traditions, Ancestry and Identity (Washington, DC: National Geographic, 2016), 8.

5. Rich Morin, "The Most (and Least) Culturally Diverse Countries in the World," Pew Research Center, July 18, 2013, https://www .pewresearch.org/fact-tank/2013/07/18/the-most-and-least-culturally -diverse-countries-in-the-world.

6. D'Vera Cohn and Andrea Caumont, "10 Demographic Trends That Are Shaping the U.S. and the World," Pew Research Center, March 31, 2016, http://www.pewresearch.org/fact-tank/2016/03/31/10-demo graphic-trends-that-are-shaping-the-u-s-and-the-world.

7. Steven T. Katz and Alan Rosen, eds., *Elie Wiesel: Jewish, Literary, and Moral Perspectives* (Bloomington: Indiana University Press, 2013), 256.

8. Ta-Nehisi Coates, *Between the World and Me* (New York: Spiegel and Grau, 2015), 70.

9. Martin Luther King Jr., "The Other America," Grosse Pointe High School, March 14, 1968, Grosse Pointe Farms, MI, transcript, https:// www.gphistorical.org/mlk/mlkspeech/.

10. Allison Plyer, "Facts for Features: Katrina Impact," The Data Center, August 26, 2016, http://www.datacenterresearch.org/date-resources /Katrina/facts-for-impact.

11. Henri Nouwen, *Bread for the Journey: A Daybook of Wisdom and Faith* (New York: HarperOne, 2006), 218.

12. Western Michigan University Archives and Regional History Col- lections and University Libraries, *MLK at Western* (Kalamazoo, MI: Western Michigan University Archives and Regional History Col- lections and University Libraries, n.d.), http://www.wmich.edu/sites /default/files/attachments/MLK.pdf.

Chapter 14: Changemakers

1. Thomas A. Nazario, *Living On a Dollar a Day: The Lives and Faces of the World's Poor* (New York: Quantuck Lane Press, 2014), 340.

Epilogue

1. Martin Luther King Jr., "I've Been to the Mountaintop" speech, April 3, 1968, https://www.americanrhetoric.com/speeches/mlkivebeento themountaintop.htm.